D0617842

The Best
AMERICAN
FOOD
WRITING
2022

GUEST EDITORS OF THE BEST AMERICAN FOOD WRITING

2018 RUTH REICHL
2019 SAMIN NOSRAT
2020 J. KENJI LÓPEZ-ALT
2021 GABRIELLE HAMILTON
2022 SOHLA EL-WAYLLY

The Best AMERICAN FOOD WRITING™ 2022

Edited and with an Introduction by SOHLA EL-WAYLLY

SILVIA KILLINGSWORTH, Series Editor

MARINER BOOKS
New York   Boston

FIRST EDITION

ISSN 2578-7667

ISBN 978-0-06-325441-1

22 23 24 25 26 LBC 6 5 4 3 2

Contents

Contents

Foreword

ONE OF THE most paradoxical things about food is the sheer infinitude of effort that can be expended—or not!—on it, with marginal effect on its intrinsic value. Some foods are celebrated for the amount of effort they require, whether in preparation (soufflé) or harvest (coconut), while others are praised for their convenience or efficiency (instant rice, Soylent). Though we rightly cheer the things that are easy—what a relief to have dinner ready in under thirty minutes, how lovely that this gas station sells prepackaged apple slices—we also value very highly the things that take a lot of effort or expertise. You can pay through the nose for dinner at a Michelin-starred restaurant, but it's dinner all the same.

Much the same can be observed of writing. The most popular stuff goes down easy,* and you get the sense that it's easy enough to produce: David Sedaris essays read as though he just rattled them off into a transcription service that sends them directly to the printer, and mass-market thrillers you can finish in one day top the bestseller lists decade after decade. But the writing that wins the most prestigious awards—Pulitzers, Nobels, James Beards—is usually a feat of reporting, research, writing, and editing. Both are highly valued, and neither is per se morally superior, though some may try to argue otherwise.

---

* Even the way we speak about writing has echoes with the universe of food: we talk of devouring books, voracious readers, and how "beach reads" resemble junk food in that they are easy to consume quickly and lack nutritional value.

Curiously, society puts a premium on hiding all that effort—"You make it look so easy!" is a common compliment for successful writers and cooks alike. Much fuss is made over making things seem effortless, to the point of illogic. I am reminded of a scene from HBO's *Succession* where Nan Pierce, the matriarch of a WASPy old newspaper family, swoops into the kitchen at the last second to escort a roast out to the dining room, to polite applause. Of course, no one in their right mind believes she actually prepared the hunk of meat, but she claims the credit nonetheless while hiding the true source of effort: a fully staffed kitchen just over the threshold.

So perhaps the paradox of effort is a false one, because even the easy stuff takes work. There's no denying it: when you eat something, even if it's just a can of Spaghetti-Os, someone—usually multiple someones—has put in a good deal of effort to bring it to you. Behind any line cook's perfect frying-pan flip are hours of practice and dozens of spills, with the forearm burns to show for it. The most successful authors put out books as regularly as once a year, which is a whole lot of work and discipline, no matter how formulaic the stories may be. But so is getting your very first byline in the local newspaper.

Furthermore, all writing is more than just one's person's work—there are editors, producers, designers, and all sorts of people who make publication possible. This goes for food, too. In restaurants you have prep cooks and sauciers and expediters, as well as servers and hosts and dishwashers, to say nothing of the people involved in growing and transporting the ingredients. And those are just the mainstream, commercialized outlets for those pursuits. Many of us write and cook for ourselves or our friends and family; just because they don't pay for it doesn't mean it isn't incredibly valuable.

Writing about food, then, is some of the most intensely social material out there, which is why I love editing this series year after year. In writing as in food, we are communicating with others, telling them something, whether through our perspective, technique, or subject. In the case of Sam Anderson's ludic meditation on chips as a snack, or in Liz Cook's lucid rationalization of how she came to taste rat repellent, food writing can be a way of expressing an opinion or a firsthand experience. Or in the case of Sam Dean's investigation into the man who *didn't* invent Flamin' Hot Cheetos or Josh Dzieza's account of the food-delivery workers who sustain New Yorkers, they are the stories that enlighten and remind us where food does and doesn't come from. But some of my favorites are the ones that use food as a narrative vehicle to talk about something else entirely: travel, love, history, family, pain.

Since this anthology first debuted in 2018, I have gotten to know so many more people who are as entranced and possessed by this topic as I am. Besides confirming, year after year, that Ligaya Mishan is consistently one of the best food writers working today, I love discovering new voices—many of whom don't necessarily have a background in food journalism—who write wonderfully about the stuff that sustains us all. I love looking off the beaten path for surprising sources of new material.

Indeed, the less we restrict ourselves to a single definition of "food writing," the better. This year, for the first time, the anthology will include a piece of fiction, as well as a piece that originally ran in the form of a newsletter. You can bet that if this series had been around in 1934, William Carlos Williams's now-ubiquitous ode to the plums in the icebox would be included.

It's fun to scour the landscape and to see the people who put in good work. And it's even more fun to tell them: Good job, I see what you've done. We should celebrate their effort, whether it is the result of six months of reporting or six minutes of feverish typing. Effort comes in many stripes, and so these things come in all forms, from all corners. Try as I may, I cannot be sure that I read it all. If you see something published this year you think deserves a nod, please send it to me by December 31, 2022, at silvia .killingsworth@gmail.com.

SILVIA KILLINGSWORTH

Introduction

AT TEN YEARS old, I did not have access to Grand Marnier, but I figured microwaved Minute Maid frozen orange-juice concentrate would make an acceptable substitute. I stirred it into a mixture of melted Nestlé chocolate chips, Country Crock, and egg yolks. It would be the base for my Soufflé au chocolat et au Grand Marnier from *At Home with the French Classics* by Richard Grausman, one of the only two cookbooks I owned until adulthood. In my early cooking years, I'd been obsessed with soufflés, omelets, and all the French things. My goal was to work my way through the entire cookbook, which had more than fifteen different sweet and savory soufflé recipes, including one baked inside pâte à choux. This was my first attempt.

It started out easy enough, but now came whipping time. What I know now that I didn't then is that not all whisks are created equal. Mine had flimsy metal loops held together with a coiled wire handle that dug into your palm. I sloshed the egg whites around the bowl until I grew tired and calloused. I guess that's a stiff peak? The syrupy omelet I ended up with didn't quite match the fluff-city Richard had promised. But don't worry, Dick, I kept going. I made that soufflé for years, then the others, and eventually every recipe in that book.

My other cookbook, *Better Homes and Gardens New Junior Cookbook,* was a gift from a friend on my seventh birthday. I spent hours staring at the two-page technique section called "Words to Cook By." It has black-and-white drawings and text illustrating kitchen basics such as how to grease a pan and test cakes for doneness with a toothpick, the difference between a simmer and a boil, and a very questionable method for cracking eggs with a butter knife. You bet I cooked through every recipe in there, too, carefully popping cans of Pillsbury dough for sheet-pan pizzas and folding slices of Kraft Singles into dense bricks ready for stuffing into mini ketchup-glazed meatloaves. This book also gave me my first recipe for a non–Betty Crocker cake mix cake. I didn't have powdered sugar for the frosting, so I swapped in granulated. We ate the entire gritty cake anyway.

Back then, I had nothing but words on a page to teach me techniques I was totally unfamiliar with. And it wasn't like there was access to a wealth of recipes like we have now, so why not keep trying? I guess the good is that I made every recipe I did have over and over again. Still, as I scroll through YouTube today and find endless videos highlighting everything from making your own lamian— hand-pulled, visually mesmerizing Chinese noodles—to all the things you could possibly do with sourdough discard (remember when we all became artisanal bread bakers?), I can't help but feel a pang of heartache for young Sohla. These days we're all just a click away from reading a thoroughly researched article about sustainably sourced chocolate, with a killer recipe for chocolate-tahini brownies attached. Food content has become an accessible and all-encompassing media juggernaut not only highlighting recipes but providing investigative reporting and meaningful and powerful insights into culture, politics, and history.

Occasionally I would wear my mom down enough that she would buy me an issue of *Gourmet* magazine. (To be honest, I was more drawn to *Food and Wine.* However, the mention of wine in the title was enough to deter my conservative Muslim parents from investing in the "scripture of heathens.") The glossy pages of *Gourmet* let me peer into a brand-new world of food and, more important, food writing. Before, I thought food content was limited to recipes and Jacques Torres roller-skating on his PBS show, *Dessert Circus. Gourmet* showed me that food writing can tell stories. My favorites were of cooks who like to suffer, because I've got a good hit of that culinary masochism in myself, too. Every time I start holiday baking, I remember Celia Barbour's harrowing spoon-cookie tale. For her self-inflicted holiday hardship, soft brown-butter cookie dough is pressed into the bowl of a spoon. Then she'd carefully slide the molded cookie dough onto a tray and repeat, one cookie at a time. After baking, the impossibly crumbly cookies are carefully sandwiched with jam. She'd work through the night, and still her recipients ended up with a sparse cellophane sleeve holding only a couple of cookies—but they are the best freaking cookies. Regardless of how fussy they were, Celia said, she made spoon cookies every Christmas and regretted it every time. I feel you, Cece. I'm always so pumped for prepping Christmas cookie boxes until I start, and the reality of what I've gotten myself into smacks me in the face.

My occasional *Gourmet* magazine indulgence just got me dipping a toe into food media. As I got older, I eventually came across the seminal works of M.F.K. Fisher. The iconic tangerine story from her first book, *Serve It Forth,* is probably the reason 90 percent of us are in this food writing hustle at all:

> In the morning, in the soft sultry chamber, sit in the window peeling tangerines, three or four. Peel them gently; do not bruise them. . . . Separate each plump little pregnant crescent. . . . Take yesterday's paper (when we were in Strasbourg *L'Ami du Peuple* was the best, because when it got hot the ink stayed on it) and spread it on top of the radiator. . . . After you have put the pieces of tangerine on the paper on the hot radiator, it is best to forget about them. . . . On the radiator the sections of tangerines have grown even plumper, hot and full. You carry them to the window, pull it open, and leave them for a few minutes on the packed snow on the sill. They are ready. . . . I cannot tell you why they are so magical. Perhaps it is that little shell, thin as one layer of enamel on a Chinese bowl, that crackles so tinily, so ultimately under your teeth. Or the rush of cold pulp just after it. Or the perfume. I cannot tell.

Since I grew up in the sunny suburbs of Southern California without steady (or any) access to snow, I'd daydream of snapping through the brittle casing to the juicy pulp of her chaud-froid tangerines. I tried to approximate the snack by letting segments bathe in LA's dry summer sun before popping them into the freezer, but it didn't feel the same. I didn't have a radiator, I didn't have fresh snow, I didn't have the terroir of the city Fisher so poetically described. Years later, when we moved into our first Manhattan apartment, I could finally do it right. I had it all—snow, radiator, and city ambience. Following her instructions like a treasure map, I carefully separated each segment, peeled off every loose pithy thread, and laid them out with precision on a single unfolded sheet of the *New York Times* resting across the radiator. While I waited for the syrupy juices to sizzle at the seams, I listened to the delicate cries of neighbors asking us to shut up our dogs and the songs of ambulances ringing in the background. I cracked open the fire escape to nestle the segments in a fresh layer of snow on the ledge, while the faint scent of urine wafted into our 200-square-foot West Chelsea apartment. It's true what they say: Manhattan does make dreams come true. The first bite gave me both a jolting, dramatic swoosh of icy citrus pulp running down my throat and the manifestation of a feeling I'd only ever experienced in my imagination. Fisher's words captured everything so perfectly, I thought I was experiencing déjà vu. Now, every year after the first snowfall, in all the various downtown apartments I've lived in, I make these tangerines. It's the way I mark how far I've come, as we've transitioned from teeny studios to slightly larger one-bedrooms to finally having an in-unit washer and dryer. We did it, Mary!

While I was always experimental with the things I prepared in the kitchen, as a kid I couldn't have been a fussier eater. Most of my childhood memories involve the vivid standoffs between me and my mother. I wasn't allowed to leave the table until I finished my dal bhat, the mixture of steamed rice and stewed lentils at the core of every Bangladeshi meal. I'd sit there for hours, even falling asleep at the table, but I would never finish my plate. Coming across Jeffrey Steingarten's *The Man Who Ate Everything* showed me that, through perseverance, I too can eat everything. My greatest accomplishment is my current love for tahini. I can easily get through a jar in two weeks, and I even had to limit myself to just three tahini recipes in my cookbook. But for the longest time I hated it, anything related to sesame, and anyone who tried to push that bitter, oily cement onto me. Once I became determined that food was my field, I just kept asking myself, what would good ole Jeff do? I started with halva (a little sugar helps the medicine go down, right?), then moved on to tahini-sauced shawarma, and now I'm straight-up slathering it on toast.

Besides turning me into a zealous eater, Steingarten made me a better cook by letting me in on his obsessions, providing a template for how I live and work today—completely unhinged, with no semblance of work-life balance, daily testing the limits of my husband's devotion. Steingarten's essay about fries, simply titled "Fries," describes a life I never knew I longed for. In an effort to learn everything possible about the crisp yet fluffy spud side, he "gathered one hundred pounds of potatoes, ten gallons of peanut oil, four electric deep fryers," and coaxed an Austrian chef to smuggle six pounds of rendered horse fat into the country. I did not know that this is what a paying job could look like. I wanted in.

Food offers a clear path to connecting with anyone because we all eat. Even though I was a thirteen-year-old girl living in the San Fernando Valley, just trying to keep my Tamagotchi alive, I could empathize with a fifty-six-year-old former lawyer from New York because we both appreciate french fries. I grew up staining my fingers by eating my mother's turmeric-tinted macher jhol, but was able to get a taste of France by cooking through Grausman's saffron-speckled bouillabaisse. I've never been to France, yet through Fisher's prose I could feel the energy of the streets of pre–World War II Alsace. Wait—that's a lot of France.

No offense to France. Who doesn't love a flaky pain au chocolat? I adore the baguette's fearless ratio of brusque crust to supple middle, and, I mean, cheese. But India is nearly six times the size of France, with twenty-two official languages, yet historically the food media has watered the nation's cuisine down to a curry. China is only slightly smaller than the whole of Europe and features eight major styles of cuisines with countless regional variations, from mild and subtly sweet Jiangsu cuisine to tongue-tingling-hot Sichuan, but we're only now getting away from orange chicken. And Africa is a whole damn continent, made up of fifty-four unique countries, and we've had only a few years of mainstream representation of the food and culture of its specific regions and nations. But hey, better late than fucking never. I deeply love the food media I grew up with: Dick, Mary, Cece, and Jeff all feel like old friends. However, there's no denying the evolution of food media over the years. For the first time, I can see a life like mine represented. If melted chocolate chips and orange-juice concentrate could connect a little brown girl to a country more than five thousand miles away, what other bridges are being built, now that we're finally hearing more from a wider variety of people?

I never thought I'd be one of those people, somehow relating to so many others with totally different perspectives and backgrounds all because of a mutually healthy appetite. I never dreamed I might have a voice that anyone thought mattered, and it's still taking some time to get used to it. When I was first asked to make the selections for this book of the best food writing of the past year, honestly, I was real iffy about it. How could I judge these writers, real writers, when I've spent most of my food career working in unventilated basements, scrubbing mussels, baking rounds of focaccia, or spinning ice cream for menus developed by white male chefs? In my old life, I was invisible. Even when I transitioned to food media, I was hired to add color to the masthead or spice up the background. It was never intended that I would take center stage. My literary agent told me that "it was an honor," so I thought about doing it for her, but ultimately I said yes for you. All of you who decided my voice mattered have given me a platform; you are the reason I can even write the phrase "my literary agent." I try every day to prove to you that I was worth it, that you all made the right call. These are stories I truly believe you will love. I'm certain that Rajesh, Bryan, Nina, and Willa will become your BFFs because through their words I get all the feels, too. Things are changing fast, and it's a direct result of the audience, writers, editors, and participants in media at all levels finally having a say in who and what they want to see represented. This shift of power away from an omnipotent, invisible corporate executive to everyone else has resulted in better and more diverse content.

I wasn't alone in choosing the articles. Thank you, Silvia, for setting me up for success with a killer reading list of essays to pick from. This series is her baby, and I can feel how thoughtfully she selected every article that was listed on a spreadsheet across two tabs. You heard me, two! I was worried that I wouldn't be able to keep track of everything I read, so I took thorough notes, typed one letter at a time on the Notes app. Here are some excerpts from my initial thoughts:

> Wow. Incredible. Honest. Wrenching. Definitely going in the book and worthy of rereads

> Starts out so fucking miserable and grim, thank god it ends on a high

> This person's nuts and I freaking love it

I have a one-track mind—it's only occupied by food. I have no other hobbies or interests. When I'm not developing recipes, I'm still cooking, baking, eating, or rewatching old seasons of *Top Chef.* Luckily, good food writing is often a Trojan horse that looks like an easy-to-swallow treat but is actually filled with tales about culture, history, and even scandal. "Revolt of the Delivery Workers" by Josh Dzieza reads like the transcript of a true-crime podcast, following a group of delivery workers as they sleuth their way into retrieving their stolen bikes. I found myself constantly drying my sweaty palms from the suspense and feeling a rush of joy when the underdogs were victorious. Dr. Cynthia R. Greenlee's deep dive into the universally craved hot fried chicken in "Innovation and the Incinerated Tongue: Notes on Hot Chicken, Race, and Culinary Crossover" slips in commentary on Black food going viral and the appropriation of Black cool amid her witty retelling of the origins of hot chicken as revenge on an adulterous partner. It left me pensive, chuckling, and inspired to fry some chicken. Jiayang Fan sent me through a gamut of emotions in "Chronicles of a Bubble-Tea Addict," hitting on so many aspects of the Asian American experience and seamlessly weaving personal narrative, social commentary, and history. Boba was an indulgence I too had to barter with my mom to get, and my heart swelled with nostalgia as I remembered all the time I spent slurping down chewy balls through that giant plastic straw. Liz Cook's "I Tasted Honda's Spicy Rodent-Repelling Tape" taught me, first, that rodent-repelling tape was a thing that existed, and more important, that it might just be the best way to rim a Bloody Mary. After a solid five minutes of nasal snort-laughing, I even went as far as to google the availability of the product, until my horrified husband convinced me otherwise.

Julia Sonenshein's "Starving Toward Deliverance" knocked the wind out of me. It evoked the same feeling of surprise I got when I read my first copy of *Gourmet,* once again making me think: this is what food writing can be. It's fun to read and write about the pleasures of eating, but there is also shame and guilt around indulgence (or the assumption of it) across many cultures. As someone who's struggled with body image and also grew up in a conservative household, I could draw parallels between Julia's and my own experience. She bravely put her flaws and fears into words, certainly helping so many people who fight similar battles. Her story ultimately left me feeling hopeful, not just for Julia but also for myself.

Even with all the representation now, I haven't seen my school lunch experience out there. Jaya Saxena's "The Limits of the Lunchbox Moment" captures a sentiment that I have been unsure how to express forever: that growing up, I didn't get made fun of for my chicken korma sandwiches. Can't I just be a loser who happens to be brown? I went to Van Nuys High in the heart of the San Fernando Valley, a school populated by a diverse group of first-generation immigrants rocking everything from bento boxes filled with soy-dressed, housemade tofu to Korean dosirak packed tight with rice and assorted banchan. And I loved the days when I swapped my lunch for a lard-stained chile colorado tamale. There's something extremely freeing about finding someone eloquently expressing a sentiment you've carried around wordlessly with a hint of rage for years.

Growing up, I felt a huge divide between what I saw represented in food media and the real food around me. Yes, both worlds were rich and delicious. I have no regrets about all the single-serving soufflés I made after school, in search of that mousse-y perfection. And right alongside those memories, I'll never forget staring into a pot of boiling basmati rice as my mother parcooked the grains just enough to steam up tender and intact in her lamb biryani. Anytime I smell kimchi I'm reminded of middle school friend Hana and her mother's fridge, which was always brimming with homemade ferments. Whenever I get too tipsy late at night, I think of when we'd drive down to Orange County for crusty bánh mis to soak up all that sneaky high school tequila. Seeing the lines blur between the life I lead and the one I read about has finally allowed me to believe I am no longer peering into a world I could never be a part of, but in a place where I finally belong.

Looks like there's room here for all of us.

SOHLA EL-WAYLLY

The Best
AMERICAN
FOOD
WRITING
2022

NINA LI COOMES

If Silence Is the Cost of Great Ramen, So Be It

FROM *The Atlantic*

NAGOYA, JAPAN—*Vegetables, vegetables, vegetables.* I am sitting in a cardboard cubicle at a counter inside a ramen shop, rehearsing my order in my head over and over again. My sister is in the next cubicle over—all I can see is the top of her head—and later I will learn that she is doing the exact same thing. Small paper signs pasted to the partitions ask us customers to tell the chef what toppings we'd like (garlic, vegetables, soy sauce, or pork drippings) in a loud, clear voice with good tempo. The kitchen is loud and the restaurant is full, so it helps if patrons can communicate in one efficient go. Like an enthusiastic movie extra delivering a single line, I *really* want to get it right. That's because it is the only thing I will say during the entire hour I spend here.

My sister and I are at Rekishi wo Kizame, a wildly popular ramen restaurant where customers are asked to refrain from basically all chatter. The silence is not a regular aspect of eating ramen here but is instead a more recent rule because of COVID-19. Usually, both the restaurant and the line of soon-to-be diners waiting outside are raucous and noisy. But Takeshi Kitagawa, the restaurant's owner, told me that at the beginning of the pandemic, the restaurant received several complaints from people in the neighborhood that the line was a potential spot for people to cluster and spread the coronavirus. So Kitagawa implemented a strict mask mandate, as well as the practice of *mokushoku,* or silent dining, to help make things a little safer. (And there's evidence that silence actually works.)

Besides specifying your toppings, only one other interaction is allowed. While we wait in line, an employee comes to ask us how many people are in our party (just two). Other than that, no one is supposed to speak—and, at least when I was there, that's exactly what happened. No conferring with your lunch-mates about what type of ramen you'll get. No delighted exclamations when your food comes. No asking what the time is or seeing whether your friend wants to get coffee afterward. Even the initial order itself requires no speech: like lots of other restaurants, Rekishi wo Kizame has a vending machine nestled inside, where customers insert cash and receive a ramen ticket corresponding to their order.

Inside the restaurant, there are several blue-and-white posters with a face, its eyes closed and one hand raised in front of its mouth in a universal *shh* gesture. It must be mass-produced, because I've seen the same poster at other restaurants and coffee shops in town with the same policy. I couldn't find any official numbers on how many restaurants in Japan are implementing a form of *mokushoku,* but silent dining seems to have really caught on in early 2021, when a curry restaurant in Fukuoka made the news for its policy. One March survey of restaurant customers in Japan found that 22 percent of diners planned to practice *mokushoku* regardless of restaurant rules, in an effort to help stop the spread of the coronavirus.

After snaking through the line outside—we spent the time making excited eyes at each other over our masks—my sister and I are ushered into the small storefront, to the counter that rings the kitchen. The distinctly homemade dining booths we are cordoned off into make it virtually impossible to have a conversation with anyone. I sit on a stool between my cardboard partitions and reach over to clip my ramen ticket (a regular bowl of the restaurant's house noodles) onto a clothespin attached to the counter. I look again at the instructions on how to order toppings. *Vegetables, vegetables, vegetables!*

A loud *crack* interrupts my concentration. The three men next to us have apparently ordered an egg on the side. Or at least that's what I deduce, since I can't eavesdrop on their orders. I understand what just happened only when I see another customer receive a shining white egg that he proceeds to whack against the counter. Though there is no chatter, the shop still feels fairly loud. There is the backbeat of cars whizzing down the busy street outside, the blare of J-rock over the speaker, and the constant whirring of several industrial fans. Water roils on a stove; metal sieves clang against bowls; soup splashes. It's a comfortable, cheery din that makes me feel even more hungry for my ramen.

Kitagawa finally asks me what toppings I want, and in a practiced shout I say, "Vegetables and garlic." The garlic is a last-minute decision, and for a split second I am nervous that I have butchered my one and only utterance. I didn't, and from over the counter descends a bowl heaped with cabbage, bean sprouts, and two slabs of glistening roast pork. Under the meat rests a nest of thick-cut ramen noodles swimming in a dark broth. I push the minced garlic into the soup and crack apart my chopsticks, breathing in the scent of alliums, soy sauce, and rich pork-bone broth.

For a moment, I am almost apathetic about the restaurant's *mokushoku* policy. Maybe it doesn't matter at all that people can't talk with one another—especially here. Americans might eat ramen like it's dinner-party food, lingering over their bowl for what seems like hours as the noodles languish and bloat. But from a Japanese standpoint, ramen is a food to eat quickly, to slurp down before the heat of the broth causes the noodles to swell up and lose their chew. Sure, it's nice to chat with a fellow diner or remark upon how savory the broth is, how impressive a slab of *char siu* teetering on a pile of bean sprouts appears. But sitting in the whirlwind of ambient restaurant noise, the forced silence gives me no choice but to inhale my noodles quickly, exactly how they should be eaten.

Still, I want more than anything to poke my head over the barrier and make a quick comment to my sister, to marvel with her at this steaming mountain of ramen we are about to devour. But there is just me and the ramen in our little cardboard confessional, staring each other in the face. I know the clock is ticking, that I need to suck down my noodles before they become heavy with water, but I want to nudge my sister with my knee. I want to clap my hands together and say *Itadakimasu!*, the traditional Japanese phrase meant to open a meal. Above me, the blue *shh*-ing icon looks down beatifically, radiating its reminder of quiet.

When I spoke with Kitagawa, he said that, generally, most customers have an experience not too different from mine: even if they might want to speak, they respect his rules and keep quiet. Sometimes he does have to dole out a reminder, but he's careful to phrase it as a request and not an order—even if it's really just that. *Could you help us out by quieting down?* He said that most people have a hard time turning down such a request.

Even though more than 60 percent of people in Japan are now fully vaccinated, he's not sure when he'll end the policy, but he can't wait for his restaurant to once again be full of laughter and liveliness. Before the pandemic, boys would visit in groups and compete to see who could eat the most ramen the fastest, leading to cheers and boos. Still, the policy hasn't been all bad. Before the pandemic, Rekishi wo Kizame was a ramen shop frequented mostly by men. Porky, garlicky, and inelegant to eat, his ramen was somewhat of a tough sell for female customers. But the silence and privacy of the cardboard dividers has led to an uptick in women visiting the shop, Kitagawa said. They no longer have to fend off any unwanted stares or attempts at conversation, and can wolf down their ramen without a thought to decorum or composure.

At the end of our meal, I catch my sister's eye over the partition and wiggle my eyebrows toward the door to ask whether she's done. She wiggles her eyebrows back, and we (quietly!) place our ramen bowls on the counter, get up, and leave. Outside, faces fully visible, we hop on our bikes and shout to each other across the lane about the food. I spot other patrons doing the same, shrugging off their quiet as they get to the crosswalk. A pair of boys wait for the red light to turn green and wistfully sum up their meal: *Rekishi wo Kizame is always good,* they say. *We'll be back soon.* They keep talking about their meal as they cross the street, walking out of earshot. I guess you can stop people from talking about their food for only so long.

JAYA SAXENA

The Limits of the Lunchbox Moment

FROM *Eater*

"BOOGER-GI" IS WHAT the kids call Justin's bulgogi in *The Invisible Boy* by Trudy Ludwig, a picture book published in 2013. Justin is new, and when the other kids make fun of his food and his chopsticks, Brian, a shy, lonely white boy who longs to be included by his classmates, decides to leave him a note, telling him *he* isn't like those kids; he'd love to try bulgogi. Justin, whose food has not kept him from making other friends in the class, starts including Brian in activities based on this act of kindness, and all ends well, all because Brian said he'd be willing to eat bulgogi, objectively an incredibly flavorful and popular meal.

As a plot device in *The Invisible Boy*, the cafeteria scene works because the structure is familiar—Brian's kindness is noticed as kindness only if the standard response is disgust. That's because the story of that interaction has been told, in fiction, memoir, and across food media, by first-generation Americans, children of immigrants, and members of various diasporas hundreds of times. The image of a child opening their lunchbox to reveal an "ethnic" lunch and immediately being bullied for that lunch is everywhere, whether it's Toula in *My Big Fat Greek Wedding* getting teased for her moussaka, Eddie Huang recalling how "no one wanted to sit with the stinky kid" when his mom sent him to school with Chinese food, or Margaret Cho joking, "All the other kids got Ho Hos and Ding Dongs. I got squid and peanuts. You can't trade that shit." It gained its own name, "the lunchbox moment," around 2016 and has become the subject of endless personal essays. Even in the video launching the "new era" at *Bon Appétit*, editor-in-chief Dawn Davis said this anecdote was part of "every memoir" she ever published by an immigrant, and she has stated plans to launch a column around the concept of "the painful experience that was lunch."

The lunchbox moment has become such a touchstone both because it's recognizable for many and because it's an editor's dream. It cleanly illustrates, in personal essays, children's books, or stand-up routines, how food that's delicious in the context of the home becomes disgusting in public, the moment a brown child recognizes this divide, and the heartbreak of the child (usually) choosing to perform whiteness rather than get bullied again. "The odd thing was that I actually loved Chinese food, especially my mom's cooking," wrote Eddie Lin about his lunchbox moment. "I just wanted to fit in, like any other kid. . . . If it was Asian, it wasn't cool." And while rejecting tradition, religion, or language in favor of white American culture is all part of that struggle, you can't find a neater, easier-to-digest example than being told your lunch looks gross.

The story of being bullied in the cafeteria for one's lunch is so ubiquitous that it's attained a gloss of fictionality. It's become metonymy for the entire diaspora experience; to be a young immigrant or child of immigrants is to be bullied for your lunch, and vice versa. Other food experiences have become almost as common in immigrant literature—the realization that your cuisine has become "trendy"; the moment when a white friend tries to explain your favorite food back to you; the decision to re-create your family's signature dish, thereby shedding the shame you've carried over your culture's cuisine—and can be sources of bonding across immigrant communities. If "you can't be what you can't see," an oft-repeated phrase about the importance of representation in media, then these stories are allowing more people than ever to be seen. But the lunchbox moment is the anecdote that's probably the most widely employed, the background assumption at the base of these other stories.

This story, in which the bullied children age into a world clamoring for the flavors they grew up with and come to embrace the cuisine they tried to reject, is true for many. But in its retelling and fictionalization, it's been filed down to its most obvious and recognizable parts. There is no nuance to the lunchbox moment, and while the trope-ification of these real-life experiences conveys trauma and discrimination to often white readers or viewers, it leaves no room for the people whose lives did not fit that template. Yes, we can't be what we can't see. But what are we seeing? And what do we lose when we reduce our culinary experiences to one story?

"As a kid, when I started reading Asian American stories, [the lunchbox moment] was always the part that struck me as bizarre," said Zen Ren, who was born in China but moved with their family to Dallas when they were three years old. Much of that is because Ren grew up surrounded by other Asians, immigrants, and people of color. "In elementary [school] my closest friends were all Chinese American . . . so of course they weren't going to make fun of our food," they said, and as they grew up, they made other friends from different backgrounds who were accustomed to trying new cuisines. "People were curious about what I ate or didn't notice at all."

The lunchbox moment is a story about norms, with the assumption that the person of color is the odd one out—which it's easy to be. According to the United States Census Bureau, 76.3 percent of Americans identify as white (with 60.1 percent identifying as both white and not Hispanic or Latino). But that doesn't account for nonwhite people who grew up around others of their background or in diverse neighborhoods where no one race is in the majority. And while most people of color have some moment of feeling othered or different, it doesn't always happen around food, nor does it happen with the same intensity. "I absolutely never [felt shame]," said Ren. "I felt bad for my white American friends and the boring-ass food they ate."

Annu Subramanian seems like the archetypal protagonist in a lunchbox-moment story. She was born in Nebraska to Indian parents, and for about ten years she and her parents lived in a small town in South Dakota before moving to San Diego. "My skin is brown and my name is twenty-one letters long. I clearly stuck out in South Dakota," she said. And yet, stories about children of color being belittled for their food never resonated with her, because they never resembled her experience. Her parents sent her to school with both Indian and non-Indian food, and her classmates responded to her Indian lunches with either genuine curiosity or "at worst boredom," not derision. They even asked for it when they came over to her house. "I never ran into that 'Indian people smell' [stereotype]," she said.

She admits she was free to pack what she wanted for lunch, so she only brought Indian food when she was in the mood for it. "I think if I had been forced to take it, it might have been different," she said, and it's not as though she didn't feel different from her peers at times. But she loved Indian food. What was more alienating were the books she read in middle school about brown people feeling embarrassment and pain around what they ate, with the assumption that this feeling was shared by all children of immigrants. "I always believed it to be universal, even though it hadn't happened to me," she said. "I'm still trying to find the words around it, but I became aware of the lunchbox moment as archetype, so I think I was always waiting for something like that to happen."

The expectation that being brown or an immigrant in America inherently meant suffering and shame was frustrating to both Ren and Subramanian. "[It was alienating] as a kid because I just thought that's how I was supposed to be and feel, because activists [and] progressives were positioned as good and insightful, and if I didn't agree, it meant I was a bad and clueless person about my own experiences," said Ren. They recalled reading *Yell-oh Girls!*, a collection of essays by young Asian American women, and feeling like none of it spoke to them. Ren was annoyed that the experiences of a certain group of Asian Americans were packaged as if they represented everybody. "I don't know a single person in real life who felt bad about their Asian immigrant food growing up, just online stories," they said.

Subramanian recognizes it may have been unusual that her white peers responded to her family's Indian cooking with curiosity and joy, but even if her experience wasn't typical, it was still hard to see media that basically didn't acknowledge her experience could exist. The lunchbox moment's prevalence "narrows the frames we can use to tell our stories," she said. "I would hate to see someone who doesn't have any shame around their food see yet another story of bullying because of it, and then believe they *should* be ashamed!"

Even for people whose lunch experiences did resemble the

archetype, certain details were fattened by the trope. Krutika Mallikarjuna, who moved to the US from the state of Karnataka in India as a toddler, remembers her first lunchbox moment. "I would sit down at lunch and I would open up the lunchbox, [and kids would say], 'What is that weird goopy thing that looks like poop in your Tupperware?' " Instead of being ashamed, she was angry. "I was like, 'How dare you? This is okra saaru. This is the most delicious meal in the world.' " However, in the interest of having a less dramatic cafeteria experience, she recognized that she had to start bringing a more American lunch, which led to a different kind of lunchbox moment.

By middle school, Mallikarjuna's mom began making her sandwiches, but sandwiches that in no way resembled anything her white friends recognized. "I'd open up my sandwich and on one slice of bread would just be plain unsalted butter, and on the other side would be orange marmalade with the skin in it, which I fucking hate," she said. Even when her lunches consisted of "Western" food, there was something different about them. But Mallikarjuna's sandwiches turned into a running joke with her friends, a joke inspired by love, not discrimination. After all, they all clamored for Indian snacks whenever they went to her house. "I'm sure in retrospect there was a little bit of, like, 'Oh, she's foreign,' which is a little gross," she said. "But at the same time, we were eleven or twelve, so I think I can let my middle-school friends slide on that." They were clumsily curious and not at all interested in ostracizing her, and instead of being a moment of exclusion, lunch became a site of fun and connection.

Others confronted feelings of shame about their family's food derived from media and culture, even if they found support (or indifference) among their peers. Food writer Karon Liu, whose parents moved to Toronto from Hong Kong when he was a baby, said he can't remember anyone getting teased for their lunch in his school full of Chinese and other immigrant kids. But it didn't take bullying to make him feel ashamed of Chinese cuisine anyway. "So much of my feelings toward food were shaped by television and pop culture," he said. The movies and TV shows he watched positioned Chinese food as "weird," full of "gross" ingredients and prone to making people sick. He began throwing out the lunches his parents packed him, even though many of the kids at school ate the same things, and asked them to cook him more Western food. But he still enjoyed himself at Chinese restaurants. Even with the discomfort, his relationship with Chinese food wasn't black-and-white.

Stories about white people finding unfamiliar food off-putting, like the scene in *A Christmas Story* where the family is shocked and disgusted at the head on a Peking duck, and about immigrants feeling shame about their food resonated with Liu as a child, but he thinks they may have limited his understanding of the breadth of the immigrant experience. During an interview, he recalls asking Elaine Lui, of Lainey Gossip, if she felt ashamed of Chinese food growing up. "I was expecting the answer where it's like, 'Oh, yeah, I was made fun of all the time, blah, blah, blah, blah, blah.' And then Lainey was like, 'No, I never resented Chinese food—it's delicious and my family made me proud of it, so no.' " Shocked, Liu realized that while his feelings of shame were very real, they were also enforced by cultural narratives implying that mortification and bullying are the only experiences an immigrant can have. "Now I'm kind of wondering if I rebuilt my childhood memories in order to ft that narrative."

In 2016, I wrote an essay about struggle and Pizza Hut's stuffed crust. In 1995, I was a half-white, half-Indian child living in Manhattan, with grandparents across the river in New Jersey and a taste for cheese. In the essay, I am ashamed of many things: of liking Pizza Hut (a chain, even though I was from the pizza capital of New York City), of the Indian food my grandma cooked, but also of not liking Indian food, even though it was the food of my family. I wrote about the things that caused that shame, too, like seeing my classmates mocked in the cafeteria for eating "anything other than standard American food." It painted a familiar arc to anyone who has read a personal essay by a child of immigrants— childhood frustration, navigating the space between two cultures, American prejudice, all bending toward the acceptance and unity of adulthood. And upon rereading it earlier this year, I realized a lot of it wasn't really true.

The truth is, I wasn't ashamed of Indian food or my Indianness. I was curious about that part of my culture sometimes, but mostly indifferent. I was pretty content in my racial identity, the way one is content with most facts. And I never saw anyone being mocked for their lunch. It wasn't like I was consciously lying through the process of writing the Pizza Hut essay. Instead, not being a good enough writer or deep enough thinker to identify what, exactly, had caused me such distress as a child, I resorted to illustrating my feelings with a more common narrative: the lunchbox moment. I didn't know how to write about being a mixed-race child of immigrants in a way that didn't involve shame or bullying, and the familiar cafeteria scene offered the structure I needed to help my story land. Regardless of whether or not it actually rang true for me, this trope felt familiar enough, and if it was true for people *like* me, some deep part of my brain assumed it must have been true for me as well.

Reading the essay now, it's clear to me I was after a sense of belonging—and so much of belonging for people in marginalized groups has to do with shared struggle. Which sucks! We are more than that! But that common experience means being able to say to people who share parts of your identity that, yes, the white people, the rich people, the colonizers hurt me too. Here is what they did. Here is what they said. This is when the kids bullied me for my lunch. This is when my boyfriend turned his nose at the food my parents served him. This is when they knocked on my door and told me the smells of my cooking were making them sick. And after the description of pain comes the eye rolling, and then the laughter, the kind that says *I know what you know* and *I've been where you've been* and *we.*

"Belonging" doesn't mean one thing. Beyond the imperative to fit in with one's white American peers and their white American food, there's the desire to belong with other immigrants, with one's classmates, or with one's family. For many, though, part of the desire to share their lunchbox moment isn't just to commiserate with other members of the diaspora but to tell a story that white people can sympathize with. In some ways, being bullied for your food *is* universal—who can't relate to the feeling of being taunted for something completely outside of your control?

And most of the time, the lunchroom drama is a story with a satisfying ending for both parties. The food in question is often now more widely beloved, so the immigrant narrator is no longer directly bullied; at the least, they've grown stronger and more self-assured. And white readers can pat themselves on the back, knowing they're too open-minded to totally dismiss another culture's cuisine. Confronting racism becomes as easy as "try new food," and they get to be the Brian who shows Justin that not all non-immigrant Americans are so prejudiced. White people, essentially, get to be the hero.

These stories are "sellable to an editor," Mallikarjuna says. She jokes that white editors love it when a brown person writes about their trauma, whether in a children's book, a personal essay, or an op-ed for a food magazine. If mainstream culture continues to downplay immigrant and POC voices, when these writers do have the chance to tell a story, it has to be a clear, compelling one. Being bullied for your lunch, only to grow up and find white people putting chile crisp on everything, is a trajectory that's easy to understand—and easy to sell to a white editor. What's more, it often operates on a personal scale that makes these issues manageable. The lunchbox moment doesn't require the reader to think about how class, religion, or caste could all change an immigrant's experience. It doesn't point out all the invisible ways immigrants and people of color are made to feel unwelcome. It doesn't allow for muted or shifting feelings, or the complications of systemic racism. It's just the hard clarity of Us versus Them, Shame versus Triumph, a white boy telling you you're gross and a different white boy telling you he actually likes lumpia. The white gaze expects brown suffering, and even if these stories of shame and bullying are true, they can also serve to enforce that suffering. Suddenly, belonging means catering to the stories white people assume we carry.

With the Pizza Hut essay, I wanted to configure my feelings into a recognizable shape to become part of that *we*. Part of that is just what writing is—highlighting certain things and ignoring others, shepherding the reader to see what you want them to see. But it was so easy to guide myself into an imagined past where I felt things like shame over my heritage, fear of ridicule, and pressure to be a version of Indian I didn't want to be. There are true things in there: my reluctance to try a lot of Indian food because I only ate it when visiting my grandparents, my frustration with the idea that any one of my identity labels was incompatible with the others, my deep love of cheese. But mostly I gave in to the lunchbox narrative, and I didn't notice, and of course no one else did either. Indian and non-Indian friends told me how relatable it was, because it is, because I made it into a story for other people.

And in doing so, I trampled over an opportunity to expand what *we* could mean.

While researching this piece, I finally experienced a sense of belonging. I felt the fluttering energy, the urge to shout "Me too!" when someone names an experience, but backward—it was the excitement over *not* experiencing the thing I thought was universal. And while it is incredibly important to acknowledge the suffering, there are so many more ways to connect, to belong. "A lot of this is just solved by sharing more voices, more honesty, more of the shitty experiences, and more opportunities to demonstrate pride," said Subramanian. Our relationship with food can be shameful but also joyful, confusing, ambivalent, and antagonistic. And there should be room for all of it, and all of us. "I never felt shame around my food and never thought to. That story should ft somewhere, too."

JULIA SONENSHEIN

Starving Toward Deliverance

FROM *Catapult*

CONTENT WARNINGS FOR THIS ESSAY INCLUDE
REFERENCES TO: dieting, anti-fatness, and eating disorders.

THE FIRST AND only time I ever felt God's arms around me, holding me to his breast like I was something very precious, I was shitting my brains out at the Target in Brooklyn's Atlantic Terminal. In the stall, I had been shivering and dripping cold sweat; now I was warmed, wrapped in spun gold. The feeling was corporeal: arms around me, rocking me slightly. Part of me panicked and part of me melted—*God is real,* I thought. *How?* In his embrace, I moved toward salvation, deliverance: I was becoming empty, my stomach concave, free.

It was Christmas Eve—my last day after a solid year with little to no food. To start the new chapter, I'd just eaten a slice of chocolate cake my partner made me buy from the Starbucks inside the store and that landed me, almost instantly, in the bathroom. We were there on a mission to buy pajamas before he drove me to Philadelphia and dropped me off at an eating disorder treatment center, where I would be fed breakfast, lunch, and dinner and made to drink a nutrition shake if I couldn't complete my meals.

After Target, we went to a movie theater and saw *I, Tonya,* anything to distract me from the place I'd found myself and to give my partner a chance to look away from me, the person he couldn't recognize. In the movie theater, I braced against the AC and ate chocolate-covered raisins, the flavor overpowering me. I didn't reach for my partner's hand but hugged myself tight. There were no other arms around my body. The God I had made of starvation—the one I had worshiped my whole life—had left me.

In *The Dieter's Prayer Book*—one of hundreds of devotionals for dieters that I find years later, scrolling mindlessly on an Instagram algorithm that continues to serve me diet content—author Heather Harpham Kopp writes, "[A] prayer a day keeps the weight away!" Her diets have failed, she writes, and it is only through a deep spiritual practice that she has managed to keep her weight off. It's God that you need, not food: "It's not coincidence that when Jesus was on earth, He declared several times, 'I am the bread of life.' "

There is an entire industry of Christian weight-loss programs. Christian weight-loss books sell tens of millions of copies to scores of adherents—who might also buy the associated fitness DVDs, nutritional supplements with questionable medical foundations, branded toothpaste, and the countless sequels and spin-offs of the bestselling titles. They might pay $19.99 a month for a video series or $69.99 for a six-week workshop or $1,495 for six weeks of individual coaching. The scope of Christian weight-loss programs is astronomical: it's estimated to be a $1 billion market. Other religions have their own weight-loss approaches but without the same scale and influence. I roll my eyes while taking in these numbers, before I redden at the memory that I, too, have spent countless dollars on fitness, supplements, DVDs, subscriptions, anything. When it comes to our bodies—and to our own salvation—we are all easy marks.

Kate Bowler explains the onset of Christian weight loss as related to the prosperity gospel in her book *Blessed: A History of the American Prosperity Gospel*. The prosperity gospel is the notion that wealth and health are divine rights afforded to the faithful who invest in themselves—especially by tithing into their increasingly corporate houses of worship. The prosperity gospel began to evolve in the early nineteenth century, going from philosophical thought to the ten-thousand-plus-person megachurches that dot the American (and world) landscape.

Divine healing requires that the supplicant both ask God to be made new and to actively accept the healing. If an ill person did not recover, it was because they did not adequately let God in. Poor health—like poverty in the prosperity gospel's wealth thread—is a spiritual failing. It was perhaps inevitable that as the prosperity gospel began to integrate with scientific advances to guarantee divine health, the spiritual imperative toward health began to overlap with the American obsession with weight loss through self-control. It is now widely understood that health and fatness are not remotely mutually exclusive, but this ideology hinged on the false belief that they were connected.

The mix of diet culture and religious judgment was easy to come by: "Teachings on food and exercise dripped with judgment as they piled up the sins of obesity: gluttony, bondage, idolatry, and moral weakness," Bowler writes. Satan came on Saran-wrapped plates—a slice of cake, a cherry cobbler. Worse, Satan was inside the faithful, for fat had a demonic root.

To exorcise the evil within came a series of options to pray—and buy—your way thin. In *Born Again Bodies: Flesh and Spirit in American Christianity*, R. Marie Griffith culls together a reading list: 1957's *Pray Your Weight Away* proclaimed any "extra" weight as being "pounds of sin." Three years later, an article appeared in the *American Weekly* that became a book called *I Prayed Myself Slim*. And then came the wildly popular, oft-copied *Devotions for Dieters*, published in 1967, which named an inability to control appetites as "dietary idolatry." The list goes on: Joel Osteen with his fitness DVD, Pat Robertson with his shake—stretching into the 1980s, 1990s, and 2000s.

But in the late 1980s, diet culture was reaching a fever pitch.

There to raise the devotees' hands up in praise or plea—higher and in masses greater than anyone before her—was Gwen Shamblin Lara.

I was not raised in the evangelical church, but it is impossible to decouple the culture in which I came of age from the church's influence: from sexuality to gender to even personality, entering young womanhood in the aughts meant living in the shadow of a certain version of Christ. You didn't have to believe in him to be punished for your sins.

This was George W. Bush's America, the surge of purity culture, of modest clothing, of compulsory heterosexuality. I forced myself to dream at night of a boy my age touching my shoulders. I hung magazine cutouts of heartthrobs on my wall; I thought of each of them as my future husband. I understood the danger in my body, that men might look. My body, which grew hips and breasts while

I still had braces and long braids, was a weapon I didn't know how to wield.

I read in the magazines that were supposed to teach me how to become a woman to swish mouthwash around in my mouth to trick myself into fullness, on pages next to wedding spreads and blow job tips. Men like gaps between your legs, they told me. Men like thin fingers to put a ring on. Men like a girl who can eat a steak (but take small bites!). Drive him crazy by wearing his white shirt the next morning before he leaves for work, the shirttails billowing out behind you like an angel. You'll look so small in his shirt. Make him breakfast. Men don't like egg whites, but you can make them taste good with enough salt and hot sauce. The way to a man's heart is through his stomach. Ten core exercises to get a flat tummy. You're not hungry, you're thirsty.

The sex educator Erica Smith works with people who have left evangelical purity culture to build their own fulfilling relationships to their bodies, desire, and sex. She draws compelling connections between purity culture and diet culture. Both assert that "your body's natural appetites are bad for you, whether your sexual appetite or your appetite for food," she says. And both purity culture and diet culture operate in the same way: they "completely disconnect humans from trusting their own bodies—from being able to trust themselves at all," she says. From assessing hunger signals to sexual desire, these systems of control take the agency out of the person's body and make it a collective decision: a decision for their families, their churches, or their country to decide for them.

Lying in bed under the taped-up heartthrobs with their floppy haircuts, I knew I hungered for something. I didn't know what, but I hoped that if I chewed enough ice like the magazine told me to, I could go to bed feeling full. Full enough.

The orientation video for the Weigh Down Basics program opens with John 4:34: "My food is to do the will of him who sent me and to finish his work." Gwen Shamblin Lara appears on-screen, unforgettable with her trademark blonde bouffant. She introduces her "medically sound and faith-based" weight-loss program that she started in 1986, one that teaches you to "learn the self-control of a thin eater, someone who can stop in the middle of a candy bar and have no desire to eat the second half."

The program started out of a mall in Memphis but moved to a

Baptist church in the early nineties. By the late nineties, the program had over 250,000 adherents scattered on every continent, especially after the 1997 publication of Lara's book, *The Weigh Down Diet.*

Her book and the videos I find on YouTube are hard to stomach—steeped in an unapologetic anti-fatness. There are, in theory, no forbidden foods in the Weigh Down Diet (which, Shamblin repeatedly asserts, is *not,* despite the title, a diet at all). Instead, restriction of quantity is key. She advises a massive reduction in intake. One should only eat when one has achieved what Lara defines as "true hunger": when one's stomach growls. ("If you are not sure that this feeling is hunger," she writes, "just wait a little longer.")

Her diet wasn't some wingnut product. She was widely accepted by mainstream media, appearing on *Larry King Live, Good Morning America, The View, The Tyra Banks Show,* and countless others. Like her predecessors, Lara is clear about the biblical mandate to be thin: God wants us thin, in control, and all of us, apparently, strive for thinness.

The Weigh Down Diet professes that God and food are antithetical to each other: "We love the master that we obey," she writes. "And we obey the master we love. We cannot love both God and food." Similarly, a woman offers a testimonial in the video: "It taught me to fall out of love with food and into love with God." (I will confess something to you now that shames me: I read this, and an old part of me says, *Could you make God real again? Could you love him more than food?*) Lara addresses a longing heart—a vast emptiness. "The truth is going to set you permanently free," she says. "The love of food will disappear—salvation!"

To Lara, to lick brownie batter from your finger isn't its own godly delight but a false idol of misdirected worship, a moment where one loses control over one's desires. As if Christians don't join hands and say grace, thanking God for the bounty of the food on their table. The Weigh Down Diet was certainly the most popular Christian weight-loss program, with 1.2 million copies of the book sold. It still has participants today, training their eyes away from the dinner table, asking God to take control.

In my first year of college, I cried most nights, lonely in the wrong city, at the wrong school, in a bout of clinical depression. There were nice girls on my floor who met down the hall every Monday night. They invited me to join them, and so I did.

It was, predictably, a Bible study. I munched on the chips and salsa and nodded along. I always told them I wasn't religious, but they kept inviting me back, and soon I joined in, debating, asking questions, expressing skepticism. They struggled with elements of self-control, especially around sex, but they always had answers for me: "I know God," they would say to me. "I know he's here as much as I know you're here."

We prayed together and I cast wishes. *Ten pounds,* I'd beg. *Make my stomach smaller. Take away my arms.* I wanted to believe—in God and in thinness, that a different body would mean a different life.

I wanted a miracle. I reached for him, but no hands received me, and I looked around as the young, slender women in that dorm room raised their hands, mouthed silently, let the spirit pour into them, speaking a shared emotional language that I didn't understand. *Why not me?* It was a loneliness I had never known, to be refused on earth and in heaven.

When the leader of the group one day asked me, "What would it mean for your life if you accepted Jesus Christ into your heart today?" all I could say was "I'm sorry."

"It's okay," she said.

But we didn't talk again after that, and I didn't go back to the group. I had failed at being godly, I knew, and God had failed me. I hadn't made myself a vessel, hadn't made myself clean and worthy, and he hadn't filled me.

But I wasn't searching for God for salvation in the afterlife, but for deliverance into a smaller body on earth. My search for God was a vehicle for an obsession, not a devotion. It wasn't until years later, when I played God in my life by denying myself food, that I found the thinness I prayed for, which I mistook for divinity.

Some years after a crisis of faith for Lara's followers, in which she broke with the typical evangelical notion of Trinitarianism, Lara died in 2021 in a plane crash with other church leaders. I wonder about her final moments, if her stomach growled, if she regretted the candy bars she'd left half-eaten.

Lara's teachings didn't disappear. Americans are still desperately trying to lose weight and are turning to their faiths for guidance. As I scroll Instagram one night many years after that day in Target, I come across the page of a woman I'll call Emily, who posts a reel about working out with skirts over her leggings. God convinced her to make a change to a more modest wardrobe, she captions a reel. Emily becomes my gateway to Christian weight-loss coaches on social media. She leads me to a woman I'll call Jenna, another Christian weight-loss coach—not a nutritionist, certified trainer, or medical professional.

I message Jenna, set up an interview. My first thought is to pitch an article, an exposé of this industry. Instead, her smile is warm and friendly, and I want to hug her. I introduce myself and hear myself say: "I am a searcher, still looking for my spiritual home."

Can an atheist have a spiritual home? I don't believe in God anymore, even as I sought him out as I became an adult, hoping for a different answer. I've long since stopped making a god of starvation, the one who I remember from the bathroom. But something pricks at me, some want that I can't define. I search for the words but come up empty.

Jenna is among the legion I find on Instagram under various hashtags: #christianweightloss, for one, or #fit4christ. She, among countless others, has what they believe is a biblical mandate toward their definition of an ideal body—that is to say, one that is thin. On their business websites where they offer their programs, they cite various quotes from the New Testament. Any number of verses can be interpreted to tell you to lose weight if you're looking for it.

Jenna tells me that she used to be fat and has since dropped 150 pounds with prayer. She's also cut out sugar and flour, foods that she said she used to worship instead of God. These foods were her sins, she says. Through what she calls "food boundaries" (banned foods) and prayer, God, she says, has delivered her into a thin body.

She offers weight-loss coaching to other women and posts to her almost twenty thousand followers questions like: "Does your relationship with food bring glory to God?"

There are so many more: men who lift weights for God's glory, countless women who pray instead of eat. There are so many people complaining of emptiness, who are searching through their Bibles for answers, who find the problem is themselves, their wants, their cravings, their desires. They are waiting for new bodies, for God to save them. To relieve them of their needs, to make them whole.

It would be easy to pin the people behind Christian weight-loss efforts as craven hucksters selling snake oil. But it's more complex than that. Yes, there is money flowing directly from the wallets of the devoted into megachurch pastors' hands. But through the interpretation of the prosperity gospel, the riches afforded to these people seem like a divine right. Even their faith, which can seem performative or convenient, rings true: God, in his infinite wisdom and benevolence, has provided these people with a path to wealth and health.

Christian weight loss hardly has a monopoly on the notion of making thinness a god. Pick up a health magazine, and you'll find headlines accusing you of worshiping sugar. SoulCycle devotees sing of their spiritual experiences on stationary bikes. It takes all of two minutes to buy a tank top that reads TRAINING IS MY RELIGION. THE GYM IS MY CHURCH.

Fail at the Weigh Down Diet? Buy more tapes or in-person workshops. Fail at Weight Watchers? Sign up for another program by entering your credit card number. Live your faith? Donate to a certain politician. Live your values? Buy "ethical" products. Christian weight-loss programs didn't invent anything that wasn't already there. They simply encapsulate a distinctly American, capitalist truth: Your god is only as good as the money you spend to worship him. Your salvation is determined by the amount of control he is able to exert over you.

Diets, like purity culture, are highly effective "systems of control" that "keep the people in power in power," Erica Smith says. Inside the church, outside the church, we are eager supplicants, thirsty buyers, ready and willing to allow someone else, someone more in control than we are, to take the wheel. *You are not your own, for you were bought with a price.*

In churches, in gyms, in America, it is not enough to feel hungry and to eat. You have to be changing yourself, investing in yourself, shrinking yourself, controlling yourself, controllable, until you are malleable and worthy.

The year after I left the residential eating disorder treatment center in Philadelphia was the darkest of my life. Without starvation to numb me, I sank into a depression so severe I thought I'd never crawl out, that I would die there, alone in a hole where no one could reach me. My entire body ached, both from what is called "refeeding syndrome" and from the despair, which clawed at my insides. Medication didn't help, and a doctor suggested electro-shock therapy, but I was too afraid.

Without being able to worship thinness, without being able to fast to prove my devotion, I was adrift, purposeless. I was lonelier than ever, divorced from my body, from my relationships, from faith in anyone and anything.

I negotiated with myself throughout those early days of re-covery: *I can always lose weight again if I want to.* But even as I am settling into years of recovery, there is a truth I have had to face more difficult than an absence of God, one that leaves me bereft, one that keeps the Weigh Down Diet and Weight Watchers alike in business: diets don't work. The control we believe we have over our bodies is fleeting. Most people gain back the weight they lose, if not more.

There was a turning point: medication that finally helped, ther-apy that was a godsend, supportive relationships that were as close to divine as I can imagine. But it was messy—it meant untangling a lifetime of worthiness and godliness and a body that wouldn't cooperate. It meant finding new ways to define worthiness, some-thing divorced from my size—to find something redeeming in this earthly form of mine. Untangling also meant divesting from the political structure of anti-fatness and grappling with the ways in which I benefit from and uphold that system.

The mess remains. When I became what in eating-disorder treatment is called "weight restored," it felt like the biggest fail-ing of my life. It may seem small to you, shallow. You might pass judgment—you wouldn't be the first. But it's simply true. I had been nurtured, like a lamb, for one purpose; mine was to be thin.

Like religion, dieting—and later anorexia—gave an organizing principle to my life, something to strive for. There was ritual in my daily calorie allotment, worship in weighing my portions and counting my ribs. It gave me a thrill of ecstasy when the scale moved in the direction I wanted it to, and it answered questions about my purpose. Like Bible study, it gave me fellowship—other people trying to lose weight in my family, my social circle, on Insta-gram. And it gave me something to fill my time: tracking calories, getting my steps in, meal planning.

But it left me lacking. No matter how devoted I was, it was never enough. And diets—and eating disorders—have an end date. The body fights back. Mine wanted to live.

When my body returned to its prestarvation size, I had to find faith in something else, something that wasn't fleeting, something that wasn't killing me.

If diets don't work, what does? I used to ask myself: *Does religion? Will God give me something that starvation won't? Is someone there to take me in? To wrap me up? Where is my body's home?* But these are the wrong questions, I know. They leave me chasing vapors, seeking something that offers no answers for me. They ask me to look outside myself, above myself, when the problem is here, deep in me, internal. The better questions are *What am I hungry for today? How can I feed it? Can I give myself the gift of meeting my own desires?*

I write this with years of distance: distance from that treatment center in Philadelphia that saved my life, distance from dieting, distance from those Bible studies in a dorm room in Boston. There are for me, now, more unanswered questions than ever, and I am comfortable with my place as a searcher. But it is not accurate that I am searching for a spiritual home like I told Jenna. Not any longer, at least.

I am my own place to come home to, my own house of worship. Eating the first ripe peach of the summer, lying next to my partner in the grass, brightening at the sound of my sister's laugh, cooking holiday meals with my friends, who let themselves into the apartment using their own keys, pressing my fingers into the softness of my stomach and feeling the abundance, the little miracles of daily life, of having a body that recovered, that fought to live. Of feeling grounded, my feet on the ground, my eyes cast forward. Joy, despair, a burnt piece of toast, homemade ricotta. That—all of it—is its own glory.

It is deliverance.

SAM DEAN

The Man Who Didn't Invent Flamin' Hot Cheetos

FROM *Los Angeles Times*

FOR THE LAST decade, Richard Montañez has been telling the story of how he invented Flamin' Hot Cheetos. The world has been eating it up.

It goes like this: he was working as a janitor at Frito-Lay's Rancho Cucamonga plant when he dreamed up a chile-covered Cheeto and believed in himself enough to call up the chief executive to pitch his spicy idea.

Corporate backstabbers tried to sabotage Montañez for stepping out of line, but he out-hustled them, driven by a hunger to succeed. Flamin' Hots became a runaway hit, and Montañez rose through the ranks and became an icon.

Watching his many recorded speaking engagements, it's easy to see why his story has taken off.

Montañez is a charismatic speaker, and his tale of a Mexican American underdog whose ingenuity conquered the corporate world is a rags-to-riches fable baked into the origin of a wildly popular snack.

With their spicy kick and neon red flavor dust, Flamin' Hot Cheetos have inspired viral rap videos, Instagram-worthy menu items, and streetwear designs. Schools have banned the snack altogether over concerns about its popularity with children. Clear revenue numbers are hard to come by, but nearly every major Frito-Lay line, from Smartfood popcorn to Funyuns, now has a Flamin' Hot variety on the market.

Montañez has built a lucrative second career out of telling and selling this story, appearing at events for Target, Walmart, Harvard, and USC, among others, and commanding fees of $10,000 to $50,000 per appearance.

His second memoir, *Flamin' Hot: The Incredible True Story of One Man's Rise from Janitor to Top Executive,* is out in June from an imprint of Penguin Random House.

A biopic based on his life, to be directed by Eva Longoria and produced by Christian super-producer DeVon Franklin for Searchlight Pictures, is set to begin filming this summer. Both the book and the movie were sold after bidding wars—Montañez's story is undeniably hot.

There's just one problem: Montañez didn't invent Flamin' Hot Cheetos, according to interviews with more than a dozen former Frito-Lay employees, the archival record, and Frito-Lay itself.

"None of our records show that Richard was involved in any capacity in the Flamin' Hot test market," Frito-Lay wrote in a statement to the *Los Angeles Times,* in response to questions about an internal investigation whose existence has not been previously disclosed. "We have interviewed multiple personnel who were involved in the test market, and all of them indicate that Richard was not involved in any capacity in the test market.

"That doesn't mean we don't celebrate Richard," the statement continued, "but the facts do not support the urban legend."

Flamin' Hots were created by a team of hotshot snack food professionals starting in 1989, in the corporate offices of Frito-Lay's headquarters in Plano, Texas. The new product was designed to compete with spicy snacks sold in the inner-city mini-marts of the Midwest. A junior employee with a freshly minted MBA named Lynne Greenfeld got the assignment to develop the brand—she came up with the Flamin' Hot name and shepherded the line into existence.

Montañez did live out a less Hollywood version of his story, ascending from a plant worker to a director focused on marketing. He also pitched new product initiatives, which may have changed the path of his career.

But Montañez began taking public credit for inventing Flamin' Hots in the late 2000s, nearly two decades after they were invented. First he talked about it in speeches at local business and philanthropy award ceremonies. Then the online media, hungry for a feel-good story, took his claims viral.

And nobody at Frito-Lay stopped him. Most of the original Flamin' Hot team had retired by the 2000s, but the few who remained let the story spread unchecked.

Greenfeld contacted Frito-Lay in 2018 after first seeing that Montañez was taking credit for Flamin' Hot Cheetos, triggering a company investigation. That process unearthed evidence calling his account into question and led the company to the conclusion it shared with the *Times*: "We value Richard's many contributions to our company, especially his insights into Hispanic consumers, but we do not credit the creation of Flamin' Hot Cheetos or any Flamin' Hot products to him."

The producers of his biopic, despite being informed of problems by Frito-Lay in 2019, announced a cast for the movie in early May.

The producers of the film and the publisher of Montañez's latest book did not respond to requests for comment before publication of this article.

The core of Montañez's story rested on the pitch meeting that he says changed his life, where he sold his idea of Flamin' Hot Cheetos directly to the Frito-Lay elite. In his new memoir, he lays out a dramatic scene, with more than a hundred people, most of them "leading executives," assembled alongside the CEO in a conference room at the Rancho Cucamonga complex to witness his presentation.

The *Times* spoke with twenty people who worked at the Frito-Lay divisions responsible for new product development thirty-two years ago, when Flamin' Hot Cheetos were first extruded into existence. None recalls anything like the episode Montañez describes taking place.

"If that story existed, believe me, we would have heard about it," said Ken Lukaska, who worked as a product manager for the core Cheetos brand when Flamin' Hots were rolling out nationally. "This guy should run for office if he's that good at fooling everyone."

The idea that grew into Flamin' Hots didn't come from Rancho Cucamonga, or California, or even Frito-Lay's home base in Texas.

Six of the former employees remember inspiration coming from the corner stores of Chicago and Detroit. One of the earliest newspaper articles about the product corroborates that detail: a Frito-Lay spokesperson told the *Dallas Morning News* in March

1992 that "our sales group in the northern United States asked for them."

Fred Lindsay, a retired Frito-Lay salesman from the South Side of Chicago, feels that he can be more specific: "I'm the one that was responsible for getting us into Flamin' Hot products."

The late '80s were a cutthroat time in corporate foodstuffs, and PepsiCo Inc., Frito-Lay's parent company, was fighting a marketing war on three fronts. In its restaurant division, Pizza Hut was clawing its way into delivery to fend off Domino's, and Taco Bell resorted to free soda refills to undercut the competition.

Pepsi's beverage business was locked in the decade-long cola wars, with its flashy CEO, Roger Enrico, pouring millions into ad deals with Michael Jackson and Madonna to peel people away from King Coke.

Frito-Lay's battle was quieter but just as brutal. The company had been the reigning champ of salty snacks for decades, ever since Frito Co. and H.W. Lay & Co. had first merged, but Anheuser-Busch had come out swinging with its national Eagle Snacks line, and Frito-Lay was losing ground.

Lindsay for years worked the sales beat in Chicago and the Great Lakes region, where he witnessed spicy products from regional competitors "just blow off the shelf" at corner stores and gas stations. So he started beating the drum for the marketing department to gin up something. "I was fighting mad to try and get hot stuff in the market," Lindsay said.

By the time he got promoted to corporate headquarters in Plano, working for the UDS business—shorthand for "up and down the street," meaning any liquor store, sundry shop, or mini-mart smaller than a grocery store—his idea had been taken up by the marketing department.

"The funny thing is, I heard maybe a year ago that some guy from California was taking credit for developing hot Cheetos, which is crazy," Lindsay said. "I'm not trying to take credit; I'm just trying to set the record straight."

The assignment to create spicy competitor products landed in the inbox of Sharon Owens, a product manager in the Single Serve group at the time. Unlike the mainline brands—Fritos, Doritos, Cheetos, and Lays—whose managers were expected to serve as custodians of just one product, Single Serve was organized around a format: individually wrapped products made for cramped mini-marts and customers with just a few quarters to spend.

Owens recalls that she assigned the project to a new employee: Greenfeld.

Flamin' Hot was Greenfeld's first project at the company when she started in the summer of 1989, fresh out of the MBA program at the University of North Carolina at Chapel Hill. Business degrees were practically required to get in the door at PepsiCo in those days, with rare exceptions made for people with BAs from Babson College, Enrico's alma mater.

Miguel Lecuona, an MBA classmate of Greenfeld's, joined the Single Serve team at the same time, working on beef sticks, sweet snacks, and other odd products that would sit by a mini-mart register. "I was on the cookie," Lecuona said, "and Lynne Greenfeld was on the small-bag business.

"We'd go on a field marketing tour and bring home fifty different bags of chips that we had never seen in our lives—they'd say we're losing sales to this kind of product line right now," Lecuona said, "and so Flamin' Hot was actually, you could call it a flavor idea."

Over the next few months, Greenfeld went on market tours of small stores in Chicago, Detroit, and Houston to get a better feel for what consumers craved. She worked with Frito-Lay's packaging and product design teams to come up with the right flavor mix and branding for the bags. She went with a chubby devil holding a Cheeto, Frito, or chip on a pitchfork, depending on the bag's contents, she recalls, a memory independently corroborated by newspaper archives.

By the summer of 1990, the product entered its test market. Frito-Lay's trademark for the Flamin' Hot name lists that August as the month the product made its debut.

A trio of Flamin' Hot snacks—Fritos, Cheetos, and Lays—hit small stores in Chicago, Detroit, Cleveland, and Houston, according to the *Dallas Morning News* article and newspaper ads for the new products in those regions.

Frito-Lay corroborated many of the details of this account, writing that "as early as 1989, there were regional competitive spicy products on the market," including a spicy, bright red potato chip from the Chicago snack company Jays.

"In response, Frito-Lay launched a test market of spicy Lay's,

Cheetos, Fritos, and Baken-ets in Chicago, Detroit, and Houston" beginning in August 1990, the company wrote in a statement.

Frito-Lay wrote that "a product or flavor extension is the work of a number of people across functions as diverse as R&D, sales, and marketing, all of whom are proud of the products they help create."

An internal promotional video for the Cheetos brand from the first quarter of 1991 serves as further proof that Flamin' Hots were already out in the world.

The nearly nine-minute video, which Lukaska shared with the *Times,* is a Day-Glo green-and-pink time capsule, with Frito-Lay execs in fashionably baggy suits touting the latest and greatest snack aimed at kids, Cheetos Paws. At one point, two DDB Needham advertising executives perform a *New Jack City*–era rap about the coolness of Chester himself. Flamin' Hots appear in the video for less than a second, in a rapid-fire slideshow set to MC Hammer's "U Can't Touch This," alongside two other minor brands of the day, Cheetos Curls and Cheetos Light.

The test markets soon proved that Lindsay's insight was right, and Greenfeld's execution worked. Flamin' Hot Cheetos and Lays rolled out across the country by early 1992 and would slowly grow to become a cult hit.

Greenfeld, who now goes by her married name, Leinmel, said she's "very proud" of leading the team that put Flamin' Hots into the world, and for coming up with the Flamin' Hot brand name.

"It is disappointing that twenty years later, someone who played no role in this project would begin to claim our experience as his own and then personally profit from it," she added.

Montañez did not respond to multiple requests for comment via email, phone, direct message, attempts to reach him through a publicity agent, and questions delivered to a family member at a home listed in Montañez's name.

Hours after initial publication of this story, Montañez posted a video to his Instagram account, addressed to "all you young leaders."

"I don't care what room you're in, there's always somebody in the room that's going to try to steal your destiny. They may even say you never existed," Montañez says to the camera. "I want you to do this: write down your history, because if you don't, somebody else will. Remember that. And also remember this, the best way to destroy a positive message is to destroy the messenger. Never allow that to happen to you. I'm certainly not going to allow it to happen to me."

The record of Flamin' Hot Cheetos first entering the market in 1990 points to an impossibility at the heart of Montañez's story all along.

In telling after telling, Montañez says he felt empowered to invent Flamin' Hot Cheetos after watching a motivational video from Enrico, the CEO of the company, that encouraged all Frito-Lay workers to "act like owners" and take charge of the business.

And time after time, he says that Enrico was the CEO whom he boldly called to pitch his idea and that Enrico flew out to Rancho Cucamonga weeks later to witness his pitch in person. In his new memoir, Montañez clearly restates this claim: Enrico's name appears sixty times in the text.

But Enrico did not work at Frito-Lay when Flamin' Hot products were developed. His move to Frito-Lay was announced in December 1990, and he took over control at the beginning of 1991—nearly six months after Flamin' Hots were already out in the test market.

When the Flamin' Hot line first entered test markets in the summer of 1990, Robert Beeby was leading Frito-Lay. Wayne Calloway was running the parent company, PepsiCo. Enrico was the president and CEO of PepsiCo Worldwide Beverages, the separate soft drink division of PepsiCo, leading the company in the cola wars.

Enrico went on to lead PepsiCo as a whole by the end of the '90s, and the first media mention of his "I Own the New Frito-Lay" campaign came in a May 1992 feature in *Ad Day*. He retired in 2001, and he died while snorkeling in the Cayman Islands in 2016. The *Times* found no public comments from him on Flamin' Hot Cheetos or any Flamin' Hot product.

Patti Rueff, who worked as Enrico's secretary for decades as he moved from the beverage business to Frito-Lay and on to the top of the parent company, vividly recalls Montañez calling her office to speak with Enrico—once he was already leading Frito-Lay, in 1992 or 1993, and after Flamin' Hot products were already on shelves.

One other Frito-Lay executive played a key role in Montañez's Flamin' Hot story: Al Carey, a Frito-Lay lifer who worked at the company for nearly forty years, rising through the executive suite to the top of the corporate pyramid.

Carey appears to be the only Frito-Lay executive who worked at the company at the time of Flamin' Hot's development to publicly endorse Montañez's version of events over the years.

In 1990, Carey was working as vice president of national sales out of the Plano offices. When Enrico came in, he promoted Carey to oversee a new vending machine and warehouse division in early 1992, and then to division president of Frito-Lay West, based in the Bay Area, at the end of that year.

Carey became president and CEO of Frito-Lay North America in 2006. In 2007, Montañez began telling his story in public, and the pair have made joint appearances at a number of public events over the course of their careers.

Montañez writes in his new memoir that he met Carey in the late 1980s, when the exec was taking a tour of the Cucamonga plant. When Montañez later called him for advice on pitching his idea for spicy Cheetos, he says, Carey encouraged him to call Enrico directly.

In an interview, Carey, sixty-nine, initially said that he first met Montañez after becoming division president for Frito-Lay West in December 1992, and that Montañez pitched him a set of products targeted at the Latino market. When asked how that timeline fits with the 1990 Flamin' Hot trademark and test market, Carey insisted that Montañez is the creator of Flamin' Hot Cheetos.

"The product that we know today as Flamin' Hot Cheetos was definitely not out in the market" before his meeting with Montañez, Carey said. "That product was developed by those guys in the plant."

When asked to explain the news clippings and former employee accounts that place Flamin' Hot Cheetos in the market two years earlier, Carey hedged his statement. "This is such a long time ago, I bet there was a spicy Cheeto in the Chicago, L.A., maybe Houston market, too," Carey said.

"Of all the people who are in PepsiCo or around PepsiCo, I have the most experience," he continued. "I can promise you for sure there was no brand development, no brand launched called Flamin' Hot Cheetos," Carey said, adding that if there was a prior spicy product on the market, it was reformulated to match Montañez's sample product. "The ingredients, that's the magic of the product," Carey said.

Frito-Lay's statement contradicted its former CEO. "According to our records, McCormick, Frito-Lay's longtime seasoning supplier, developed the Flamin' Hot seasoning and sent initial samples to Frito-Lay on Dec. 15, 1989," the statement said. "This is essentially the same seasoning Frito-Lay uses today."

Carey said he was unsure how to account for that contradiction. "I'm sure if you went back into the Frito-Lay history, OK, there's probably something in 1990 that was a test market on a spicy product," he said. "I'll be surprised if it was this same ingredient, but it could have been, I guess."

When asked about the pitch meeting central to Montañez's account, Carey said that Enrico was not in attendance.

"Of course stories grow, and the longer we get away from the date, the stories evolve," Carey said. "I'll bet Richard's added a little flavor to it."

He said that he "suggested strongly" that Montañez retire when he did, in 2019, if he wanted to pursue his career as a motivational speaker, memoirist, and film subject.

"You're theoretically not supposed to be giving a speech and being paid for it if you're still a part of the company," Carey said. "I said, this is a fun story; this shouldn't be a controversial story; your inclination to dramatize the story a little bit, you've got to keep away from that."

But he repeated that Montañez was key to Flamin' Hot Cheetos' success. Lots of products have grown into hits, he said, only after a charismatic leader comes along. "They may have not invented the ingredient, but they invented the energy that goes behind this thing and the positioning, and then it becomes successful," he said.

"Without Richard, this thing would not be out there," he concluded.

Beneath Montañez's story about Flamin' Hot Cheetos, visible through its inconsistencies and supported by the documented timeline of events, there is a real story of a man rising up the corporate ladder from factory floor to marketing executive, pitching some products along the way.

Montañez was born in Ontario to a Mexican American family

that lived in the unincorporated community of Guasti, a cluster of buildings and shops centered on vineyards east of Los Angeles, where some of the men in his family picked grapes for a living.

He dropped out of school—but not, as he has claimed in past media appearances, after the fourth grade or, as he claims in his new memoir, before the sixth. Montañez appears to have made it to at least the ninth grade—he is listed in the freshman class section of the Chaffey High yearbook of 1972 but disappears from the area's yearbooks after that.

Montañez got a job at the Frito-Lay plant in Rancho Cucamonga in the late 1970s. Although Montañez has at times said he was working as a janitor when he pitched Flamin' Hot Cheetos, Frito-Lay said its records show he was promoted to machinist operator by October 1977, shortly after his hiring. In that role, he writes in his new memoir, he spearheaded a program to reduce waste along the assembly line.

After Enrico moved to Frito-Lay and the motivational "I Own the New Frito-Lay" campaign rippled across the company, a single news clipping featuring Montañez provides a window into that moment in his career.

The *U.S. News and World Report* article from December 1993 focuses on businesses finding success by empowering their employees. The section on Frito-Lay talks about the plant in Rancho Cucamonga, where manager Steve Smith had taken up Enrico's initiative and gotten more front-line workers thinking about how to improve the business as a whole.

"Veteran machine operator Richard Montañez, thirty-seven, became so energized by Smith's new operating style that after listening to salesmen he developed a new ethnic-food concept aimed at the Hispanic market," the reporter writes. "After testing recipes and outlining a marketing strategy, Montañez burst forth with a kernel of an idea: Flamin' Hot Popcorn, which will soon make its debut."

An industry news wire announced that Flamin' Hot Popcorn did in fact hit shelves in March 1994, as an extension of the Flamin' Hot line that Greenfeld and her colleagues had rolled out four years earlier.

Around that time, Montañez began working on a line of products pitched specifically at the Latino market in the Los Angeles area: Sabrositas. Images that Montañez has posted to his Instagram account show that the Sabrositas line included Flamin' Hot Popcorn, two types of Fritos—Flamin' Hot and Lime and Chile Corn Chips—and a Doritos variety billed as buñuelito-style tortilla chips.

Roberto Siewczynski worked on the Sabrositas test market in 1994 as an outside consultant for Casanova, a Latino-focused wing of the ad agency McCann, and remembers Montañez being deeply involved in the process.

Siewczynski's recollection of the Sabrositas marketing campaign aligns with what Montañez describes in his memoir—though Montañez attaches his story to Flamin' Hot products, not the Sabrositas launch.

"I did go to Rancho Cucamonga," Siewczynski said, where he was surprised to learn that the Sabrositas project was being led by production and distribution workers, not the marketing department, as a community-driven campaign focused on the Latino market in Los Angeles. "It was, 'Hey, the plant really wants to do this; Richard really wants to do this,' and they cut out a lot of the traditional management."

He remembers Montañez as a colorful, engaging storyteller, well-liked by all of his coworkers at the plant. And he remembers a creation story, but one that focused on Lime and Chile Fritos, not Flamin' Hot Cheetos.

Montañez "told the whole story about how when he was a kid he would put lime and chile on his Fritos, and that was sort of the impetus for the product design," Siewczynski said.

In his new memoir, Montañez writes that he tapped into the local network of women hosting Tupperware parties to get Flamin' Hot Cheetos out to customers in Southern California as a way to bolster the struggling test market.

Siewczynski recalls the same story—for Sabrositas. "The product was rolled out without any mass media or advertising," he said. "We did a strategic partnership with Tupperware, where they would take the product to their parties," he added, recalling a mortifying presentation that he made as a twenty-two-year-old ad man to a room of hundreds of Tupperware ladies, who ribbed him onstage for being so young and handsome.

Frito-Lay records shared with the *Times* show that Montañez was promoted to a quality-control tech services specialist from 1998 to

2002, then left the plant and rose to a director-level position. He received a number of accolades from both community groups and PepsiCo CEOs along the way.

He's now retired in his early sixties, after a full career climbing the corporate ladder. Montañez made it, from rags to riches, from factory floor to corporate suite. He just didn't make Flamin' Hot Cheetos.

Flamin' Hot Cheetos became a cultural phenomenon in the 2000s. As early as 2005, school administrators considered banning them in the classroom because of their distracting popularity with students; Pasadena schools eventually prohibited them in 2012. Their first meme moment came in that same year, in a 2012 viral rap video, "Hot Cheetos and Takis," a song written and performed by a group of kids as part of an after-school program in north Minneapolis. The years since have seen pop-up restaurants and fashion lines, and countless Instagram-ready Flamin' Hot Cheetos menu items at restaurants across the country.

Montañez's story of the janitor who had invented Flamin' Hot Cheetos picked up traction, serving as fodder for blog posts and online videos. Montañez's own Instagram account accumulated tens of thousands of followers, and his TikTok following now tops 100,000.

But the people who had worked on the original Flamin' Hot line weren't watching viral videos or reading food blogs targeted at young audiences. Most of them had already left the company by the early 2000s. Most had already retired.

Greenfeld, the Flamin' Hot team leader, didn't see the story of the scrappy janitor who invented Flamin' Hot Cheetos until the summer of 2018, when she happened upon a blog post on the *Esquire* website.

Greenfeld was shocked to see someone taking credit for a product that she had worked on. She reached out to an acquaintance who was still working at Frito-Lay, according to emails viewed by the *Times,* asking if they had ever heard of the Montañez story, and if they knew anyone she could alert in the legal department that someone was claiming to have invented Flamin' Hot Cheetos.

Michele Thatcher, chief counsel in PepsiCo's global human resources department, wrote that she and the legal team "know Richard well," were aware of his book and movie projects, and were unsure what problem, if any, there might be with his story. Over the decades, the institutional memory had been lost.

Further email correspondence shows that the company launched an investigation into the question of Flamin' Hot's origin after Greenfeld's initial email.

In a December 2018 message, Leanne Oliver, general counsel at Frito-Lay North America, wrote that she didn't think there was "any question" that the Flamin' Hot test market predated "the Cucamonga meeting" where Montañez pitched some kind of product.

In a later email, another Frito-Lay lawyer, Susan Chao, wrote, "We know you and the Law Dept worked together to trademark 'Flamin' Hot' " but asked Greenfeld if she remembered who had invented the name. "I came up with the Flamin' Hot name on my own," Greenfeld replied.

The investigation soon came to an effective dead end. Montañez retired in March 2019. Carey, his corporate mentor, retired that same month.

The next month, Oliver wrote in an email that "Frito-Lay will continue to take the position that Flamin' Hot Cheetos was created by a team of people and, as with all of our products, we do not credit one person with a product invention or flavor extension."

Carey and Montañez appeared together soon after, at a June 2019 ceremony where Carey accepted a lifetime achievement award from the East Los Angeles Community Union. In a video created for the event, Montañez shifts his story, saying that it was Carey, and not Enrico, who created the motivational video that inspired him to create Flamin' Hot Cheetos in the first place, though he has since returned to his version of the story featuring Enrico.

Carey currently sits on the board of the Home Depot, serves as executive chairman of the North Carolina textiles company Unifi, and is on the board of a blank-check vehicle, Omnichannel Acquisition Corp.

Indra Nooyi, who was chairman and CEO of PepsiCo while Carey was running Frito-Lay and the Pepsi beverage business, has blurbed Montañez's new memoir, calling it a "tour de force." (Nooyi also retired in 2019.) Tom Greco, who took over at Frito-Lay once Carey moved to Pepsi, has also blurbed the book. Nooyi joined PepsiCo in 1994, and Greco worked in Frito-Lay's Canadian division until the early 2000s.

Montañez has spent much of his time since retirement working the speaker circuit, according to his social media accounts, delivering keynotes at in-person and virtual events for organizations such as Prudential Financial, the Philadelphia Eagles, recruitment tech company Indeed, call-center technology company Genesys, and at PestWorld 2019, the annual conference of the National Pest Management Association.

After the investigation and his retirement, Montañez has also repeatedly posted to his social media accounts photographs of what he claims are original design materials for Flamin' Hot Cheetos. Many have recently been deleted.

One photograph, posted to Instagram in October 2019 but now deleted, shows four pieces of lined notebook paper, labeled "mild," "reg," "hot," and "extra hot," with Cheetos piled on top of each. At the bottom of one, Montañez signed his name and wrote the date "1988."

In another post, now deleted, he wrote that he worked on the Doritos Salsa Rio flavor in 1998—a product that first hit test markets in 1987, according to *Advertising Age* articles from that year.

In public statements since conducting its internal investigation, Frito-Lay has struck a cautious tone.

In an August 2019 interview with *Fast Company* about Montañez's biopic, Frito-Lay Chief Marketing Officer Jennifer Saenz said that the company helped the film's producers piece together the historical information that exists on Flamin' Hot Cheetos.

Saenz then substantially repeated the statement that the company had sent to Lynne some months earlier: "At Frito-Lay, and PepsiCo, a product or flavor extension is the work of a number of people across functions as diverse as R&D, sales, and marketing, all of whom are proud of the products they help create."

In April 2020, a new chief marketing officer, Rachel Ferdinando, appeared in a CNBC video feature about Flamin' Hot products. She stops short of calling Montañez the inventor of the product.

But she does name Montañez, saying that "Richard's insights into the Hispanic consumer really helped us shape and think about how we should talk to that consumer," adding that his thinking insight "was something we relied on very heavily."

The filmmakers behind Montañez's biopic were informed of potential problems with his story two years ago. In April 2019,

Frito-Lay's legal team forwarded a letter that Greenfeld wrote outlining her version of events to Franklin, whose production company, Franklin Entertainment, is coproducing Montañez's biopic along with Searchlight Pictures.

It's unclear whether the producers ever informed Longoria, who's set to direct the film. And like many Hollywood projects, the movie could use Montañez's story as a jumping-off point for a fictional story.

In early May, Longoria announced that she had chosen the actors to play Montañez and his wife, and that the film would begin shooting this summer in New Mexico.

She told *Variety* that it has been her "biggest priority to make sure we are telling Richard Montañez's story authentically."

JIAYANG FAN

The Gatekeepers Who
Get to Decide What Food
Is "Disgusting"

FROM *The New Yorker*

IN THE SPRING of 2019, Arthur De Meyer, a twenty-nine-year-old Belgian journalist, toured the Disgusting Food Museum, in Malmö, Sweden. As with the Museum of Sex, in New York City, and the Museum of Ice Cream, in San Francisco, the Disgusting Food Museum is conceptually closer to an amusement park than to a museum. There are eighty-five culinary horrors on display—ordinary fare and delicacies from thirty countries—and each tour concludes with a taste test of a dozen items. De Meyer, the son of a cookbook author and a food photographer, told me that he'd always been an adventurous eater. As a reporter, he also prided himself on his ability to maintain his composure. "But the taste test was war," he said. "The kind where you're defenseless, because the bombs are going off invisibly, inside of you."

An Icelandic shark dish called hákarl was the first assault on his stomach. "Eating it was like gnawing on three-week-old cheese from the garbage that had also been pissed on by every dog in the neighborhood," he said. Next up was durian, a spiky, custard-like fruit from Southeast Asia that "smelled like socks at the bottom of a gym locker, drizzled with paint thinner." But worst of all was surströmming, a fermented herring that is beloved in northern Sweden. De Meyer said that eating it was like taking a bite out of a corpse.

He vomited ten times, topping the museum's previous record of six. Mercifully, admission tickets are printed on airplane-style barf bags.

The Disgusting Food Museum, which opened in 2018, is the brainchild of Samuel West, a forty-seven-year-old psychologist who was born in California and has lived in Sweden for more than two decades. In 2016, during a trip to Zagreb, Croatia, he wandered into the Museum of Broken Relationships. As he studied the remnants of strangers' failed romances—photos of hookup spots; a diet book that a woman received from her fiancé—West came up with an idea for a museum dedicated to failed business products and services. A year later, in Helsingborg, Sweden, he opened the Museum of Failure, where the takeaway was simple: blunders are the midwives of success. One example on display at the museum was the Newton, a personal digital assistant released by Apple in 1993. Its shoddy handwriting software and exorbitant price nearly torpedoed the entire company, but its sleek black design eventually inspired the iPhone. The exhibits also included Bic for Her, a line of pens, from 2011, that were designed for women; DivX, a 2003 trademark for "self-destructing" DVDs that could be watched for only forty-eight hours; a collection of Harley-Davidson perfumes, from the mid-nineties; and Trump: The Game, a Monopoly rip-off released in 1989. (The game was pulled from shelves after Trump said that it was "too complicated.")

The Museum of Failure was a resounding commercial success, attracting visitors from across the world and attention from the *Times,* the *Washington Post,* and *National Geographic.* By 2018, though, West was on to his next project, after reading an article about how reducing beef consumption could slow climate change. The piece explained that a dire problem could be eased by a simple solution—eating insects, a good source of protein—but that the First World had rejected this idea out of disgust. West realized that if the experience of failure had expedited human innovation, then the experience of disgust was potentially holding us back. Could that aversion be challenged or changed? "I just wanted to know, why is it that even talking about eating certain things makes my skin crawl?" he told me, animatedly, over Zoom.

The planning for the museum began with a more basic question: what counts as food? West recruited his friend Andreas Ahrens, a former IT entrepreneur and a foodie, to help him choose which items would qualify for exhibition. The men ruled out artificially flavored gag gifts—such as Rocket Fizz's barf soda and Jelly Belly's booger jelly beans—and novelty foods like deep-fried Oreos and a Polish beer that had been brewed with a woman's vaginal yeast. Four hundred items made it through the initial screening, after which they were culled based on four criteria: taste, texture, smell, and the process by which they were made. Foie gras "failed" the taste, texture, and smell tests, which is to say that West and Ahrens found it inoffensive on those fronts. But the dish, which is typically produced by force-feeding ducks until their livers swell to ten times their normal size, easily passed the process test, earning itself a place at the museum. (According to Ahrens, many visitors, after reading about the process, swear to never eat foie gras again.) The winnowing of the foods was spirited and combative. West emerged as the bigger wimp; he threw up so many times that he lost count. Ahrens found plenty of the foods unpleasant, but he got sick only after tasting balut, a Filipino egg-fetus snack that is eaten straight from the shell—feathers, beak, blood, and all.

After the men chose the items, they had to contend with customs and transportation. Svið, a traditional Icelandic dish in which a sheep's head is cut in half and boiled, was impossible to procure, for "logistical reasons," Ahrens said. The food is instead represented by a photo of the head next to helpings of mashed potatoes and pureed root vegetables. The same goes for ortolan, a nearly extinct French songbird, which is prepared by blinding the bird and then drowning it in brandy, a practice that is now banned in the European Union. Raw monkey brain, which was supposedly served at Chinese imperial banquets, is represented by a type of wooden table that would have been used to hold down a live monkey while the top of its head was sliced open and spooned out. ("It is unclear whether it's an urban legend, or something that's still being served in China," an accompanying sign says.)

Even the foods that appear at the museum in their real forms posed unusual difficulties. To make cuy, a Peruvian dish, West had to watch several YouTube videos on how to skin and boil a guinea pig. "I sent my wife and children away the day I did it," he recalled. "It just felt wrong, bordering on criminal." For a South Korean wine that demanded the "fresh turds" of children, Ahrens found himself scooping up his eight-year-old daughter's excrement and fermenting it with rice wine. The final product is on display at the museum, in a gallon jug, though Ahrens has not mustered the will to try it.

On Tripadvisor, the Disgusting Food Museum is ranked No. 1 on a list of ninety-four things to do in Malmö, the third-largest city in Sweden. Visitors are often surprised to find that the museum is situated on the first floor of a shopping mall, between a furniture store and an art gallery. Daniela Nusfelean, a Romanian college student who visited the museum in January, said that one of the first things she noticed was the absence of any odor. "This place is supposed to have so much food," Nusfelean remembered thinking. "How can food not smell?"

The stinkier items are secured under bell jars, Ahrens, the museum's director, said, when he gave me a tour over Zoom, earlier this year. Most foods, such as kale pache—an Iranian soup made from a sheep's head and hooves, which are boiled overnight to eliminate any smells—were displayed in bowls or pots that sat atop a series of white tables, illuminated by long-necked lamps. (Some of the foods are made fresh every week; others, like the poop wine, have a lengthy shelf life.) The museum, whose walls were bright and bare, looked as sterile as a science lab, until Ahrens, who wore a T-shirt that bore the museum's logo and the word *Yuck!*, gestured to a chalkboard that read 2 DAYS SINCE LAST VOMIT. "This is the scoreboard," he said, grinning.

We went on to the exhibits, each of which was accompanied by a placard that, in English and Swedish, noted a dish's history and its country of origin. First stop: dried stinkbugs from Zimbabwe, which vaguely resembled the buds of microgreen sprouts. Then there was kungu cake (East Africa), a dessert made from millions of crushed flies; fried locusts (Israel), the only insect that the Torah considers kosher; frog juice (Peru), a frothy green beverage containing frogs and quail eggs; and mouse wine (China), a jug of rice wine infused with two hundred baby rodents.

Eventually, Ahrens led me to a Warhol-esque wall of yellow and red cans. "Our most popular selfie destination," he said, adding that the cans, which were full of surströmming, the fermented herring, had induced more vomiting than any other item in the museum. ("Surströmming is one of the worst-smelling foods in the world," a placard read.) The exhibit featured a smell jar, inviting visitors to lift the lid and to take a sniff. Before the pandemic, one of the highlights of the museum was a photo booth that sprayed jet streams of various scents—durian, stinky tofu (a fermented bean-curd dish)—and captured visitors' facial expressions as they inhaled. "Instagram," Ahrens explained.

The term *disgust* entered the English language more than four hundred years ago, from the Old French word *desgouster,* meaning "to put off one's appetite." But disgust wasn't considered worthy of scientific examination until 1872, when Charles Darwin defined it as a reaction to "something revolting, primarily in relation to the sense of taste . . . and secondarily to anything which causes a similar feeling, through the sense of smell, touch and even of eyesight." Darwin theorized that disgust is a basic human emotion—like anger, fear, or sadness—and that it is expressed with a universal "disgust face." If you are presented with a glass of sour milk, you will almost certainly scrunch up your nose, purse your lips, and blow out air between them, making an "ack" or "ugh" sound through clenched teeth. If you are forced to drink the milk, you might open your mouth wide, tense your brows, and retract your upper lip to decrease inhalation, pinching your features into the likeness of the vomit-face emoji (all of which is often a precursor to the act itself).

There is a reason that we find certain foods offensive. A prehistoric human who scarfed down decomposing meat or bacteria-ridden feces wouldn't have lived long. "Life would have been simpler if we were koala bears," Daniel Fessler, an evolutionary anthropologist at UCLA, told me. Koala bears eat only eucalyptus leaves, so there isn't a lot of hand wringing about what's for dinner. But humans have made it a lot further in life than koalas, in large part because of our diet. Eating meat has allowed our digestive tracts to shrink and our brains to grow in outsized proportion to our bodies, because the animals we consume have already extracted the nutrients we need. Meat consumption, however, has also entangled our species in the omnivore's dilemma: we must be flexible enough to consume a variegated diet, yet wary enough of novelty to avoid accidental death.

Evolutionary psychologists often cite the Swiss Army knife as an analogy for the mind, because both have all-purpose tools designed to cope with an unpredictable world. Disgust is simply one

blade of many. If the blade is kept sharp, it helps you avoid disease, but if it becomes too sharp you might not ingest enough
calories. "Evolution has optimized this trade-off so that priority is
placed on the more urgent goal," Fessler said. If you're starving,
then the blade is dulled: you may be more likely to eat something
that you'd otherwise find disgusting, such as rotting leftovers. (As
Cervantes wrote in *Don Quixote,* "Hunger is the best sauce.") "The
key point here is that people do not need to make conscious decisions about these trade-offs," Fessler said. Evolved psychological
mechanisms do the work.

Disgust may have originated as a food-rejection system, Paul
Rozin, a psychology professor at the University of Pennsylvania,
told me, "but it has expanded into a vehicle for perceiving the
social and moral world." Rozin is the pioneer of a subfield called
disgust studies. His favorite experiment involves dropping a cockroach into a glass of juice. Most people, of course, refuse to drink
the juice, citing the dirtiness of cockroaches. "What's amazing is
that even if you disinfect the cockroach and convincingly demonstrate that the juice is harmless, people still won't want to drink it,"
Rozin said. The juice has been irrevocably contaminated.

The concept of contamination is one example of how biology
maps onto cultural systems. Both Islam and Judaism forbid the
consumption of pork; many cultures avoid other kinds of meat.
These taboos may have been provoked by disgust (pigs are thought
to be unclean, raw meat tends to be slimy and unappetizing, and
both can cause disease if prepared incorrectly), but disgust can
also be perpetuated by taboos. Lebanese Christians are technically
allowed to eat pork, but many of them abstain, owing to the influence of their pork-avoidant neighbors in the Muslim-majority
country.

Like a regional dialect or a style of dress, most food taboos ad-
vertise and affirm membership within a group. Humans evolved in
tribes, and food taboos helped to define coalitions. In a Hobbes-
ian past, a cohesive tribe would have had a better chance of dom-
ination. Chimps know this just as well as high school cliques do. A
show of strength intimidates the loners—by making them feel like
losers. It's not an accident that minorities with unfamiliar customs
can pique our suspicion, Mark Schaller, a social psychologist at the
University of British Columbia, told me. Our behavioral immune
system, much like our biological immune system, is meant to de-

tect danger. But it can go into overdrive. Schaller compared it to a smoke detector. "It's designed to be hypersensitive for a reason," he said. "In the wild, it's OK to make small errors by overestimating a threat, but, if you underestimate, you are dead."

When I was a child in Chongqing, in the nineteen-eighties, food forged the rules and the language of existence. To be fed was to be loved, and to live was to taste the world. (In Chinese, the character for *life* contains the component word *tongue*.) I grew up on an Army compound—my mother was in the military—and the adults I knew had a habit of pinching the round bums of young children, appraising them as "great juicy cuts of meat for dumplings." Many of those adults, my father included, had lived through the worst famine in history, during which some villagers had cannibalized one another. When I wondered, at the age of four, if human flesh tasted like pork, it did not occur to me that the thought might be disgusting.

As a young Army recruit, my mother ate the rats that scurried outside the granary she guarded, and for years she ate kernels of rice that she found on the ground—something I was told by other adults never to do. To be the first member of my family spared the pangs of hunger was to live through an epochal transition that felt like cultural transformation. Still, the threat of deprivation hung over our lives like the dangling carcasses in the village wet markets.

At those markets, my mother traded her extra grain coupons—which she began to receive after becoming an Army doctor—for eggs, an expensive protein in the hierarchy of foods. Shortly before I began first grade, my mother stopped feeding me the rice porridge and the pickles that she and my grandmother ate every morning and started me on a special breakfast of what she called "brain foods": a warm, viscous puddle of milk, bobbing with chunks of raw egg yolk. My Swiss Army knife was already being honed. Disgust welled up in me, but it contended with other blades that were necessary for survival: the shame of ingratitude, and the fear of disobedience. I ate the brain foods every morning for two interminable years.

Even so, disgust did not leave a lasting mark on my psyche until 1992, when, at the age of eight, on a flight to America with my mother, I was served the first non-Chinese meal of my life. In a tinfoil-covered tray was what looked like a pile of dumplings, except that they were square. I picked one up and took a bite, expecting it to be filled with meat, and discovered a gooey, creamy substance inside. Surely this was a dessert. Why else would the squares be swimming in a thick white sauce? I was grossed out, but ate the whole meal, because I had never been permitted to do otherwise. For weeks afterward, the taste festered in my thoughts, goading my gag reflex. Years later, I learned that those curious squares were called cheese ravioli.

Olives were another mystery. In Chongqing, I had been introduced to them as a fig-like snack, dried or cured, that had a sweet-tart kick. In the US, I placed a dark green drop onto my tongue and, for the first time in my life, spat something out of my mouth and into my palm. Salty and greasy weren't what I was expecting, and my reaction was born as much of disgust as it was of having been deceived.

To be a new immigrant is to be trapped in a disgusting-food museum, confused by the unfamiliar and unsettled by the familiar-looking. The firm, crumbly white blocks that you mistake for tofu are called feta. The vanilla icing that tastes spoiled is served on top of potatoes and is called sour cream. At a certain point, the trickery of food starts to become mundane. Disgusting foods become regulars in the cafeteria, and at the dinner table.

Recently, I joined a few Asian American friends at a restaurant in Queens to have hot pot, a fondue-like communal meal in which ingredients are dipped in a shared pot of boiling broth at the center of the table. By the time I arrived, bowls of sliced pig arteries, pig intestines, cow stomach, duck feet, and pale pink brains of unidentified provenance already sat around a burbling vat of broth, spices, and chili oil. All of these would have made it into a Westerner's encyclopedia of disgusting foods, but everyone at the table knew that the gusto with which we consumed the entrails and viscera connected us.

I asked my companions if they'd had any memorable encounters with disgusting food. Nearly all of them named dairy products that they had tried for the first time in the United States. A Chengdu native recalled the chalky taste of a protein shake, making the classic disgust face as she spoke. "The first time I had pizza was bad," Alex, a forty-year-old network engineer, said. It was margherita pizza, and he thought that the little white splotches of melted burrata were fresh vomit. "I couldn't believe that there were people who ate this regularly," he continued. "But Americans told me this was a very common food here." He bit into the muscled leg of a bullfrog.

"And?" I asked.

"And I just learned to get used to it."

I had had almost the exact same experience with a Sicilian slice some three decades before. Assimilating requires you to adopt a foreign tongue, in more ways than one. But when the choice is between annihilation and assimilation, you assimilate. This was as true for prehistoric humans as it is for a young, deracinated Chinese immigrant in America. One of the wonders of the tongue is its sheer malleability. New tastes are acquired and seamlessly incorporated into the tapestry of one's gastronomic predilections. I don't remember the exact moment when I began relishing Western olives, but the change felt natural; with each new experience, the tapestry is rewoven.

Shortly before my virtual tour of the Disgusting Food Museum, I had received a temperature-controlled package in the mail. It contained goat-stomach cheese, fermented shark, surströmming, and several other items from the museum's taste test. I arranged the food in small saucers around my laptop and launched Zoom, where Andreas Ahrens was waiting for me. Before I dug in, he suggested I check that the items had made it through their transatlantic journey OK. "Maybe smell them just to make sure they haven't gone bad," he said. But, wait, I said, weren't most of them supposed to smell bad? He laughed. "Good luck, then."

I opened a pouch of German sauerkraut juice. Its putrid gray color reminded me of stagnant gutter water. By way of encouragement, Ahrens said, "Very few people try nothing. Most try more than they thought they would." I had skipped lunch to prepare for the taste test, and by then my stomach was growling so loudly that I felt obliged to apologize to the screen.

The juice tasted cool and refreshing—a blend of pickles and kimchi. Next was bagoong, a Filipino fermented shrimp, which tasted so much like a beloved Chinese fish sauce that I was tempted to spoon it over some leftover rice. Things started getting real with hákarl, the Icelandic shark. My head cocked back at the taste of ammonia, but the chewy texture reminded me pleasantly of squid. I moved on to the insects, beginning with grasshoppers from Oaxaca, Mexico, which had been marinated with dried chilies. They were delicious—crispy, sour, and spicy, like lime-tossed tortilla chips. A bag of dehydrated mixed bugs contained mole crickets and sago worms. The hardest part was knowing that you were eating something that you last saw crawling on the bathroom floor. Crunchiness, I discovered, was a crucial factor in palatability; the crickets could have passed for salty granola. The worms, which looked like deformed prunes, were denser and nuttier. Everything tasted considerably better than it looked.

While I sniffed and chewed, periodically watching my features contort on-screen, I couldn't help but think of De Meyer, the hapless Belgian. My lack of disgust felt like cheating. The Chinese pidan, for example—a clay-preserved egg with a swampy blue-green hue—has been one of my comfort foods since childhood. The thought of stinky tofu makes me salivate. Durian was more complicated. I don't like its smell, which some describe as a mix of turpentine and onions, but I've eaten enough durian-flavored desserts to reflexively separate the fruit's odor from its taste, which is simultaneously creamy, sweet, and savory—like chives, garlic, and caramel, blended into a butter.

It was time to try the surströmming, which Ahrens had packed in a vacuum-sealed bag. I used a teaspoon to scoop out a moist, grayish morsel. It was so salty that it tasted bitter. But it was the smell—of rotten eggs brined in raw sewage—that made me jerk my body back like Keanu Reeves dodging bullets in *The Matrix*. The fish's scent is so foul, Ahrens told me, that a German man was once evicted from his building after leaving surströmming in the stairwell to annoy his neighbor, with whom he was engaged in a petty dispute. (The man sued his landlord, but a judge ruled in favor of the eviction, stating that "the disgusting smell of the fish brine far exceeded the degree that fellow tenants in the building could be expected to tolerate.") Ahrens said that, of all the items in the taste test, he'd found the smell of surströmming the most objectionable. The fact that the two of us—a Swede and a Chinese American—more or less aligned on this pleased me. Disgust, at least in this instance, seemed to unify rather than divide.

The final item was Lakkris Djöflar, a type of salmiak, or salty licorice candy, that is popular in Nordic countries. Easy, I thought.

I don't love licorice, but its herbal taste reminds me of the medicinal soups that my mother fed me as a child. One second after I put the candy in my mouth, though, I spat it out with such force that it left a sticky mark on my screen, where Ahrens's mouth was curled into a smile.

There was a bowl of the vile confection on his countertop. He ate two, emitting a satisfied "Mmm" as he chewed. "It's one of my favorite things," he said.

"But isn't it horribly salty and bitter?" I asked, incredulous, clutching my glass of water. When the candy was in my mouth, I'd felt as if I were drowning in brackish seawater.

"That's what makes it good," he said. "People naturally like foods they grew up eating."

After finishing the taste test, I called up De Moyer. It had been two years since his visit to the museum, and from what I could tell via Zoom—he was slouched on a sofa, chain-smoking Camels—it looked like he had mostly recovered from the experience. "I feel lucky that I was able to go," he told me. It had been "refreshing" to be taken out of his comfort zone, even if it had involved going through a dozen barf bags.

After a pause, he recounted how he'd recently cooked onions in a miso-butter glaze for his six-year-old niece. "She hated it the first time," he said. But he kept encouraging her to try it, telling her that it wasn't weird, and, by the fourth bite, she was fully on board. "That's why it was a privilege to go to the museum," he said. "It takes ten tries for people to like something new. But, if you don't start somewhere, how else would you expand your reference point? How else would my niece learn that she loves miso butter?"

Ahrens's goal is to replicate such experiences on a large scale. He recently took over the Disgusting Food Museum, and, later this year, he will open two more locations, in Bordeaux and Berlin, that will feature site-specific exhibits, such as Berliner schnitzel made from cow udders.

The museum in Malmö has been mostly well received by tourists, but it also has numerous critics, who have accused it of cultural insensitivity and, in some cases, of outright racism. In 2018, the *Los Angeles Times* columnist Lucas Kwan Peterson argued that the museum reinforces prejudices by oversimplifying the customs of other countries and reducing their foods to clichés. A museum's use of the word *disgusting* in its name implies an endorsement of the term, he wrote.

When I asked Ahrens about his use of the word *disgusting*, and whether he'd considered using a different name for the new museums, he nodded. " 'Disgusting' is a controversial word, but if we used 'unusual' or 'strange' it's just not the same," he said.

" 'Disgusting' calls attention to itself," I said.

"Exactly," he replied. "And we are a museum that relies on public support. That is how we survive."

As Peterson wrote, "The museum is trying to have it both ways—poking the bear, then backing away, hands raised innocently." Even those who believe in the museum's statement of purpose question whether it can be put into practice. The trouble with cultural institutions, Casey R. Kelly, the author of *Food Television and Otherness in the Age of Globalization,* said, is that those who run them can't always control what's being communicated. "On the one hand, the museum is introducing visitors to new foods," he said, "but, on the other, there's a cosmopolitan sanitization process at work," in which foods are being stripped of their cultural context and then presented at a museum that keeps track of how many people they make vomit.

At the Disgusting Food Museum, I felt both like a tourist and like one of the exhibits. Twenty-nine of the eighty-five dishes on display are Asian, and twelve are from China. Despite Ahrens's reminder that Asia is underrepresented at the museum compared with its population, seeing stinky tofu, century eggs, and other staples of my childhood branded as "disgusting" stung me with self-consciousness. Those foods were in my fridge at that very moment. Turtle soup and dog meat, also among the exhibits, were dishes that I'd eaten in Chongqing; though I'd likely never revisit them, I knew them well enough as communal holiday fare. Meanwhile, mouse wine, monkey brain, and virgin-boy eggs (eggs boiled in young boys' urine) were as foreign to me as surströmming. Ahrens and West's decision to categorize them all under *China* felt simultaneously alienating and reasonable: the Westerner in me understood the urge not to differentiate them, while the Chinese rebelled at the notion that they would ever belong together.

Just as Michelangelo's David represents the height of the Italian Renaissance, and cobalt porcelain the cultural apogee of the Ming dynasty, the exhibits at the Disgusting Food Museum, divided as they are by geography, perform an act of synecdoche, with the foods standing in for individual places or peoples. This makes sense as a method of cataloguing exhibits, but it can obviate the obvious: foods in the premodern era were often disgusting—at least to the uninitiated palate—but they were also ingenious. Why is hákarl the token food of Iceland? The Vikings wanted a way to eat sleeper sharks, which are plentiful but poisonous; consequently, they invented a technique for purifying the two-thousand-pound beasts.

When food is available only to a select few, it becomes a symbol for one's social position. The reason that the French aristocracy once ate ortolans is probably similar to the reason that monkey brains would have been served at royal banquets in China. Across cultures, the elite gravitate toward foods that are inaccessible to the masses, owing to price, scarcity, or difficulty of preparation. It was in part the pursuit of "exotic" spices that led to Western conquests in Africa and East Asia, which in turn created asymmetries of power that surface in the modern sociological concept of "taste," or in a worldly palate informed by various cultural or class-based rituals. (By using the phrase "in good taste," one invokes the gastronomically satisfying to connote something that is socially sanctioned.)

In the twentieth century, powerful nations seemed to reinvent food by processing the disgust out of it. At the Disgusting Food Museum, the US is represented mostly by calorie-packed, nutritionally deficient snacks, such as Twinkies, Spam, and Pop-Tarts. The element of disgust, as detailed by the museum's placards, exists largely in the factory farms, the economies of waste, the misuse of growth hormones, and the exploitation it takes to produce these items. Kelly said that Americans are generally uninterested in knowing where their food comes from: "There is entitlement in this willful ignorance—to be in a place where you don't have to think about how to make the feet and beak of a bird palatable."

At the beginning of the pandemic, many Americans were suddenly confronted with the threat of food insecurity, as the virus exposed the fragility of our supply chains. Restaurants shuttered, bottled water was rationed, and egg prices rose threefold overnight. I asked Ahrens if his view of disgust or of the museum had changed during the pandemic. (Although Sweden did not shut down, 99 percent of the museum's visitors disappeared overnight.) In slow, methodical tones, he spoke to me about the health impact of food. "The more foreign foods I come across, the more I realize how little I know about the food I eat, and the more I want to know," he said. The museum is planning a temporary exhibit on dangerous foods, in which danger is defined as everything from "poison or toxin, like fungus, to manufacturing errors that cause the end product to be injurious." What's dangerous is what we don't know, Ahrens told me. The horseshoe bat, which early in the pandemic was thought to be responsible for the transmission of the coronavirus in China, will be prominently featured in the exhibit.

Last spring, shortly after Donald Trump referred to COVID-19 as the "China virus," I received a Twitter message from a stranger. "Y'all Chinese ppl want eat bat soup & alive mice no wonder this coronavirus started y'all dirty asses eating shit wit rabies," he wrote. "Get the fuck out the us go back to China with the rest of y'all eating animals alive ass family members." This was also when photos of bats began arriving in my social media inboxes.

One afternoon, while I was talking on the phone at a grocery store, a passerby, hearing me speak Mandarin, hissed, "Nasty Chinese." Another day, when I was riding the subway for the first time in months, a man called me a "disgusting Chink" over and over until he reached his station and left the car.

Something happens when you discover that you yourself are "disgusting." It does not matter whether you believe it to be true. Shame and fear flood your body, as involuntarily as the disgust face, until a kind of self-disgust takes root. The origins of self-disgust have yet to be fully understood, but scientists speculate that the emotion likely arises from the internalization of others' disgust. It is also a unique form of torture; to be perceived as repugnant is to live inside that repugnance, desperate to expel you from yourself.

"Have Americans always been like this?" my mother's Chinese health aide, Ying, asked me the other day, as she showed me a news story about yet another unprovoked attack on an elderly Asian woman in Chinatown. Ying was wearing a hat and a mask, not only for COVID safety, she told me, but also because she was anxious about being identified as Asian—an abstract feeling that, in recent weeks, had concretized to an acute fear.

Perhaps this is what terrifies me the most about disgust: its ability to weaponize one's gut in service of the outlandish. The idea that all Chinese carry the coronavirus because it could have originated from eating bats is risible. But COVID's invisibility has lent credence to the tribalist notion that disgusting-food-consuming Asians must surely be the ones who are carrying and spreading the virus.

If only nature were so straightforward. In food, funky smells raise an alarm that warns against ingestion; respiratory droplets expelled during a conversation with an asymptomatic carrier of the coronavirus raise no such alarms. Disgust can't protect us from this particular virus. If anything, it leaves us more vulnerable than we were before. Many people who contract the virus lose their senses of taste and smell. A friend of mine who got COVID in March of 2020 can smell and taste again, but can no longer eat meat. "Hamburgers, ground turkey"—foods that were once staples of her diet—"it's all become gross," she told me. Pamela Dalton, an experimental psychologist who studies the interaction between emotion and odor perception, told me that many COVID patients have reported a distortion of their senses of taste and smell while recovering from the virus, resulting in disgusting sensations. "The olfactory system is playing a protective role here," Dalton said. "It's not surprising that if parts of the system have gone awry due to COVID the default setting is to turn tastes and smells unpleasant, so as to help us avoid high-risk foods." Like meat.

If COVID is, in some ways, a failure of disgust, it is also a breeding ground for it. The question—similar to the one that inspired West to open the Disgusting Food Museum—is whether this disgust, particularly as it pertains to other people, can be swallowed for the greater good. Kevin Arceneaux, a political scientist at Temple University, told me, "Your intuition may tell you that the immigrant across the street smells weird, cooks weird food, and therefore does not belong. But we also possess the capacity to reflect and override our intuitions with conscious reason. This second step is harder, but the capacity to do so is also what makes us uniquely human."

To be disgusted is natural, but to understand why we are disgusted requires us to reconfigure the way we see the world. "Human beings are accustomed to protecting themselves and their own," Arceneaux said. "But a pandemic is the kind of unprecedented event that requires people to reframe the threat." The purpose of wearing a mask is not to protect yourself but to protect others around you. "The only way to save yourself from a contagion *is* to save the strangers who may disgust you," Arceneaux said.

One day this past winter, when my mother's nursing facility was locked down, her aide, Ying, turned up on my doorstep with a bag that refused to stay still. A dozen crabs were squirming inside. My mother had told Ying (accurately) that I had been living on ramen and takeout for a while and that I loved steamed crabs, though I almost never cooked them at home. Both of them assumed that this was because I couldn't deal with the inconvenience, but the truth was more complicated: the prospect of boiling the crabs alive, as my mother had done while I was growing up, disgusted me. Ying would not have understood this. My refusal to accept the food probably would have struck her as callous and rude. I thanked her and took the crabs. "Boil them quickly or they will die and no longer be fresh!" she admonished.

As I stood in my kitchen, a few minutes later, agonizing over what to do, I became aware of my hypocrisy: I was ready to eat the crabs when they were served by someone else, but I was too cowardly to do the killing myself. Still, if I left them in the bag on my kitchen floor, they would die, and I would have squandered Ying's effort. Reluctantly, I dropped the crabs' writhing bodies into a pot, covered it with a lid, and turned on the stove. Outside, two ambulances sped by, sirens blaring.

I poured vinegar and chopped ginger and tried to think about anything besides the crustaceans in my kettle. Egocentric pain. This was what evolutionary biologists would call my uneasiness. Our ability to empathize with animals is a function of their phylogenetic proximity to us; we can see the emotions of a dog much more clearly than those of a crab. And yet there was an unbearable scratching and scraping inside the pot—a mad scramble for life.

It occurred to me that what I felt was not disgust with the crabs or with the process but with myself, and what I had the power to do—or not to do. The doomed fight for survival is what the crabs and I had in common. Steam and the smell of the ocean had begun to fill my kitchen when the phone rang. It was Ying, and there was an impossible tenderness in her voice when she asked about the dinner: had I cooked it yet?

Fruits of Empire

FROM *The New York Review of Books*

IN A BUSY market in Ceylon, now Sri Lanka, the botanist David Fairchild, sporting a pith helmet, white suit, and large white mustache, ate a halved bael fruit with a tiny spoon. He examined betel nuts and grabbed the arm of a passing vendor to inspect the large bunch of coconuts balanced on his head. It was 1925, and Fairchild was leading an expedition to Ceylon, Sumatra, and Java on behalf of the United States Department of Agriculture in search of foreign plants to introduce to American growers, a trip documented in a silent film. After the market, the plant explorers visited a village where locals demonstrated various uses of the Palmyra palm, "a handsome and extremely valuable plant," and carved open gigantic jackfruits.

Fairchild was the head of the Office of Foreign Seed and Plant Introduction, a section of the USDA founded in 1898 to search the world for plants that could boost commercial agriculture at home and reduce economic reliance on imports. Atelier Éditions recently published a book documenting this project to expand the American palate: *An Illustrated Catalog of American Fruits & Nuts*, a sampling of watercolors from the department's pomological collection. In a time before color photography was widespread, USDA artists, many with decades-long careers at the agency, created 7,584 technically accurate illustrations to record this cornucopia of the new. Along with short essays, including excerpted musings on fruit from Michael Pollan and John McPhee, the catalog contains the most visually striking of these images, from the incandescent King tangor to the dusky, green-fleshed Tragedy plum.

While fruits have never contributed as much to the economy as staples like soybeans, which last year brought $25.7 billion in exports as a result of varieties found by USDA explorers, they evoke more passionate cravings. Pineapples, native to South America and costly to grow in hothouses in northern climates, became a status symbol in Europe and colonial America; it was possible for middle-class households to rent individual fruits to show off as centerpieces at dinner parties, even if they could not afford to eat them. Until recent methods of refrigeration and transportation, fruit cultivation could defy even royal command: Queen Victoria was fixated on tasting a mango, but the fruit could not survive the six-week sea voyage from India.

Though we now eat fruits from every part of the globe in every season, the selection we enjoy is far more limited than the one promised by the USDA's mouthwatering collection. The concerted efforts of plant explorers, researchers, breeders, marketers, government officials, entrepreneurs, and giant corporations enabled fruit to flow around the globe—but at a human, ecological, and ultimately gustatory cost.

North America is the original home of cranberries, salmonberries, huckleberries, chokeberries, elderberries, serviceberries, thimbleberries, and buffaloberries. The largest native fruit is the pawpaw, whose custardy flesh has a tropical flavor incongruous with its ability to survive harsh midwestern winters. Pecans received their name from the Algonquin word *pecane*, which referred to any nut too hard to crack without a stone. The American persimmon is smaller and spicier than its Asian cousins; our grapes include the large, musky, thick-skinned Scuppernong, Muscadine, and Fox (the latter an ancestor of Concord grapes). Other domestic gems include black cherries, crabapples, and as many as thirteen plums. Around the time that fruit explorers went abroad, the USDA also pushed for the cultivation and distribution of some of this native bounty: in 1910, the agency published a bulletin calling growers' attention to a "strangely overlooked" perennial, the blueberry.

Nearly all the other fruits grown in the US today are transplants. Citrus, originally from Southeast Asia, was established in the Mediterranean by around the second century BCE and brought to Florida and California by the Spanish. Cultivated apples, "American as pie," are from the mountains of Kazakhstan. Peaches are from China, and watermelons from northeastern Africa. From the nation's earliest days, long before Fairchild's Division of Pomology, gaining mastery over valuable plants was considered important to state building. While in Europe, Benjamin Franklin would frequently exchange seeds through the mail with agriculturally minded friends back home—in one letter from London he described sending rhubarb seeds, a variety of pea "highly esteemed here as the best for making pease soup," and soybeans, which he called "Chinese garavances," mistaking them for a variety of garbanzo bean. Thomas Jefferson experimented in his garden at Monticello with methods to grow crops from northern and southern Europe alongside African plants brought over by enslaved people, and asserted in 1790 that "the greatest service that can be rendered any country is to add a useful plant to its culture."

Through the nineteenth century, the diets of American settlers were heavy with meat, carbohydrates, and dairy, which could be produced and stored more reliably than fruits and vegetables. But this began to change with the spread of the steamship and railroad in the 1870s, as Daniel Stone describes in his 2018 book on David Fairchild, *The Food Explorer*. The banana, native to Southeast Asia and unknown to most Americans, debuted at the 1876 Philadelphia World Fair, wrapped in foil and served with a knife and fork. New rail lines linking Florida to northern markets brought "orange fever," as people flocked to the state hoping to cash in on the citrus gold rush. In 1917, Fairchild wrote that "the whole trend of the world is toward greater intercourse, more frequent exchange of commodities, less isolation, and a greater mixture of the plants and plant products over the face of the globe."

In this time, USDA plant explorers had tremendous success in bringing new fruits within reach. Fairchild himself was responsible for introducing over 200,000 varieties of plants to the United States, including the flowering cherry trees that grow on the National Mall, marketable mangoes, and navel oranges. On a trip to Chile, he sent a shipment of nearly a thousand avocados to Washington, DC; from the few that survived the journey, the California avocado industry took root. Dates and nectarines he found in Baghdad were similarly profitable.

This collecting project was, at best, of no benefit to the countries being explored, as the food writer and historian Adam Leith Gollner notes in the introduction to the *Illustrated Catalog*: "The

USDA's undertaking, in terms of plant introduction, was itself an actor in the complex legacy of colonialism—one in which countries from the global North and West have extracted materials of value from the South and East in an exploitative, non-compensatory manner." At worst, it was part and parcel of US imperial expansion taking place around the turn of the century. President William McKinley, asking Fairchild to carry out a survey of the agricultural potential of the Philippines in 1900 in the midst of the brutal Philippine–American War, wrote that "an American military presence might work in your favor." Though Filipinos' guerrilla tactics made a comprehensive assessment impossible—"They are not yet sufficiently pacified," Fairchild complained—he still managed to snag a Carabao mango, which was critical to the US mango industry for the next century. After the US decisively gained control over the country in 1913, having committed numerous military atrocities there, the new colonial government invested heavily in agricultural production. Land devoted to coconuts expanded from one thousand acres to 1.4 million by 1934, making the Philippines the world's largest exporter of coconut oil, much of it going to US markets.

Most tropical fruits cannot adapt to colder or drier climates and must be imported. This basic horticultural fact underlies a brutal history of American extraction, as companies established industrial-scale plantations in Latin America and the Caribbean. Plantation labor was surveilled and violently policed; workers lived in company dwellings and were paid in scrip, creating an essential continuity with earlier slave production of commodities like sugar. In Honduras the United Fruit Company took enormous land subsidies from the Honduran government in exchange for the construction and operation of a railroad that provided ample transport between agricultural regions and ports but did not connect to the capital city. The company was complicit in the Colombian military's massacre of hundreds of striking plantation workers in 1928, and successfully lobbied US officials to overthrow the president of Guatemala in 1954 after he instituted land reforms. All for the ubiquity of the banana, which was aggressively marketed to Americans in the 1940s—the Chiquita jingle, instructing consumers how to eat and store bananas, was played on the radio as many as 376 times a day.

The Kingdom of Hawaii, led by Queen Lili'uokalani, was overthrown in 1893 by a group of businessmen and sugar planters who felt that it would be beneficial to be annexed by the country that imported the bulk of their agricultural products. The leader of this coup and first governor of the new territory, Sanford Dole, was the cousin of James Dole, who would soon establish the world's largest pineapple company on the islands. A list of the places to which David Fairchild's seeds were sent to be cultivated—Cuba, Honduras, the Panama Canal Zone—provides a revealing map of US influence and control around the world at the turn of the century, a time when the US was using dubious legal devices to create de facto colonies while maintaining plausible deniability about its status as an imperialist power. The USDA opened experimental stations in Hawaii and Puerto Rico to receive shipments of tropical plants that wouldn't survive at headquarters in Washington, DC.

By the dawn of World War I, public enthusiasm for colonial administration was waning, and backlash to an era of rapid globalization stoked nativist fears about foreign contamination. The entomologist Charles Marlatt frequently clashed publicly with Fairchild—the men had been childhood friends before their feud—as he argued that the import of so many exotic plants was causing America to become overrun with disease and "foreign insect enemies." Invasive pests were indeed a problem: Marlatt had seen the San Jose scale, an insect, decimate fruit trees in California in the 1880s after it was accidentally introduced on Chinese peach trees (he later traveled to China to find the scale's natural predator—and returned with the ladybug). The US was one of the last wealthy nations without any restrictions on importing live plants, until Marlatt's efforts paid off and the Plant Quarantine Act passed in 1912. Though the law was relaxed somewhat after World War II, when the global mood again swung toward internationalism and trade liberalization, it effectively put an end to the unregulated heyday of the plant explorers.

Fairchild's dream of bringing the boundless variety of the world's fruits to Americans went unrealized in other ways. An unforeseen consequence of his work was the rise of industrial monoculture to grow the most profitable varieties in the cheapest locales, at the expense of native and heirloom varieties. In the 1860s, New England was in the grip of a "pear mania," an enthusiasm for amateur horticulture which irked Henry David Thoreau, who felt pears were

a finicky and "aristocratic" fruit compared to the apples he loved.
"The hired man gathers the apples and barrels them. The proprietor plucks the pears at odd hours for a pastime, and his daughter
wraps them each in its paper," he wrote. "Judges & ex-judges &
honorables are connoisseurs of pears & discourse of them at
length between sessions." He might have been less judgmental had
he known that Bartlett pears would soon become available by train
from California, where trees could bear heavier crops than in the
East. Of the 2,683 pear varieties recorded in use between 1803
and 1903, 88 percent were extinct by 1982. Indeed, the US grows
far fewer commercial varieties of most fruits than it did one hundred years ago. It is dismaying to flip through the *Illustrated Catalog*'s abundance of grapes—including the inky Memory, oblong
Rose d'Italie, and maroon Requa—and think of the two options
available in the supermarket: "red" and "green."

Fairchild was eager to see his favorite fruit, the "indescribably
delicious" mangosteen, available in the US, but in addition to re-
quiring the moist, humid growing conditions of Southeast Asia,
it bruises easily and won't ripen after being picked. The pawpaw
is also considered too fragile to make the bumpy truck journey
to stores. While it is now possible to ship intensely flavorful mangoes from India, as Victoria once dreamed, it's too expensive to
be worthwhile at anything larger than a boutique scale. Instead,
we are stuck with the insipid red-and-green Tommy Atkins, which
was rejected numerous times by the Florida Mango Forum Variety
Committee when it was first discovered, in the 1950s, for being
bland and fibrous—"not a connoisseur's mango." But the fruit was
disease resistant, difficult to damage, and visually appealing: a tri-
fecta that, in the global market, nearly always trumps taste.

The greatest success of fruit mass production, and perhaps its
greatest cautionary tale, is the banana. There are more than a
thousand varieties of banana, but 99 percent of those exported
to the US and Europe are the hardy Cavendish, and all Cavendish bananas are clones, propagated from cuttings that can all be
traced back to one original plant (as are Granny Smith apples,
navel oranges, and many other commercial fruits). Unfortunately,
being genetically homogeneous and grown in the tropics makes
the Cavendish highly susceptible to disease. In the 1950s, a fungus
known as Panama disease rapidly spread through United Fruit's
empire and virtually obliterated the Gros Michel banana, once

as widespread as the Cavendish (and said to be more flavorful). United Fruit researchers' efforts to find a fungicide that could control Panama disease, though unsuccessful, ushered in a new era of rampant pesticide use. The application of the pesticide DBCP between the 1960s and 1980s caused the sterilization of plantation workers in five countries, and other chemicals continue to cause high rates of cancer and respiratory disease among banana workers.

Agrobiodiversity is in stark decline worldwide. To hedge against an increasingly precarious food supply, the USDA now conserves many wild or discontinued varieties in seed banks and germplasm repositories, including one of the world's largest collection of apples in Geneva, New York. The Fairchild Tropical Botanic Garden in Miami, founded in 1936 and home to many plants Fairchild personally collected, has changed its mission from the introduction of new plants to the preservation of endangered Floridian species, and protects the genetic diversity of a large tropical fruit collection. Many of Fairchild's samples are no longer grown anywhere else, having been crossbred out of existence. After decades of hybridization in pursuit of new cultivars, there is now some dawning recognition of what has been lost in the shuffle.

Seed banks alone, of course, can't restore local foodways: in the US, that work is being done by groups like I-Collective, a coalition of Indigenous chefs, herbalists, seed keepers, and others working on projects related to food sovereignty. There are also organizations like the Neighborhood Planting Project, a group in Bloomington, Indiana, that goes door to door offering to plant native fruit-bearing shrubs and trees like pawpaws, crabapples, hazelnuts, and persimmons in front yards at no cost. (So far, they have given away over seven thousand plants.) Next year the artist Sam Van Aken will plant an orchard on Governor's Island in New York, each tree with a number of native or lost heirloom species grafted onto its branches. The fruits will be shared with the public, "giving everyone a chance to see and taste fruits that, in some cases, haven't been available for centuries."

Decades of Red Delicious dominance in the produce aisle have left customers looking for better. On the one hand, this has led to a movement of local agriculture; on the other, to ever more rigorous breeding and genetic engineering programs to create produce better suited for the industrial food system, like apples that won't brown when exposed to air and can be sold presliced in plastic bags. It's possible such new technologies will find ways to avoid the trade-off between taste and the unlimited accessibility we have been promised, but markets tend to cater to our simplest desires, for the shiny, the seedless, and the sweet (two of the most successful recent designer fruits have been Honeycrisp apples and Cotton Candy grapes). It is easy to forget that fruit is not a commodity first, but part of a living organism that, when bound to a place and season, can both surprise and satisfy.

In his 1862 essay "Wild Apples," Thoreau describes an apple-picking walk through the Massachusetts countryside in November as a full sensory experience, in which the fruit can only be appreciated as part of the environment that produced it—as a way to taste late autumn. "These apples have hung in the wind and frost and rain till they have absorbed the qualities of the weather or season, and thus are highly *seasoned,* and they *pierce* and *sting* and *permeate* us with their spirit. They must be eaten in *season,* accordingly,— that is, out-of-doors." Wild apples, randomly cross-pollinated by bees, have a wide range of flavors, sometimes even when grown from the same tree, and a love for them requires a palate that can tolerate the occasionally sour, gnarled, irregular, intense. This is a kind of novelty that has been eradicated in our quest for endless choice. Thoreau himself predicted that "The era of the Wild Apple will soon be past . . . I fear that he who walks over these fields a century hence will not know the pleasure of knocking off wild apples. Ah, poor man, there are many pleasures which he will not know!"

JIAYANG FAN

Chronicles of a Bubble-Tea Addict

FROM *The New Yorker*

I FIRST DISCOVERED *zhen zhu nai cha*, as bubble milk tea, or boba, is known in Chinese, when I was ten. It was the early nineties, and I'd been in the United States only two years, living and going to school in Connecticut towns so uniformly white that soy sauce was still considered exotic there. A few times a year, my mother and I would take the Metro-North an hour south to New York City for the sole purpose of stockpiling Chinese groceries. These were not leisurely shopping trips but carefully strategized plans of attack, during which my mother practiced bargain hunting as blood sport. Behind her I'd trudge, up Canal and down East Broadway, a weary foot soldier weighed down by growing satchels of fish tofu and Chinese cabbage and hoisin sauce. Invariably, our last stop was Taipan Bakery, which offered an end-of-day discount on goods such as red-bean buns and sponge cake, my favorites. At some point, it also began selling a newfangled drink, served in plastic cups with jumbo straws and what appeared to be shiny marbles piled on the bottom. An order cost about three dollars, half of my mother's hourly wage cleaning houses. Yet every time she relented and let me buy one, and the victory tasted as sweet as the drink itself.

There was only one flavor of boba back then—black tea with sweetened condensed milk and balls of tapioca—and the cups had annoyingly flimsy lids that leaked at the slightest jostle. This provided a solid excuse to sit down at one of the bakery's unwiped chrome-rimmed tables, where I'd sip my tea and indulge in my second-favorite activity in Chinatown: people watching. It didn't

matter that the bits of chatter I picked up were not exactly juicy—
the crowd at Taipan was mostly elderly grandmas or weary parents
and their children—or that I had to contend with my mother's
complaints about my indulgence. ("Why are we wasting money
when I can just pour sugar and gummies in your tea?") What I
savored was the illusion, ever so rare for a bewildered young immigrant, that we, too, could afford a few pearls of leisure.

At school, a fancy one that my mother toiled to afford, we were
reading *A Tree Grows in Brooklyn,* Betty Smith's semi-autobiographical
novel about a family fighting indigence and hard luck in early-
twentieth-century Williamsburg. Francie Nolan, the teenaged
protagonist—nerdy, plain, and secretly ambitious, like me—loved
the smell of coffee, one of the family's few luxuries, but she seldom drank her serving—"at the end of the meal, it went down
the sink." It was Francie's mother's comment, in particular, that
stayed with me: "I think it's good that people like us can waste
something once in a while and get the feeling of how it would be
to have lots of money and not have to worry about scrounging."
Unlike Francie, though, I gulped down king-sized cups of boba
without leaving behind a single drop. When only melting ice cubes
remained, I hunted the last tapioca balls stranded among them as
if on a search-and-rescue mission, and savored how their gummy
vestiges would remain stuck in my molars long after I'd thrown the
empty cup away.

Like me, bubble tea was a recent immigrant to the US. It had
originated, sometime in the eighties, amid the vibrant snack culture of Taiwan, although exactly how and when is a matter of
dispute. One story goes that a Taichung tea house whimsically
blended iced black tea with *fen yuan,* a traditional Taiwanese
dessert of sweetened tapioca pudding, only to discover that the
combo outsold every other offering. It wasn't long before the new
beverage traveled overseas with the waves of immigrants from Taiwan who were arriving on California's shores; before there were
specialty boba shops, Taiwanese restaurants would offer it as an
off-menu item for those in the know. Today bubble tea is rampant
in China (the term "boba" is also Chinese slang for "big breasts,"
though the name isn't popular on the mainland), but the Taiwan–
US pipeline is how the trend first traveled. When I went back to
China as a kid, during summer vacations, I was astonished to dis-

cover that my extended family living in third- and fourth-tier cities had never even tasted the drink.

If it were up to me, my mother and I would have moved next door to Taipan Bakery, and I could have grown up on a diet of tapioca, gawking at the Chinese American boys with their gelled hair and baggy denim. (At twelve, I crushed hard on the "wannabe gangsta" look.) But my mother knew, in a way a child could not, that a life in New York would have also meant life in government-subsidized housing, in an urban school district whose quality she couldn't ascertain. It was better for us to be interlopers among affluent strangers while quietly chipping away at the American dream.

After college, in 2007, I moved to New York, and lived in stamp-sized apartments on the Upper East Side and in Murray Hill—neighborhoods dominated by the elite, white demographic of my youth. But four years later my mother was diagnosed with ALS, a progressive, neurodegenerative illness that was destined to paralyze every voluntary muscle of her body. She was still living in Connecticut, working the same nanny job she'd had for a decade; the prospect of losing independence petrified her. But the disease left her with few options; her doctor warned that she would need a caretaker. So she scoured New York City for affordable apartments that the two of us could share, employing the same hard-nosed diligence she applied to grocery shopping, and settled on a place in Elmhurst, Queens, one of the most diverse and immigrant-dense neighborhoods in the city. I would have preferred a newer building with fewer cockroaches in the kitchen sink and a more handicap-friendly lobby, but it did not escape my notice that there were two bubble-tea parlors within a five-minute walk of our apartment.

Ten Ren, on Elmhurst's main drag, was an old-timey place specializing in loose-leaf tea in gilded canisters. Founded in Taiwan, in 1953, by the son of a tea-farming family, it had introduced boba as the trend accelerated in the late nineties. There, I'd skip milk tea in favor of the classics—ginseng oolong and High Mountain tie guan yin, which had a quietly earthy fragrance. The place reminded me of my childhood in China, with middle-aged saleswomen who spoke no English and cracked sunflower seeds between their teeth.

A block away, the second shop, Quickly, delivered me into another scene entirely. Founded in Southern California, in 2002, by a Taiwanese entrepreneur who billed her café as "New Generation Asian Fusion," Quickly offered pearl milk tea in Americanized flavors— chocolate and coffee and caramel—and simplified the operation, doing away with traditional hot brewed teas altogether. I patronized Quickly more often, because it was closer to my subway stop and because, in the right mood, I enjoyed a coffee-flavored tea instead of my usual taro. Waiting for my order to arrive, I'd watch coteries of Asian teenagers slip in and out, laughing and chatting in a mixture of Chinese idioms and English slang.

The contrast between Ten Ren and Quickly was the first sign, for me, that the world of bubble tea was changing. Riding the wave of upscale coffee bars, boba shops in the following years would proliferate, moving outside ethnic enclaves to claim real estate on main city thoroughfares. Before the pandemic engulfed New York, I liked to travel forty-five minutes from where I live now, in Harlem, to St. Marks Place, which boasted, at one time, six bubble-tea shops on a single block. I am well into my thirties, but in my sweats and sneakers I'd convince myself that I could pass for one of the Gen Z students who are increasingly the target boba demographic, even if the panoply of novel bubble-tea offerings felt increasingly estranged from the drink as I knew it. Why go to a boba shop if you want panna cotta, or chia seeds in place of tapioca balls? My favorite haunt, Mi Tea, a spacious, well-lit outpost of a Chinese chain, specialized in "cheese tea," a viral sensation featuring layers of foamy milk and salty whipped cream cheese. The drink, which originated in a Taiwanese night market around 2010, costs anywhere between five and eight dollars a cup, but before the pandemic, when I'd hunker in Mi Tea working for hours at a time, I'd notice many orders abandoned half-consumed on unoccupied tables. This was an altogether different kind of waste than what Francie practiced with her coffee. Boba and I had spent our adolescence as scrappy, enterprising immigrants at America's periphery. But it had evolved into something different: the boba shop was now a sort of social club for Asian youth, a snacky sanctuary of belonging, and bubble tea a ubiquitous, Instagram-friendly accessory for a new generation of upwardly mobile Asian kids.

*

In 2018, boba's new status was enshrined in a Facebook group called Subtle Asian Traits, a forum created, as a lark, by Asian Australian high-schoolers, to collect observations and memes about the Asian diaspora. Along with experiences such as strict parents, or a familiarity with the question "Where are you *really* from?" a fondness for bubble tea was, according to the group, a signature trait of Asian youth; one meme shows an Asian baby being baptized with bubble tea instead of holy water. The phenomenon of Subtle Asian Traits, which has since swelled into one of the internet's largest Asian communities, with almost two million members (and has inspired such spin-off groups as Subtle Asian Leftovers and Subtle Asian Dating), suggests how hungry young Asians were to find a knowing, unifying language of their shared experience. Reading through the group's posts, I felt as if I were at one of the middle-school sleepovers I'd never got invited to as a kid, laughing at insidery jokes whose punchlines, for once, did not have to be explained. By publicly cataloging the habits and quirks of Asian identity, though, Subtle Asian Traits in effect, perhaps inadvertently, issued a definition of what—and, by extension, who—counts as Asian. The group became a subject of debate, criticized for being elitist and skewed toward the East Asian experience, and for otherwise treating a narrow, consumerist version of Asian-ness as somehow universal. In a long piece about boba for *Eater,* from 2019, the writer and critic Jenny G. Zhang wrote that "there is something irredeemably maddening" about defining one's cultural identity in terms of commodified objects, "as young Asian Americans have done with bubble tea."

On social media, such frustrations had found expression in a new coinage, a sort of intra-Asian put-down for the bubble-tea generation: "boba liberalism." According to the Twitter user @diaspora_is_red, an Asian American who was among the first to use the term, a boba liberal is someone who centers her Asian identity in buzzy cultural objects and "trend-chasing spectacle" but lacks true engagement with the politics of her Asian identity. It's the Asian who can't stop talking about *Crazy Rich Asians* as a breakthrough in Asian representation, or who posts boba selfies as a way to prove her Asian bona fides while, elsewhere, seeking acceptance within white culture. For the boba liberal, politics is as much a performance as is one's choice of beverage, a cultural prop in the theater of identity. I had seen the label lobbed back and forth on social media, but I never paid it much mind, until, last October, I noticed it attached to my own name. I had written a food diary for *New York* magazine's Grub Street, in which I mentioned enjoying, among many other Asian (and occasionally non-Asian) foods, boba in popsicle form. A few days after the article came out, I discovered, to my bemusement, that a fellow Asian American had linked to it on Twitter, with the caption "boba lib idiot queen."

I am admittedly vocal about my obsession with bubble tea; in fact, the editors of the Grub Street piece had cut several other mentions of it, on the ground that it was boba overkill. I also write for a mainstream, left-leaning American publication, and it's true that I once wrote a Profile of the *Crazy Rich Asians* star Constance Wu. It hadn't occurred to me that such proclivities made me a quintessential boba liberal (much less an idiot queen)—aren't I too old, anyway, to be implicated in a younger generation's negotiations over the meaning of bubble tea? But my intentions don't quite matter; as my mother has always been fond of reminding me, an identity is as much about how you are perceived as it is about what you mean to project.

The boba-liberal label made me think back to my first year of college in New England, when I joined an Asian American campus organization. (Another hallmark of the boba liberal: placing excessive value in Asian student groups.) The first Chinese American I encountered at the group's meeting had been born in the US. Another didn't speak Chinese at all. They were comfortably middle class, with parents who worked white-collar jobs. I don't recall much about our activities—I had been appointed the PR rep, a role I performed lackadaisically at best—except that, at a campus-wide spring-festival event, we decided unanimously to offer bubble tea as a way of "sharing our Asian American heritage." Looking back, I wonder whether serving this ostensibly exotic drink to our predominantly white classmates effectively engaged their cultural curiosity, or whether it was exactly the kind of superficial, flattening display of Asian-ness that the term "boba liberal" was coined to critique—"all sugar, no substance," as @diaspora_is_red put it.

On the other hand, a group of college freshmen could be forgiven for assuming that compromising our complexity was a condition of survival as minorities in a majority world. Part of being Asian American—a subtle trait, if you want to call it that—is the fear of being judged for losing one's Asian-ness while failing to earn acceptance as a real American. Assimilation, in other words, is an impossible process of pouring oneself into another while holding on to a sense of self. It is tricky to judge from the outside a transformation that largely takes place within.

The whole trajectory of my life in America has involved navigating cultural symbols, most of which were far more intimidating than boba. When I was young, my mother thumbed through the *U.S. News & World Report* college rankings as if it were the Bible, until its pages went dirty and ragged. She knew that an elite education functioned as a trophy on the mantel of cultural capital, and that accruing me such capital was the surest way to ensure my success in this country. It was only years later, once I'd achieved the higher education she'd painstakingly engineered for me, that I recognized how my mother's diligence was intertwined with a deep cynicism, a search for validation in a world whose ingrained racism and structural inequities she accepted as inevitable. What arrogance must I possess, she'd say, to believe that the system could change? Better to learn the rules of the game and submit. Practice this sort of pragmatism long enough and it becomes a kind of complicity: *everything* is merely a performance, a bending of oneself to the warped shape of America. And yet, my mother's very journey to this country was a gamble premised on the possibility of change.

In adulthood, I've sought out boba most obsessively during the times when my life has felt most beyond my control. As the roles reversed between my mother and me, something about the syrupy, caramelized milk fortified—or perhaps anesthetized—me against the sight of her shrinking body, which weakened a little every day until she could no longer survive without a hospital's round-the-clock care. The day she had a feeding tube inserted, because she'd lost the ability to swallow, I nursed a green milk tea with red beans and tapioca balls while waiting for the liquid food supplement to drain into her stomach. See, we both have our *zhen zhu nai cha,* I told her. Last March, when the pandemic hit New York City, and it was unclear whether I'd be able to continue visiting my mother at the medical facility where she lives, I hurried down to Chinatown to stock up on quarantine groceries. A rainbow-colored package

that had never tempted me before suddenly called out: black tapioca pearl, ready in five minutes! I threw it into my shopping cart
and hoped that I would not have to resort to using it.

The packet spent most of last year deep in the recesses of
my kitchen cabinet, among my collection of dried seaweed and
pickled tofu. To pass the fearful, lonely months of quarantine, I
splurged on boba delivery, often several cups at a time. (When I
went for an endoscopy recently, the first of my life, a mysterious
gummy substance was detected in my gut.) But one night in December, too late to order in, I was overcome by the familiar crav-
ing. I fished out the emergency boba provisions and tore open the
package. The shriveled balls inside looked like rat droppings, with
a whitish powder clinging to their surface. Dismayed that I hadn't
checked the expiration date at the time of purchase, as my mother
would have surely done, I saw that the tapioca had expired some
months ago. I googled the dangers of consuming expired bubbles
and was assured, by an entry on a site called talkboba.com, that "if
you consume expired tapioca starch or other starches and flours,
you most likely won't get sick." Good enough. I took a handful of
the pebbles, dropped them into a pot, and turned on the stove.
The balls vibrated in the water as they became bloated, and took
on a transparent sheen. A thick honey smell filled the air. Before
they were fully cooked, I couldn't resist scooping out a spoonful,
gulping them down so quickly that I could feel their dark, sticky
heat long after I swallowed.

LIGAYA MISHAN

Let Them Eat Fakes

FROM *The New York Times Style Magazine*

WHAT DO YOU feed a king, dulled to every luxury beyond want? In the city-state of Venice in 1574, the young Henry III, then king of Poland and en route to becoming king of France, was welcomed with a banquet, just another in the hundreds of his life. But when he reached for his napkin, it shattered, a handful of dust. The whole setup was fake—the drape of tablecloth, the platters and knives. All were molded out of a powdered sugar paste likely made with rose and orange blossom water and tragacanth, a resin from a plant indigenous to the Middle East and Asia: the yields of trade and Western expansion. A year before, Venice had ended a war with the Ottoman Empire by grudgingly ceding Cyprus, the site of its cane plantations, and the price of sugar was high. To waste so much of it was a show of power. It hardly mattered, then, that this was a feast of nothing, too sweet to eat. The pleasure lay in the surprise, the beautiful lie.

For centuries, the West has delighted in the treachery of food in disguise, from the intricate sotelties of the Middle Ages, presented to aristocrats between dinner courses—a pastry stag, say, with an arrow in its side, which when plucked let loose a gush of bloodlike claret—to the grand edible monuments and landscapes erected for public festivals in Italy in the sixteenth through eighteenth centuries, with swooping arches of bread and cheese crowned by suckling pigs and mock trees hung with fruit and haunches of game. Part of the entertainment was inviting the public to ransack the displays and scrabble for mouthfuls among the ruins, while nobles of the court applauded from afar: a literal hunger games.

These fever dreams were meant to evoke the mythic Land of Cock-aigne, a utopia that first entered European literature around the thirteenth century, where custard rained down from the sky, roofs were tiled in bacon, and garlic-roasted geese and stewed larks, tasting of cloves and cinnamon, flew straight into your mouth—where no one, highborn or low, had to suffer to make a living to ease their hunger. It was a fantasy of abundance at a time when, for much of the population, food was no certainty. (Inevitably, a disapproving tone crept in, and by the sixteenth century, Cockaigne was a cautionary tale of gluttony and sloth.)

Centuries later, we're still mesmerized by these little duplicities, the more so in our compulsively visual culture, where food is increasingly consumed without actual eating, experienced through a screen. Between or even in lieu of meals, we sate ourselves on the theater of ever-proliferating TV cooking shows while trawling Instagram for brightly staged still lifes of brimming-over burgers and neon macarons. This disembodiment was exacerbated during the pandemic, when many restaurants were forced to shut down, and dining with anyone beyond immediate family—eating as occasion, as opposed to mere sustenance—all but ceased. What a happy distraction, then, when last summer, BuzzFeed's *Tasty* shared a video on Twitter that opened on a close-up of a knife looming over a red Croc sandal with its bulbous toe box. There was barely a moment for the viewer to register the banality of the shoe before the knife, wielded by a black-gloved hand, cut it brusquely in half, revealing layers of yellow and pink cake.

More objects followed, each the work of the pastry chef Tuba Geckil of Red Rose Cake in Istanbul, and each startlingly realistic: a roll of quilted toilet paper; a bar of soap, frothy as if just used; two ripe bananas, black-flecked and joined at the stem. All fell to the blade.

Other pastry chefs in recent years have made a fetish of illusion, from Cédric Grolet at Le Meurice hotel in Paris—whose rough-skinned lemons turn out to be white chocolate shells sprayed with gold powder, masking interiors of poached lemons and yuzu ganache—to Sarah Hardy of the Edible Museum in Colchester, England, with her anatomically precise chocolate brains and hearts. But Geckil's objects, so staid and ordinary, struck a chord. Within days the video earned nearly thirty million views, and some commenters shot their own videos, thrusting knives into objects in their own homes, wondering if everything was secretly cake, even themselves. (One meme appropriated a clip from Ben Cullen, the self-appointed BakeKing, of Chester, England, showing a tattooed hand holding a knife and slicing into another tattooed hand—cake!—before blithely chopping up the arm.)

Yet no one was really fooled. *Tasty*'s tweet introducing the video gave the game away from the start: "These are all cakes." The knife is the focus, disrupting the illusion before it even has a chance of duping the viewer. Left intact, the objects would remain just objects, latent and unexceptional, beneath notice. Only once exposed as fake do they take on value. The awe is all in retrospect. And this may be why these camouflaged cakes charmed so many, that what appears to be a small-scale but still subversive undermining of reality—at a time when we're contending with far bigger and more dangerous deceptions, the widening gyre of disinformation, a stock market unmoored from actual worth, the ever more remote promise of social mobility—is in the end no threat at all. The point is not the trick but our seeing through it, which confirms the human capacity for recognizing truths and our dominion in interpreting and shaping the world around us. Maybe nothing is real; maybe everything is a joke. But at least we're in on it.

The earliest cakes were distinguished by a lack of dimension. To the ancient Greeks, they were plakous, from the word for flat. Archaeologists have found remnants dating back 6,400 years, in a lakeside Neolithic village in what is today Switzerland, where the seeds of the opium poppy were crushed into a paste (some have theorized for narcotic use) and smoothed over hot stones to bake. For millennia, so-called cakes were basically bread, save for a faint sweetness (from milk or honey, for example) and a plumping-up with some form of fat. Not until the mid-nineteenth century, with advances in flour-milling technology and the invention of baking powder—which bypassed the need for leavening with yeast—did cakes gain the buoyancy we know today.

Nevertheless, sweetness and fat were enough to lend cakes an aura of the extraordinary and earn them a ritualistic role in our lives. In *Cake: A Global History* (2010), the British cultural historian Nicola Humble notes a shared lineage with religious offerings: cake is essentially a compacted form of the rich ingredients—grain, nuts, milk, honey—that were traditionally poured out on altars to be devoured by the divine. Nutritionally unnecessary and yet more than a dessert, it's almost always celebratory, present at major life events, marking the passage of years as well as the binding contract of marriage. "Cake is one of those foodstuffs whose symbolic function can completely overwhelm its actual status as comestible," Humble writes, although it is also emphatically and often excessively sensual, smeared with icing and disgorging creamy fillings: "food layered on food."

Icing, and with it the prospect of ostentatious design, came late to the party, an innovation of the mid-seventeenth century as sugar production increased and prices dropped—a direct result of human trafficking, as native Africans were forcibly shipped to the West Indies to work the cane plantations. White cakes were explicitly favored, the British social anthropologist Simon R. Charsley has written, because the whiter the icing, the higher the amount and quality of sugar, bespeaking luxury. This was true for all cakes, whatever the occasion, until the color, historically deployed in the West to evoke cleanliness and purity, eventually became the signature of weddings in the nineteenth century, with the snowy cake standing in for the bride in her immaculate gown and the ceremonial cake cutting reenacting the loss of virginity.

And so attention shifted from the cake itself to its facade. British royal weddings set the standard with fluted columns, cathedral arches, swags, and filigrees all rendered in royal icing, a compound of powdered sugar and egg whites that clung like cement and stiffened into a shield over a layer of almond paste or marzipan. Cakes could be homey comfort, piped with impressionistic buttercream flowers whose lax edges practically begged to be smudged, or a pageantry of precision—a divide that widened toward the end of the twentieth century with the rise of fondant, also known as sugar paste, plastic icing, and ready-to-roll icing: a modern version of a traditional French confection of boiled sugar, today typically mixed with liquid glucose or corn syrup and gelatin and glycerin for pliancy, and as supple as clay.

The trouble is, fondant is undelicious, chalky, and chewy, particularly in commercially premade form, so much so that diners often just peel it off the cake. But apparently that is the price of artistry. For with this kind of moldable icing, a cake can become anything: the Colosseum, an Hermès Birkin bag, a Croc. Above all, fondant makes it possible to hide a cake's *cakeness*. The crumble, the yielding, the sumptuousness, the sheer joy of cramming it into your mouth as quickly as you can—all are sealed off under that smooth, perfected surface, which invites touch but allows no entry, no gratification. The cake has disappeared.

Deception as an art form goes back to at least the fifth century BC, when the Greek painter Zeuxis is said to have produced a picture of grapes so vivid, birds pecked at the canvas. European painting from the Renaissance through the mid-nineteenth century was committed to faithful representation, in part as a way of honoring God's manifestation in "the smallest detail of earthly creation," the German art historian Sybille Ebert-Schifferer has written. But trompe l'oeil, French for "deceive the eye"—a genre born in the Netherlands in the seventeenth century as a subcategory of still life—took this a step further, from representing to being, depicting objects so convincingly, a viewer might be persuaded that there was no painting; that the thing painted was the thing itself.

"Might" is the operative word, for no evidence suggests that viewers were ever truly conned. Nevertheless, the whiff of uncertainty was titillating, and trompe l'oeil proved hugely popular, even as critics scorned it as a gimmick and worse, a morally suspect enterprise, whose goal was simply to replicate the most mundane and trivial of items without the edification of beauty or heroic narrative. "The mind . . . derives its pleasure, not from the contemplation of a truth, but from the discovery of a falsehood," the English art critic John Ruskin declared in the first volume of *Modern Painters* in 1843. Not long after, with photography ascendant and painting shifting away from straightforward mimesis, trompe l'oeil lost its hold on the public imagination.

Yet here it is today, resurrected in sugar, and arguably once again crystallizing the anxieties of an era. For trompe l'oeil was never just a gotcha. Emerging around the same time as bourgeois capitalism, ultrarealistic still lifes both reflected and abetted a culture newly bewitched by commodities. As the Canadian American art historian Emily Braun writes in the catalog for *Cubism and the Trompe l'Oeil Tradition,* an exhibition she is co-curating that will open next year at the Metropolitan Museum of Art, sometimes these paintings were small frauds that pointed to larger ones, "from government sleight of hand with paper currency to false promises of advertising."

We remain in thrall to our purchasing power and how it defines us, especially as commodities have become untethered from reality, mediated through shop windows and iPhone screens. Part of the appeal of trompe l'oeil cakes, notably those modeled not on luxuries but on plebeian goods, is how they recalibrate value. Technically, it's the cake that undergoes transformation, cut into shape and camouflaged, but for the audience, the narrative goes the other way. What we think is merely utilitarian is exposed as something else entirely—a provocation, an exercise in the ridiculous, an unasked-for treat.

"If you can eat it, it's not art," the American humorist Fran Lebowitz once said. Yet art has historically used food as both subject and, in recent decades, materials, like the ink of boiled-down Coca-Cola in paintings by the Chinese conceptual artist He Xiangyu or the bed carved out of more than five hundred loaves of bread by the British sculptor Antony Gormley, who used his teeth to bite and shape, then ate the leftovers. In turn, chefs have claimed the mantle of artists and cast plates as staged tableaux. Trompe l'oeil was a fixture of molecular gastronomy, which gained renown in the 2000s with tricks like dropping olive juice into a bath of sodium alginate, creating an olive-like orb that trapped the juice at its center, ready to burst in the mouth—the Spanish chef Ferran Adrià's famous liquid olive.

But where in traditional trompe l'oeil attention is drawn to the materials—the paint, the canvas—in avant-garde cooking the opposite happens: the ingredients are often broken down beyond recognition and assigned startling new textures, leaving only flavor as a clue. In detecting the deceit of a trompe l'oeil painting, you become an accomplice to it; your perceptive powers are validated by your ability to decipher the artist's scheme. (This is Ruskin's critique, neatly summed up by the literary scholar Caroline Levine: "Imitative art is dangerous because it teaches us to enjoy our own authority.") Presented with a liquid olive, lacking knowledge of its origin story or the tools that make it possible, you are nothing but a witness. You aren't invited in with a handshake and a wink; you're supposed to be mystified.

The riddle of the trompe l'oeil cake is simpler. It's solved in an instant, with a stroke of the knife. And the materials matter: the cake is a cake, whatever its makeover, with a primal promise of comfort. Maybe the lure isn't the cleverness of the deception at all, but the cake as endgame—the reward that makes all the absurdity (of a cake that looks like a bottle of hand sanitizer, of life in general) worthwhile. "You will be baked, and then there will be cake," says the singsong robotic voice midway through the video game *Portal* (2007), as you run a gauntlet of puzzles and try not to die; later, the voice taunts, "I'm going to kill you, and all the cake is gone," and it's not clear which fate is worse.

So while some commenters framed last summer's cake video— in jest, but only just—as an ontological crisis, calling into question the nature of reality, it's more interesting to read it as a jubilant shattering of illusions and illusion-making itself. The knife destroys the pristine veneer of fondant and, in so doing, liberates the cake within. Already, a small subculture of bakers have started defying the norms of cake decoration and the quest for seamless, tranquilizing Instagram perfection (what the Korean-born German philosopher Byung-Chul Han calls "art in the age of *Like*"). As the essayist Alicia Kennedy writes in "On Cake: And the Shifting Aesthetics of Perfection," bakers like Bronwen Wyatt of Bayou Saint Cake in New Orleans and Joey Peach of Flavor Supreme in Chicago shun artificially smooth and impeccably finished surfaces, instead topping their cakes with thick ripples of buttercream as tall as Elizabethan ruffs, shards of pomegranate studded with seeds, pulp spilling viscously out of a passion fruit's cracked shell and even cryptic scraps of lettuce.

Of course, most of us will never taste the trompe l'oeil cakes enshrined on Instagram. Fulfillment is forever withheld. Yet something else is gained: reality is destabilized, but instead of proving hollow and empty of meaning, it's flooded with possibility. Nothing is fixed; transformation awaits. Braun notes that our relationship to our possessions has intensified during the pandemic, as we've been "pushed into proximity" with them in lockdown and isolation. With our worlds shrunk, "our imagination has to dwell within the things around us." We are left to commune with the inanimate, to uncover its secrets. Just a little nick with the knife, because you never know. Oh, let it be, let it be cake.

The Queen of Delicacies

FROM *The Bitter Southerner*

"WHERE THE HELL is this grave?"

Late on an afternoon when the heat index hovered near second-degree murder, I stood on a slope overlooking hundreds of squat white headstones descending row by regimented row to the railroad tracks at the verge of Rose Hill Cemetery in Macon, Georgia. Each marked by a dollar store battle flag stuck in the ground. A plaque erected by the Ladies Memorial Association identified the plot as Confederate Soldiers' Square.

I was clearly in the wrong place. No guitar hero here.

"Go ask someone," shouted my husband, Bronson, answering his phone when I called home for guidance.

A man walking his pit bulls finally pointed the way, and I scrambled across a series of overgrown terraces, apologizing to the forgotten dead, in an effort to find the man nicknamed Skydog, who adopted an empty glass Coricidin bottle as a slide for his Fender Stratocaster.

Established in 1840 as a final resting place and parkland for Macon's elite, Rose Hill contains a multitude of neoclassical mausoleums and obelisks, punctuated by specimen trees choked with climbing ivy, the ideal hideout for broke young musicians who wanted to get high on mushrooms and scribble song lyrics.

Helium balloons floated from the fence protecting their graves. Jasmine enveloped one corner where the first of the original band members lay at rest. A car pulled up on a pathway and several grizzled men climbed out. All lit up smokes and shambled to the brick terrace leading to the plot. They looked like bikers long past a last ride. One spotted me.

"Do you know where Elizabeth Reed is buried?" he asked.

I shrugged.

Another bent on creaky knees and scrabbled in the dirt, hunting for a rock to carry away as a memento. (Fans used to steal the decorative mushroom statuettes studding the graves until the family erected the fence.) After they drove away, I paid respect, texting pictures to my husband, the true believer, who should have been there with me.

The Allman Brothers Band formed during a volatile era of Vietnam War protests and the Civil Rights Movement, and the release of a live double album, *At Fillmore East,* which included the song "In Memory of Elizabeth Reed," propelled them to fame in 1971. Before lead guitarist Duane Allman died at age twenty-four in a motorcycle crash, and was interred here later that same year, *Good Times* magazine journalist Ellen Mandel interviewed him.

"How are you helping the revolution?" she asked.

Skydog's reply would become Southern rock legend.

"Every time I'm in Georgia I eat a peach for peace."

Peaches arrived in Georgia by way of a circuitous route from China. (The earliest fossilized peach pits, discovered in the southern province of Yunnan, date back 2.6 million years.) The stone fruit known as táo was conveyed to the West by Silk Road trade caravans, gaining its Latin name, *Prunus persica,* from a stopover in Persia—then arrived elsewhere as persik, pesca, pêssego, pêche—and finally across the Atlantic sometime after 1539, when Hernando de Soto, who apparently carried pits among the seed stores on board his vessels, landed in La Florida. Peaches proceeded along de Soto's trail from Tampa Bay to the Mississippi River. At least, this is one of the accepted narratives, since expedition chroniclers failed to mention peaches specifically. Another has peaches introduced by missionaries first to St. Augustine, and then St. Simons and Cumberland Islands, later in the sixteenth century.

Once on the ground, peaches propagated so effectively that by the time naturalist John Lawson published *A New Voyage to Carolina* in 1709, he labeled them a pest:

> We have a great many sorts of this Fruit, which all thrive to Ad-
> miration, Peach-Trees coming to Perfection (with us) as easily
> as the Weeds. A Peach falling to the Ground, brings a Peach-
> Tree that shall bear in three years, or sometimes sooner. Eat-
> ing Peaches in our Orchards makes them come up so thick
> from the Kernel, that we are forced to take a great deal of
> Care to weed them out; otherwise they make our Land a Wil-
> derness of Peach-Trees.

Lucky the pest tasted good. Peach butter, peach leather, peach
cobbler, peach pie, peach sonker, peach marmalade, brandied
peaches, pickled peaches, peach sherbet, peach cordial, peach
bread, and an archaic curiosity, peach quiddany, all appear in the
earliest Southern journals, household diaries, and cookbooks. A
recipe for ratafia dating from 1830 calls for one thousand peach
kernels to be soaked in madeira wine. Lettice Bryan, author of
The Kentucky Housewife (1839), provided an elaborate method for
a jellied confection she titled "A Dish of Peaches," the successor
of quiddany (fruit jellies) and precursor to those Jell-O molds laid
out on picnic tables at family reunions.

And peaches were a rare sweet fruit available in abundance,
even to enslaved people.

That's before peaches became an agricultural crop more valuable than cotton. In 1844, a London Horticultural Society botanist
stumbled on the Chinese Cling growing in a walled orchard south
of the city of Shanghai. Peaches are generally classified as freestone
or clingstone, and fall into two further categories, depending on
whether they have white or yellow flesh. From these traits come
a world of varieties, but when the Chinese Cling, also known as
Shanghai's Honey Nectar, was subsequently imported as a potted
plant in 1850 by nurseryman Charles Downing, it quickly caught
on in American pomology circles for its size and flavor, equally balanced between tart and sweet, with a distinct almond note.

Then the Civil War changed everything and nothing. Cotton
faded a bit. Peaches flourished a bit more. Somebody still had to
pick the crops.

From the Chinese Cling comes the daughter peach we most
often visualize neatly arranged in baskets at roadside stands or on
the jacket of a Capricorn Records album dedicated to a deceased
guitar hero. In 1875, Georgia peach grower Samuel H. Rumph

crossed an open-pollinated Chinese Cling with Early Crawford, and the resulting juicy yellow freestone was characterized by a crimson blush on its cheek. He named it for his wife, Clara Elberta Moore. One of the earliest paintings in the splendid US Department of Agriculture Pomological Watercolor Collection is a Chinese Cling by Deborah Passmore Griscom from 1893. Her 1902 cross-section study of an Elberta affected by leaf curl sings of fruit gone bad. Yet Elberta became the commercial standard, so much so that Southern growers still identify the ripening season of other varieties either as days before, or days after, this *prunus* goes sploosh on the ground.

Lawton Pearson yanked open the door to his silver pickup and a peach rolled out. More were scattered on the dashboard, piled in the center console cup holder, and tossed on the back seat, hues from sunny yellow to muddy magenta, in stages of decay and ferment. His office manager, Vicki Hollingsworth, calls these "seat peaches." The fifth-generation farmer holds a law degree from the University of Georgia but returned home fifteen years ago to manage the family business.

"One day, when I just came back, I asked my dad, 'What do you do for a living? What do you do? What do you *actually* do?' "

Pearson climbed behind the wheel.

"He told me, 'I ride and look at peaches.' "

Lawton Pearson adjusted his blue-and-white trucker hat over sweat-damp hair and rolled down the windows so the baked-cobbler smell in the hot cab swirled as we peeled out of the parking lot at the Pearson Farm packing shed.

In 1885, Moses Winlock "Lockie" Pearson and his wife, Emma, moved to Crawford County, Georgia, during the postwar era that could be loosely termed the Peach Rush. They switched from milling timber to growing fruit, but he died at forty-eight, leaving his widow with a dozen children. By 1917, their oldest, John W. "Papa John" Pearson, expanded the property with the purchase of a larger farm that included a boarding hotel for seasonal workers, a company store, a packing shed, and post office. At one point, he had five thousand acres under cultivation. Pearson also patented a peach. According to his great-grandson, that didn't go as well.

"Papa John found an Early Hiley sport in 1946," Pearson said, turning down a dirt lane. "And an Early is always more in demand;

you'd get better prices for them. He wouldn't share, so everybody
was mad at him for patenting it. But then the market up North
figured out that it was a miserable eating peach. The story goes he
got a telegram that said, 'Have received your shipment of Pearson
Hiley peaches. When will you send sugar?' "

"What happened?" I asked.

"If a peach ain't sweet, there's no point in it."

Pearson passed a row of crew houses opposite the old boarding
hotel. Men done with picking for the day waved from the porches.
Like other orchards in the South, H-2A visa holders from Latin
America have replaced mostly Black sharecroppers, and at the
height of the season, the farm employs seven crews, each consist-
ing of sixteen pickers, two tractor drivers, and a crew boss; fathers
and sons, who have crossed the border for multiple generations.
Harvesters walk from tree to tree, scanning fruit for color and size,
gathering the best in a picking bucket strapped to their chests.
Pearson currently has forty-five varieties, and fifty others in experimental trials on seventeen hundred acres; the daily yield at the
height of the season is almost ten thousand half-bushel boxes.

"There's yet to be a mechanized way to picking peaches," he
said. "And it's going to be real difficult to teach a robot which one
is ripe."

"When do you know which varieties are ready?" I asked.

"It's in my head. Have to be out there every day."

Pearson steered between rows of trees bowed with fruit, close
enough so he could reach out and grab peaches as low limbs
whipped the side of the truck. He yanked several, took bites, and
discarded them. Handed me a couple as well. One had a distinctly
boozy aftertaste.

"I'm always trying to root out the good-tasting from the bad. I
don't want to ship something that somebody gotta spit out."

Pearson cut another open with his pocket knife, grimaced, and
pointed to a split pit caused by frost.

"Cold weather in March is what just makes or breaks us every
year, so we're real particular about where we put orchards. Sometimes all I need is one degree. Just *one* degree. It's the difference
between profitability and loss. If you think too hard about it, you'll
go crazy."

He talked about altitude, airflow, and the equipment used to
keep an orchard warm during a killing snap. Back in the day, hay

bales were set ablaze. Now, it's wind turbines. Husbandry still relies to a certain extent on acute observations a peach farmer makes among his trees every day.

"The birds will tell you where the sugar is," Pearson said. "Jays are mad for them. You'll see crows, too. A lot others you don't realize are here, like brown thrashers and mockingbirds. Although they don't like some varieties, they have preferences."

A pecan grove cast shade on one side of the orchard. The Pearsons started interplanting three generations ago, because a fall nut crop keeps the lights on and bills paid after the twelve-week peach season ends.

"That's some really good peach dirt right there, but it will never get back in peaches."

"What makes good peach dirt?" I asked.

The sweet spot for growing peaches lies in a twenty-mile swath of rolling hills known as the Fall Line, a geological transition zone between the Piedmont and Coastal Plain. Stretching from middle Georgia into upcountry South Carolina, this sandy, loamy soil essentially parallels what would have been beachfront in the Mesozoic Era. It runs straight through Peach County and is home to Georgia's "big four" peach growers: Pearson, Lane Southern Orchards, Dickey Farms, and Fitzgerald Fruit Farms.

Pearson parked next to his heirloom block, a grouping of tightly clustered trees less pruned than his commercial blocks. Oddball trees, nearly obsolete, just for the heck of it.

"Most of these peaches we grew at one time or another, but they didn't have enough red color. Because now the consumer thinks red means ripe, and that's sad."

He pointed to each tree.

"This is Southland, one of the best eating peaches there is, and nobody grabs it. That's a Topaz. It often doesn't set well, goes all cattywumpus, still it's delicious. There's the Virginia series: Jefferson, Monroe, Washington, all the presidents. We also have a block of Elberta that can be traced back to the original tree."

"Hands down finest peach to eat?"

"Probably an August Prince or Scarlet Prince."

"Pie or cobbler?"

"Cobbler."

Both our seats were piled with fruit; a few more landed on the rubber floor mats. I reached out the passenger window and pried loose a desiccated peach wedged in the crotch of the rearview mirror.

"And this one?"

He beamed.

"Sun-dried."

"I always think about young trees as small babies," said Dario Chavez. "When you first plant them in the field, you want to actually take care of them like a newborn."

Born to a family of dairy cattle farmers in the Ecuadorian Andes, Chavez first studied blueberries, then switched to stone fruit for his doctorate. Since 2014, he has served as the peach specialist at the University of Georgia's Department of Horticulture, where he was offered his pick of land parcels to build a research station specifically devoted to nursing peaches. He chose Dempsey Farm, an overgrown twelve-acre plot near the Griffin campus, an hour north of Peach County. Every major peach grower in Georgia has his cell number on speed dial; his phone kept jangling in the pocket of his cargo shorts as we hiked through the orchard on a sweltering morning.

"How many varieties are you growing?" I asked.

"About 185. All of these trees that you see here basically were grafted and propagated by us."

He bent to lift a limb loaded with fruit that was weighing down his new trials of dwarfing rootstock. Originally, all peaches had white flesh. Yellow is a genetic mutation.

"The flavor of a white is different, milder; it also has more florals," he said.

The Chavez Lab conducts experiments on pollen, germplasm, rootstocks, and the brix (sugar content) of peach juice.

The flesh of peaches can be classified as either melting, non-melting, or stony hard. This means some varieties have a firmer texture than others, more suitable for canning or cooking, while the mouthwatering "melters" are most anticipated when signs advertising ripened fruit appear along the road during their all-too-fleeting midsummer season.

I began to melt a little as well. We found shade in a mixed-variety block, where the red soil was littered with brown pits from last season's fruit.

"If you want to grab some, you're welcome," Chavez said.

Several trees had white tape floating from their branches.

"We mark the plants that are ready for people to harvest. Anyone from UGA can just come pick. When we're doing research trials on yield, we actually gather all the fruit and truck it to campus. We don't send an email or anything, people start telling everybody, and in an hour or two, the trucks are empty."

I reached up into a tree.

"Which is this variety?"

"Flavorich."

One of the pretty, freckled peaches came away wet in my hand. Then I heard plop-plop-plopping among the leaves.

"Oh my gosh, it's raining juice!"

Chavez laughed.

"That's the difference from getting one in the store, right?"

"So, pie or cobbler?" I asked.

"Ice cream. OK, cobbler, because I can put peach ice cream on top. The growers sell it at their fruit stands. Cannot make a mistake buying a little of it."

Chavez walked ahead, happy to be among his babies. After standing too long under the obstinate sun, I sucked that Flavorich dry.

"What's the difference between a peach and nectarine?" asked Jeff Hopkins, the farm manager at Clemson University's 240-acre Musser Fruit Research Center.

"Fuzz?" I said.

"What else?"

Caught off guard, I squinted at specimens arranged in cartons on a lab table.

"Uh, nothing?"

"Right. That was a trick question."

We were joined by pomologist Greg Reighard, who thumbed through his first edition of U. P. Hedrick's *The Peaches of New York* (1916) to show me illustration plates of nineteenth-century varieties favored by fanciers on the Eastern Seaboard, including some cultivated in the Carolina Piedmont centuries earlier. Family Favorite, Late Crawford, Old Mixon Free, Summer Snow. Lemon Cling. Blood Cling. Before 1897, Blood Cling was also known as Indian Blood, Indian Redmeat, Indian Cling. An astringent peach with dark red flesh mostly good for fruit leather or pickling.

"Peaches were really a common fruit crop for Indigenous Americans from the 1600s onward," said Reighard, whose specialty is disease-resistant rootstock.

"Historically, this was a peach-growing area?" I asked.

"Well, it was for the Cherokee. But they didn't have the diseases we have now, and the climate had to be different, because they planted their orchards along the Seneca River. That's a low spot. We plant on a high spot."

The Musser orchards occupy Oconee Point on Lake Hartwell in Seneca, South Carolina, and lie above the Fall Line in the Piedmont region. The Upper Road of the Occaneechi Path passed through here; this Indigenous trade-route network was a conduit for furs, shells, seeds, and other valuable commodities. Those peach pits, too, soon after de Soto marched to his vainglorious death on the banks of the Mississippi. The Muscogee Creek and Cherokee became the continent's first true peach orchardists. (The Cherokee word for peach is IOᵛ, or qua-na.) Accounts by European explorers and botanists describe villages along the great trading paths surrounded by fruit trees, which thrived until white settlers coveted those autonomous territories and treaties got trashed.

When President Andrew Jackson signed the Indian Removal Act into law, Cherokee leaders protested. On July 24, 1830, the *Cherokee Phoenix,* the tribal newspaper, published these words of Going Snake, a respected Speaker of Council, ". . . orders may arrive to prevent us from working in our fields, planting Orchards, or putting down wood to make our fires." Resistance proved futile. Land confiscated, livestock looted, farms and towns destroyed. Compensation paltry, if at all. Between 1830 and 1850, almost 100,000 Indigenous people in the Southeast were forced on a genocidal march across the Mississippi. The Cherokee named this deadly journey ᎤᏃᎯ ᏓᎾᏠᎯᎸ, Nv-no-hi dv-na-tlo-hi-lv, or the Trail Where They Cried.

Their peaches went feral.

"No one was maintaining those orchards," said David Anderson, tribal horticulturalist for the Eastern Band of Cherokee Indians, when I asked for clarification. "But this is where the nurserymen of the South came to get their genetic stock to work with, here in northern Georgia, western North Carolina.

"You find these peach trees scattered on Appalachian homesteads, freaks planted on tribal land for preserving and fresh eating, isolated in western North Carolina," he said.

Greg Reighard concurred.

"When I started here in the '80s, my predecessor collected a lot of what they call Tennessee Natural and Indian Cling peaches," he said, turning pages in his book to find the Blood Cling plate. "These were wild peaches growing in the forest or on fencerows. We also selected samples from some trees in the mountains two years ago. Someone told us about a pocket of them, but you don't find peaches as an invasive species anymore. Most times when I see wild peaches now is along roadways where people throw out a pit."

We talked about how different peaches got their names. Unlike heirloom apples, modern peach varieties lack the same hype, although that wasn't always the case. In the late nineteenth century, the American Pomological Society had final approval of new name releases, and after the Civil War, the focus shifted from presidents and generals to hue and character, with an emphasis on sunshine and pretty ladies, hence the Belle of Georgia, introduced by Lewis A. Rumph, uncle to Samuel of Elberta fame.

"Hedrick wanted to stop these ridiculous multiple names that were coming up, like Stump the World," said Reighard. "He hated that name."

We left him in the lab, and on the way out to the orchards, Hopkins stopped at the walk-in cooler in the farm's post-harvest room. The potpourri scent inside reminded me of the perfume counters at the old Davison's department store on Peachtree in Atlanta.

"How are you testing for aroma?" I asked.

"With peaches, it's interesting," he said, examining bins of plums, apricots, and nectarines collected that morning. "Once you cool a peach, the aroma gets locked up. Fresh off the tree it's always going to smell like peach; if you get one out of a cooler, it takes a day or two on the counter to recondition and have that nice peachy aroma again."

Georgia put peaches on license plates and the tails side of quarters. South Carolina branded itself the "tastier peach state." The rivalry remains as deep as that between certain bulldogs and tigers. No contest, Carolina grows more. Both states are dwarfed by California, and China still produces the most by volume.

We walked across a sloping field into the advanced-selection block on the high point of a hill facing a sluice pond. Birds chattered in the still summertime air. Hopkins explained they evaluate hundreds of varieties for flavor and aroma.

"But these are ones that, you know, for one reason or another, may become the future of the Southeast."

He pulled several fruit off a random tree, rubbed one on his Clemson Tigers shirt.

"One of my personal pleasures is to browse the variety trials when everything's tree ripe. I mean, just as ripe as they can get; perfect peaches. And they'll have flavors of coconut, pineapple, black pepper, lemons, limes."

Hopkins shook his head, wonderingly, and handed me one.

"How can there be so many flavors in a peach?" I asked.

We both took bites.

"Um, this is gorgeous," I said.

"Best lunch of the week. You're one of the select few that'll ever try this one."

"What's it called?"

He made note of a tag on the trunk.

"It's SC-10."

"Needs a better name than that," I said.

Later that afternoon, the woman responsible for the SC-10 hybrid hopped on a golf cart handed down from Clemson's athletic program and drove out to the mother block. A Lowe's tool apron tied at her waist, Ksenija Gasic is Clemson's peach breeder and geneticist. She consulted her phone and counted down the row until we reached a couple of sorry-looking, buggy specimens. While commercial growers tend to keep heritage peaches as novelties, she hangs on to them like an ancestral portrait in a treasured family album.

"These are the oldest tree varieties at Clemson?" I asked.

"Old Mixon Free and Late Crawford. I got the germplasm from the USDA prunus repository in California."

She walked down the row, checking for disease.

"I need to have a block where I can put the material, or cultivars, that I like as the 'parents.' I can get pollen from anywhere around the world, but I need a mother tree, you know, with the good qualities that I like."

Born in Serbia, Gasic emigrated to the States in 2001, and was hired by the university to kick-start a breeding program for peaches compatible with current Carolina growing conditions.

"Serbia has a different environment," she said. "The issues for peaches are different. That was a learning curve, because everything here is a month earlier, even the ripening times, you know?"

"How many trees have you planted at Clemson?" I asked.

"Around thirty thousand over the years," she said. "Every year we would put in four thousand trees; then in 2010, we put in ten thousand. When they all started ripening, I said never again, because I would basically be eating peaches the whole week, and by the time I got to the end of a block, I had to start over again on Monday."

"I haven't had anything else today, and my stomach feels it," I said.

"The first week this year, I ate so much that my teeth acidified," she said. "Early peaches are not sweet, so I had to neutralize the pH in my mouth. A lingering taste on the palate can throw off the flavor of the next sample. But I couldn't stop, I just love them. That's insanity."

Then I mentioned the fantastic white peach. She brightened, climbed into the golf cart, and went looking for it. We picked and picked, trying not to be greedy, two short women entangled among branches, arms stretched for really ripe ones inches beyond our reach. Pinky orange, the color of smudged rouge. Bins on the back seat of the cart filled with fruit.

"You cannot beat the white ones," Gasic said, "because the carotenoids that get spent creating yellow flesh, they all stay in the white ones and that's what gives them the aroma."

She took a breath, and coughed sharply.

"Too much fuzz in the air."

"Oh! This cobbler is so *good*," said Sydney Dorsey, politely covering her mouth while juggling a plastic bowl, spoon, microphone, and the rhinestone tiara wobbling on her head.

Miss Georgia Peach had the first taste of the "World's Largest Peach Cobbler"—75 gallons of peaches, 70 pounds of butter, 150 pounds of sugar, 150 pounds of flour, 32 gallons of milk—baked in a brick oven lined with school-bus floor panels next to the county courthouse during Fort Valley's annual peach festival. The line for free cobbler wrapped around concession stands and down the block.

It's a long day for Dorsey, from flipping breakfast pancakes to signing autographs at one of the orchards outside town. The nineteen-year-old pageant winner and her sister queens gathered early in the lobby of the Austin Theater, an opera house that had seen better days, where the five girls changed into semiformal dresses and reapplied makeup already melting. Dorsey wore a peach-orange pleated chiffon minidress and glitter ankle boots. The youngest, Tiny Miss Georgia Peach, was six years old. She had a loose front tooth, and proudly wiggled it for the others.

"Where did you leave your sash, Ava?" Dorsey asked, helping to bind her hair into angel wings.

Their mothers, one dad, and two pageant chaperones bundled the court off to parade vehicles parked on a side street. A field tractor with bins of fresh fruit. One Shriner, no go-kart. The deputy mayor in a flatbed. A lemonade van. A ladder truck. Convertibles for the girls. When the fireman burped his siren to signal the start, the peach queens rolled.

The Miss Georgia Peach pageant was revived in 1996—after a hiatus for lack of participation—and a talent segment was mandatory back then, even for the youngest titles. Now, the emphasis is on poise and charm. Scholarships, not swimsuits. Contestants don't wear hairpieces, cupcake gowns, or false teeth, known in the glitz trade as "flippers." For the pageant this year, pandemic masks were mandatory offstage, and the audience was limited to immediate family. The winners serve as industry ambassadors during their yearlong reign while attending community events—the Georgia Peach Festival in Fort Valley, a Peaches & Politics rally sponsored by one of the "big four" farms, the District 8 GOP fish fry, even the Peach Blossom Cluster dog show. According to certified judge and board president Donna Long, the girls receive invitations for all sorts of things related to peaches. The pageant is also a gateway to bigger competitions. Two peach queens have gone on to win the Miss Georgia title.

"How do you keep the tiaras on their heads?" I asked, sipping peach ice tea with the queens and their mothers at the Peach County Historical Society luncheon.

"See these clips?" said Long, holding one up. "We take pantyhose and thread it through holes in the base before we crown them. So when you put it on, the snap clips got something to attach to."

"Pie or cobbler?" I asked.

"Pound cake."

Having changed into IT'S A FUZZY THING festival logo T-shirts, the girls poked at their plates of chicken salad. Took selfies. Shared concession-stand candy and kettle corn from the midway. Their mothers talked about the cost of pageants, hair and makeup artists. Tiara carrying cases. Favorite couture-knockoff seamstresses and the brisk trade in secondhand evening gowns. Dorsey's mother, Tanisha, a former pageant queen herself, operates an online clothing boutique.

Is a fruit queen any different from head cheerleader or debutante? Maybe. Peaches and feminine beauty have been conflated across cultures since the Taoist legend of Xiwangmu, Queen Mother of the West, who tended the Peaches of Immortality in her palace garden and decided which gods would be permitted a taste of the fruit that granted life everlasting; she hosted the chosen at an elaborate banquet known as the Feast of Peaches. Mystic peaches aside, what about the mundane kind baked into a giant soupy cobbler? Easily the subject of far too many sexy love songs. Search for Georgia+peach+lyrics, and it gets raunchy fast.

Sydney Dorsey knows about body image. The reigning peach queen was awarded additional titles for prettiest dress, smile, hair, and eyes. But pretty girls can be bullied, and after her freshman high-school year, Dorsey switched to home schooling.

"There's not a lot of [body] positivity in my county," she said.

When you wear skintight gowns, ample curves can receive comments by judging panels. And they're not always kind. Stubbornly upbeat, she cited model and size-acceptance advocate Ashley Graham as inspiration.

"That's the thing about pageants, as my mom reminds me; it's just a set of opinions on a certain day."

The court returned to mingle on the midway. A little girl with hair tied in bunches stopped Dorsey at a lemonade stand and begged for a pose, face flushed with excitement to be close to a real queen. As Dorsey bent to give her a hug, the mother caught the moment on camera.

"What's your daughter's name?" I asked.

"Scarlett."

Several days later, back home in Swainsboro, two hours east of Fort Valley, Dorsey showed me her collection of tiaras. She has over a hundred, some mothballed in storage, the most ornate dis-

played in a converted gun case painted white and gold. In a hall-
way off the family room, she opened the glass door for a better
look at the trophies, satin sashes, and rhinestone crowns.

"This is my *shrine*," she laughed.

"What is Miss Real Squeal?"

"A barbecue festival pageant."

Her path in pageants, as Dorsey explained, started as a baby.
She has reigned as Teen Miss Southeast Georgia Soapbox Derby,
Miss Uvalda Farm Festival Queen, UNM Georgia Teen, Miss Tatt-
nall Shrine, Pinetree Festival Queen, Teen Miss Peach State. Her
biggest win, Miss USA National Teen, came with a $140,000 prize
package. This year is her second go-round as a peach queen; in
2018, she held the title of Teen Miss Georgia Peach.

"I'm a big festival girl," she said, straightening the sashes in the
case. "And I love [organizers] Miss Donna and Miss Diane. They
continue to follow your journey, whatever it may be. It's not like
you give up your Miss Georgia Peach crown and you never hear
from them again."

Dorsey learned hair and makeup with YouTube tutorials, and
practiced on her pageant friends. In the fall, she's enrolled to study
cosmetology at Southeastern Technical College, and then her
mother will help set up a hair salon in town. Their boutique operates out of a spare bedroom in her parents' brick-and-clapboard
ranch. Her gowns were temporarily hung between racks of casual
wear they sell at pageant pop-ups.

"Red is my power color," she said, unzipping garment bags to
fluff silk and chiffon dresses.

One had sheer side panels and a train.

"This is my baby. I wore it at Miss Georgia Peach."

A costume feather headdress hung on one of the racks.

"I don't know why this is in here, but I have Cherokee heritage."

"You do?"

"On my mom's side. For one of my senior pictures, I wore this
with a black bodysuit and jeans."

She tucked it away.

"You seem to have a clear vision of what all this can do."

"Yes, ma'am. But a lot of people think it's girls prancing in fancy
dresses, and there's definitely a stigma around it."

"People make fun because you're in pageantry?"

"You can get on social media, especially TikTok, and they'll make fun of girls onstage or, you know, talking on the microphone, announcing who they are and where they're from."

"Well, that sounds like more bullying."

"My first year of college was completely paid for through the pageant scholarships I've earned. That alone should just make people zip it."

Dorsey walked into the kitchen, where her pet chiweenie, Ellie, demanded our attention. The peach queen flipped open an album and pulled out a childhood snapshot. A heart tiara tangled in her hair, she held a bouquet while perched next to a trophy.

"This is baby pageant me."

"How was that giant peach cobbler, honestly?"

"Well, my grandma makes the best cobbler," Dorsey said. "I know to go over to her house with a bucket of ice cream."

Before leaving, I opened my phone's music app.

"Have you ever heard of the Allman Brothers Band?"

She looked at me blankly.

"They produced an album called *Eat a Peach* in 1972."

Dorsey listened to the final track, Duane Allman's acoustic guitar duet "Little Martha," which he reportedly composed after a vivid dream about Jimi Hendrix teaching him the melody in a motel bathroom. The song's namesake, Martha Ellis, was a twelve-year-old girl who died in 1836. (It was also the nickname of his girlfriend Dixie Lee Meadows.) Visitors still tuck flowers in the stone hands of little Martha's memorial statue at Rose Hill Cemetery.

"Almost sounds like something you would hear in a Lifetime movie," Dorsey said.

"Did you eat a peach?" asked my husband.

"One or two."

"I meant in Macon."

Now would be a good time to admit that Bronson and I attended the farewell concert at the Beacon Theatre in New York City, one of the Allman Brothers Band's favorite residencies over its long touring career, just before Gregg came back home to rest beside his older sibling. The final encore on the set list that night in 2014 was a cover of Muddy Waters's "Trouble No More." A live recording of the song from the original Fillmore East sessions was included on *Eat a Peach*.

So here at the end, parked under a loblolly pine between the shrine to the Allmans and those Confederate graves, I scrambled for a seat peach of my own. Might have been from Pearson, or UGA, or Clemson, or any of the roadside stands in between; not really sure, because by then quite a few rolled around in the back of the car, escaping their paper bags after jolting from Seneca to Swainsboro. The peach juice dripped on my last clean shirt. Then the pit flew out the car window. Maybe a feral will grow in the peaceful confines of Rose Hill Cemetery.

Can someone please name a peach for Skydog? And Sydney Dorsey, too? Until that happens, let's relish this passage from naturalist James Alexander Fulton, who wrote *Peach Culture* (1870), a baseline textbook on the stone fruit that has come to define the often terrible but persistent beauty of the South.

> It ripens in perfection only in the glow of a midsummer's sun; and the hotter the weather, the more delicious are its rich cooling juices. It is eminently suited to the season. When the weather is so hot that even eating is a labor, the peach is acceptable, for it melts in the mouth without exertion.
>   It is the Queen of Delicacies.

That's a title worth a tiara.

TOM FINGER

Ghost Acres: Tulare Lake and the Past Future of Food

FROM *Pipe Wrench*

ON MAY 11, 1880, Walter Crow was shot in the back as he ran through a wheat field. Two tendrils of smoke wafting from a stand of oak and sycamore behind him gave away the location of his killer. Minutes prior, Crow had murdered four others in fifteen seconds with a brutally efficient double-barreled shotgun.

Earlier that day, farmers from around the countryside had gathered to hear Judge David Terry, who was scheduled to speak on the tangled mass of land and water rights that had piled up in California over the previous twenty years. As the farmers picnicked, United States Marshal Alonzo Poole prepared for his day's task, a land grab: serving eviction notices to farmers along a patch of land called Mussel Slough to make way for a railroad. As an armed group coalesced around Poole, rumors of the evictions washed over the farmers. They grabbed their own guns and rode off.

The two armed groups met by Henry Brewer's farmstead. The marshal dismounted and stood; heated words were exchanged. Suddenly, two men—farmer James Harris and pro-railroad Mills Hartt—opened fire on each other. Harris's bullet hit Hartt in the groin. Seeing his friend Hartt fall, Walter Crow raised his shotgun. A noted marksman, Crow hit Harris in the chest, killing him instantly, before turning and opening on Iver Knutson, dropping him as well. Next, he swiveled and unloaded on farmer Daniel Kelly "so that the charge entered [his] side and practically blew it off," then jumped off his wagon and ran toward Archibald McGregor, who was using the marshal's horse as a shield. Crow wheeled around the horse and shot McGregor twice in the chest. Farmer John Henderson had managed to jump off his horse and aim at Crow; they rushed each other and exchanged four shots, and Henderson was dead. Crow then ran toward the maturing wheat, crawling to remain hidden as two unknown settlers pursued. As Crow neared his house and what he thought was safety, he stood and broke into a sprint. Two shots rang out and Crow fell.

Every man who fired a shot that day—except Crow's anonymous killers—lay either dead or seriously wounded. (Harris died of his injuries four days later.) The initial volley of gunfire had lasted less than twenty seconds. Neither Wild Bill Hickok, Wyatt Earp, nor Billy the Kid ever killed as many people in a single incident as Walter Crow.

Today the field where Crow died lies in modern-day Hanford, California, about thirty-five miles south of Fresno in California's Central Valley. Among the ghosts of Crow, Hartt, and Harris, you'll find another, much larger one: shrouded by fields of soybeans, alfalfa, and corn, Tulare Lake lies hidden. What was once the largest freshwater lake west of the Mississippi River is now rows of grain crops and vegetables. These crops feed millions of people across the world on the stored wealth of an ecosystem cultivated over generations by the Yokuts people.

The shootout was no simple competition between farm and railroad. It was, rather, a culminating flash of violence as settlers wrested land from Indigenous peoples and plugged it into the global food economy—less an Old West story than one about the origins of our food systems.

The Mussel Slough Tragedy drenched the dry, maturing wheat fields with blood, but violence was already endemic to the land. During the second half of the nineteenth century, an abundant landscape of tule marshes and oak stands that fed Yokuts peoples transformed into a giant wheat field feeding industrialization in England. This involved human violence as well as ecological collapse, creating a landscape that historian Kenneth Pomeranz refers to evocatively as ghost acres: acres of land outside the UK hijacked to produce resources to fuel industrialization and population growth with*in* the UK. Ghost acres are in a state of suspended animation—complex seasonal networks of food production homogenized into uniform suppliers of Western capitalism.

Modern food is not just the products on the shelves, but the acres and people transformed so we can consume those products. The nineteenth century laid the groundwork for those new places, and Tulare Lake, a ghostly landscape, is an example of the violence written into them. Its history can help us wrestle with the full brunt of food choices, and how the health of bodies is entwined with our current food system, its past—and its future. Each jar of peaches or glass of milk produced on Tulare bottomland owes a portion of its nutrients to the land and water management of the ancestors of those who live and work almost within sight of the dried lake, and its existence to layers of violence. Understanding those histories can help guide the ecological and human reanimation of ghost acres.

Let me take you now to Ciau, a village just north of Tulare Lake, in 1840. The now-disappeared Nutunutu band of the Yokuts people migrated around their central village, making use of the valley's rich ecological diversity and seasonal patterns of productivity to forge a healthy and resilient diet. Nearby, a seasonal channel later called Mussel Slough moved water back and forth between the Kings River and Tulare Lake. Here, Yokuts women migrated to find food according to the pulses of seasons.

The women of Ciau understood this was a place of dramatic variation in water and temperature. Prior to the late nineteenth century, the San Joaquin Valley surrounding Tulare Lake was a patchwork of niches, running the ecological gamut from alkaline desert to lush riparian forest. The western portions of the Tulare Basin lay in the rain shadow of coastal mountain ranges and were the most arid regions of the valley. Moving further east, alkaline flats gave way to short grasslands. These grasslands in turn transitioned to salt marshes that thrived along the lake's wavering shoreline. Tall grasslands predominated as the land rose from lake to foothills covered in oak parkland. Tendrils of sycamore forest clung to waterways that cut toward the lake.

Tulare Lake itself filled entirely from snowmelt in the Sierra Nevada Mountains each spring, and would shrink considerably in the hot, dry summer months. Dimensions changed dramatically from season to season, and year to year; the lake measured only forty feet deep at its deepest location, and in many places it was shallow enough for someone to wade out a mile and still only be up to their shoulders. In wetter years, Tulare could cover as many as 1,800 square miles. Early surveys record the area around the lake as "overflow and swamp," and early white settlers recorded extremely wet years in 1852, 1858, 1860, and 1868. Despite this, the lake almost dried completely in 1854. One local newspaper reported in 1890 that the lake had spread out a full fifteen miles during the spring season at a rate of about a mile and a half a week. Another early settler remembered "the shore lines of Tulare lake changed and shifted a great deal. If a strong wind came from the north, as it often did, the water would move several miles south, and would move again when the wind changed. Then when the water level in the lake changed the shore line shifted a long distance." This hydraulic metabolism created a rich diversity of ecological niches surrounding the lake, including Mussel Slough and nearby Ciau.

The environments of the Tulare region produced what ecologists call the portfolio effect: no matter what the season or weather conditions, some resource was experiencing peak productivity. The area must have been beautiful, and certainly was bountiful. One white settler recalled wistfully, "I have always remembered that place as one of the most ideal I have ever seen. The tall green grass, the cool clear water, and the trees with their fresh leaves made as pretty a sport as one could wish . . . for my own part, I have never seen anything equal to the virgin San Joaquin Valley before there was a plow or a fence in it."

Before the latter nineteenth century, we know the inhabitants of Ciau rarely—if ever—went hungry. As one early settler history of Tulare County recounts, "Acorns, of course, were the staple, but it is a mistake to suppose that the Indians' diet lacked variety. In addition to game of all kinds and fish, there were various kinds of seeds, nuts, berries, roots, and young shoots of the tule and clover." There were once actually mussels in Mussel Slough, which the Nutunutu collected and boiled in fine-woven baskets filled with hot stones.

As temperatures cooled in the fall, Yokuts women left Ciau for their seasonal camp in the oak-studded foothills some forty miles to the east. Here, acorns dropped from oaks fertilized by fires delicately managed by the village's men a few months prior. Women would collect piles of acorns at the creekside and break them down into a rough flour using a mortar and pestle fashioned from a tree trunk and large branch before pounding the flour into a cake and letting it dry on a rock.

With abundant food, there was little open conflict between the Tachi, Nutunutu, and many other Yokuts bands migrating around their central place. Then came consecutive blows to the Nutunutu and larger Yokuts communities in the first half of the nineteenth century. First was the expansion of the Spanish mission chain up the Pacific coast. Because Ciau sat well inland, the major impact from the missions was with the introduction of grazing animals, whose ranging contributed to the collapse of native grasses and reintroduction of foreign species. As Spanish and Mexican cattle herds fanned out across the valley, native plants died and the Nutunutu saw some strands of their dietary network collapse. Throughout the early nineteenth century, they, like many other Yokuts bands, made up for the loss of native species by adopting the horse to ride, raid, and eat.

Even as they made these adaptations, other forces conspired. In the early 1830s, malaria swept in, carried by traders for the Hudson Bay Company. Finally, in the 1840s came the cataclysm of gold mining and Anglo settlement. The next half century would see the remaking of this place as a depot for global trade, a place where violence shook food systems that had before been marked by self-reliant sustenance.

As the Nutunutu found their dietary network stressed, halfway across the world so too did the poor workers of Manchester, England, suffer. The two communities were eventually linked by the flow of wheat grown on stolen Nutunutu land in California and shipped overseas to feed the industrial English workers with cheap bread. Manchester qualified as a village at the beginning of the 1700s and was given representation in Parliament only in 1832. But as the Nutunutu reeled from disease, it became a fast-growing city of shanties, warehouses, and manufactories. The centrifugal forces of land dispossession and food commercialization forced people to migrate from farm to cities. Manchester was a city of hungry refugees.

Across England in the nineteenth century, many working-class women felt the daily brunt of these systemic changes to their food economy. Subsistence landscapes transformed into commercial farms. Growers became eaters. The life of an English rural family prior to being kicked off their land would have been seasonal in nature, not terribly unlike that of the Nutunutu. Families would have lived in the same houses year round, their lives dictated by fallow-rotation farming. They fished in local creeks and used forests, fens, and unplowed fields as sources of game, herbs, and root vegetables. But accelerating enclosure consolidated land rights in the hands of a country gentry, and portions of the English rural foodway began to crumple. Long rows of turnips, barley, and oats turned into geometric wheat fields. Forests were felled and plowed into fields. Experts drained fens, devised new labor-saving machines, and innovated fallow patterns designed to feed cities bulging with the very people who had once worked the land.

Just like the Nutunutu, unsettled English people in the nineteenth century moved around a central place. Crucially, though, this was a migration born of desperation, not seasonal forage. Most would come to work in burgeoning towns like Leeds, Birmingham, and Manchester, but hunger and housing prices kept them ever on the move. These industrial settlements were places of work opportunity but little dietary resiliency, as people worked all day in foodless environments; there was little room for gardens in tightly packed neighborhoods. Women often bore the brunt of these problems: not only would they shoulder the stress of obtaining and cooking enough food for their families (and anyone else who might be living in their crowded quarters) while also often supplementing the family's income through wage work, they were often expected to be the first to forgo food in times of shortage, leaving sufficient food for the male "breadwinner" and the children, supplementing their diets with energy-packed, nutrient-deficient sips of tea and bites of candy. Women's mental and physical health suffered.

This situation reached a crisis point in the 1840s. For so many English working-class women in the nineteenth century, universal suffrage and politics in general were "knife and fork" questions about eroding the power of the landowning class, who, through enclosure, had simultaneously cast people from traditional lands and made them dependent on the whims of the market. Merchants and laborers in newly industrial cities rose to the cry of suffrage and cheap bread. Atmospheric conditions over the North Atlantic pumped a depressing slate of cool, wet weather over northern Europe. Crops failed. Women and their families went hungry everywhere in the British Isles and northern Europe. While the "hungry forties" are most well-known from the Irish Potato Famine, the poor all over Europe found their dietary stress dip into outright starvation. And so, England—and the poor of Manchester—cast a hungry eye out across the world.

At the same time, Yokuts women noticed strangers in their oak stands. American settlers in the 1840s and 1850s preferred to settle in the oak-blanketed foothills of the eastern slopes of the Tulare region not because of the acorns they contained, but as refuge from the floods and seasonal swampland that characterized much of the valley's bottom. Here, settlers began planting wheat and alfalfa, girdling or cutting down so many of the acorn trees those of Ciau had worked so hard to keep. Much of this crop went to feed magnate Henry Miller's vast cattle empire, sprawling as it was across the central portions of the valley. These crops were consumed by both cattle workers and their charges, which, slaughtered and butchered, fed hungry miners toiling on busted claims high in the mountains.

Later arrivals moved into the marshlands below. Businessmen lurked for profit and new passions inflamed old land disputes. Failed miners and desperate emigrants rushed to the Tulare region to make quick cash from cheap Native land, often just given away by the new state government. What couldn't be taken legally was taken by force.

In a story of violent place-making that repeated itself thousands of times across the globe in the nineteenth century, newly arrived white farmers in the Tulare region went to war with the remnants of Ciau and other Yokuts communities in 1856. Farmers formed a militia after drumming up an excuse, intent on asserting their settler campaign. The few remaining Yokuts living in remnant villages scattered throughout the Tulare region rightly saw that the settlers' preparations would lead to a punitive expedition. They headed into the foothills for protection. Ciau emptied, never to be filled again.

The militia group chased the refugee community to the foothills and sought to dislodge them. Their first attack was unsuccessful, but aid from a federal cavalry unit stationed just south of the valley ultimately helped them overwhelm the Yokuts, sending survivors scattering into the mountains. For weeks after, the militia

and federal cavalry rode across the countryside, alternatively killing or gathering any Native person they found and incarcerating
the survivors at the Kings River Indian Reservation just south of
Fresno. And so, through the cumulative force of disease, environmental change, and state violence, the landscape of Tulare became
unmoored in the global economy, its people killed or captured.

Into this scene stepped Isaac Friedlander, a six-foot-seven,
three-hundred-pound German immigrant whose shadow would
loom large over the Tulare Valley for the next twenty years. Friedlander was at first as unmoored as the Tulare landscape he would
come to own. After a series of failed business ventures on the East
Coast, he came to California in 1849 hoping to strike it rich. He
failed some more, and tumbled back to San Francisco in 1852 to
reevaluate his business prospects. He read reports streaming back
from the interior of "wars" that were clearing the Yokuts, Wappos,
Miwoks, and Patwins from their lands. He also happened to meet
two very important businessmen, banker William Ralston and land
lawyer William Chapman.

Together, Ralston, Chapman, and Friedlander hatched one of
the most crooked land schemes in American history, sowing the
seeds of Tulare Lake's demise by connecting it to Manchester. No
longer would the food ecology of Tulare be controlled by temperature and moisture, but by account balances and inter-firm competition.

Ralston bankrolled the operation with gold-backed securities
from his Bank of California; Chapman massaged the law. With
these partners, Friedlander looked hungrily to the southern valley and the Tulare region. He obtained his land in ethically dubious or outright illegal ways; in the late 1850s, you might've seen
Friedlander waylaying drunken Tenderloin saloon patroons, plying them with a scheme. Friedlander would ask them to accom-
pany him to the public land office. Land law limited the amount
of dispossessed land one person could buy from the state, so Friedlander would slip the man enough money to make a purchase and
then immediately buy it back from him once he stumbled out. The
next day, you might find Friedlander in his office of the University
of California, using his membership on the Board of Regents to
privately buy and sell land nominally reserved for public schools.
Finally, he'd walk over to the state land surveyor's office and whis-
per into the ear of one Isaac Chapman, who just happened to

be land lawyer William's brother. Isaac Chapman would declare some portion of the Tulare Basin to be "swamp or marshland," and Friedlander would use Ralston's credit to buy it for pennies on the dollar. To hide these spurious land deals, Friedlander and his associates would resell the land in various parcels back and forth to each other, burying the original deal in a mountain of paper in what could only be described as a land-laundering operation. Friedlander came to own 500,000 acres in the Central Valley by the late 1860s.

As Friedlander and his cronies bought and sold land, small-time settlers came to occupy it. These settlers set to work transforming Yokuts land into wheat fields as a method to protect their squatter's rights. Many of these new settlers were displaced ex-Confederates from the American South. They came to dig irrigation ditches and plant wheat. The ditches were the improvement upon which they could base land claims or be paid for their years of occupation, while the wheat provided the cash infusions they needed every year to keep their farms running. It was these ditches and wheat plants that would eventually suck up water that normally coursed down from the mountains and came to settle in Tulare Lake. The seeds of its destruction were being planted right along Mussel Slough and beside the ghost of Ciau.

Here, significant ecological transformation was accompanied by continued human tragedy. The land around Mussel Slough had been taken so quickly, so lawlessly, that it was bound in a jumble of conflicting claims. Friedlander and associates, cattle magnate Henry Miller, railroad companies, and squatters all claimed some portion of land and water rights in the area. These overlapping claims created bizarre scenes and comical cat-and-mouse games. Dry farmers who planted wheat were never sure they would hold on to the land long enough to make improvements profitable. Often, they simply stored their grain in whatever structures they managed to build, and slept in tents. Others stored sacks out in the open, praying that the rain would hold. Families formed mutual-aid societies that often took the form of armed vigilante groups roaming the countryside. Railroad agents scoured the countryside serving eviction notices. The families would often hide at their approach so these agents, finding empty houses, would place all the furniture outside and padlock the house. Hiding families returned to break the lock and replace the furniture.

People continued to die for land along Mussel Slough in the 1870s and 1880s. Vigilante groups became more militant. Railroads locked up claims in court battles. The situation escalated until, in 1880, Walter Crow's shotgun blasts echoed across the Brewer Farm. What only a generation before was a verdant landscape tightly ordered by customary rights was now a landscape of disorder and violence increasingly controlled by a syndicate of conmen and racked by gang violence.

The settlers were not acting in a vacuum. Rather, they operated in a global drama that not only found them agents in an expansionist agenda for the country but tied them to a continent an ocean away. As white settlers transformed Mussel Slough, British factory workers looked hungrily around the world for their own daily bread. Cities like Manchester were simply growing too fast for domestic farmers to feed them. At the same time, Friedlander came to own too much wheat. He had filled his vast estates with tenant farmers who paid their rents in wheat. By the 1860s, Friedlander was holding so much that he could set prices across the entire valley, so much that hungry miners in the Sierra and sailors in San Francisco Bay couldn't eat it all.

He sought to offload the sullied bounty by chartering ships to take his wheat to whoever would buy it. His first attempt had the ships docking in far-flung settlements around the Pacific: Oregon, Hawaii, the Philippines, Chile. But there was so much that such an ad hoc approach could never sell it all . . . and the hungry markets of England started to look appealing. Friedlander began traveling every other year to Liverpool to set up business deals for his California wheat. For years, until his death in 1878, Friedlander would send a "grain fleet" of two hundred to four hundred ships to Liverpool laden with wheat grown alongside Mussel Slough and countless other creeks across the Central Valley.

By then, the Tulare region—and the larger Central Valley—was one vast field of wheat that stretched from coastal ranges to the Sierra Nevada foothills. Its new shape began to look like the modern world's epitome of agricultural productivity. Wheat pumped out of the valley in railroad cars and steamship holds where sailors loaded bags of it onto bulky sailing vessels. The wheat would breathe with heat and cold as it crossed the tropics, hitting the Antarctic Cape Horn passage before reentering the tropics and crossing into the North Atlantic. After the fourteen-thousand-mile journey, it would enter the gigantic port of Liverpool before being milled into flour and eventually sold to a small baker in downtown Manchester. It was there, sitting on a shelf of a Manchester bakery, that the bread would wait for a tired woman to enter, buy it, and carry it home to her hungry family for dinner. In this journey that would repeat itself thousands of times during the second half of the nineteenth century, Tulare now fed Manchester.

The world Friedlander helped create lived beyond his death. By the 1880s, the Manchester working-class family was no longer as hungry as their parents and grandparents had been in the 1840s, but they were just as unhealthy: their new diet was high in energy but nutrient-deficient. What's more, their sapped immune systems had to live surrounded by the digestive tracts of thousands of other people. The global system engendered by developments in California and places like it meant these people found just enough food at regular intervals to finally settle down. The European industrial class no longer had to migrate constantly for food and work; they could simply walk to the corner bakery. Bacterial diseases exploded as human waste flooded inadequate privies and sewers.

Manchester's eating patterns also helped destroy Tulare Lake. The next century saw an acceleration of the patterns of land use developed around Tulare. White settlement, for instance, accelerated when land titles became clear in the valley, with the best land snatched up before the end of the 1800s. Many new settlers shut out from lucrative valley plots bought land in the foothills—once the center of the Yokuts acorn-based food system. They grazed sheep on grasses between now-untended oak trees. When deep droughts destroyed these animals, some desperate farmers began planting orange trees. By the turn of the century, irrigation ditches snaked across foothills and laced valley bottomland, all feeding plants that would in turn feed humans thousands of miles away. Tulare Lake itself began to buckle under the pressure of so much withdrawal.

A new assault came as fishmongers in San Francisco looked hungrily south. The lake sat relatively undisturbed until the spring of 1884. In that year, the *Tulare Daily Register* reported that "the rivers ran into the lake in a flood that spring and the fish met the fresh water in solid masses. Standing at the mouth of King's river, one could see a wave come landward, a wave produced by the motion of a mighty army of fish . . . the ditches of Mussel Slough country were choked by them." Fishermen swarmed, and the Tulare fishery was dead by the early 1890s.

An irrigation craze swept over the Tulare district toward the end of the century as land titles cleared and global demand for wheat and oranges soared. Farmers began to dream of turning the lake itself into waving fields of wheat, a dream that was growing into reality when the Buena Vista reclamation levee was completed in early 1899. Its builders hoped to repossess thirty thousand acres and seed them all with grain. Soon, cotton, melons, and alfalfa joined wheat to grow on what was once lake bottomland. By the 1920s, over a million bags of grain and fifteen thousand bales of cotton were annually collected from the dead lake.

But by then, Tulare was cut from spring snowmelt and no longer breathing with hydraulic metabolism. It was suffocating. The local paper trumpeted, "Tulare Lake Disappearing: large and fertile farms where lake once stood. Tulare Lake is drying up. Its waters are constantly receding. Like the dawning of a new creation, pleasant groves and fertile fields take the place of its former wastes of waters." Another paper reported that "Tulare Lake is as dry as a chip. For the first time in recent history, the pelican, geese, ducks, snipes, mud hens . . . as well as the many fish have found that there is no longer a home for them." Looking back with quick retrospection in the 1930s, the *Fresno Bee* wrote that "the lake has only been a puddle since 1920, having not really existed since 1917 and not having had its customary size since 1906."

Ecological collapse was everywhere. The disappearance of Ciau and the murder of Yokuts people laid the groundwork for a new world of commodities. It hadn't happened by chance. Migrating settlers, Friedlander's crooked land scheme, and wheat purchases by English millers were all predicated on one another. Each decision was made with a fleeting understanding of what was happening elsewhere. Settlers and capitalists often emphasized how they made "improvements" to nature with a seemingly rational design of food economy. But the disappearance of Tulare Lake told another story, one connected to the plight of surviving Yokuts held on reservations. With the deck cleared by midcentury, agents, fishermen, irrigators, and levee builders dealt the lake a final blow. In a new, spectral place—these thousands of ghost acres—Tulare

Lake traded death for life. The bread that so many relied upon came from the demise of people, of landscape, and of nutrients. Their histories cannot be unbound.

Tulare no longer feeds Manchester, but American and Asian supermarkets. You've likely consumed a part of that place. As of 2018, the region is among the nation's largest producers of dairy products, fruit, and cotton, all grown from generations of genocide, land dispossession, and ecological collapse.

The Yokuts have witnessed it all; the Tachi Yokuts of the Santa Rosa Rancheria endure in the face of such momentous change. The land—and its ghost lake—occupies a central place in their culture and memory. As tribal historian Raymond Jeff recounts, settlers "killed the whole San Joaquin valley. I've never even seen the lake," he laments, "all I did was read about it." Importantly, however, the future of this story can be one of rebirth, not death. As the tribe proclaims, "Now, we rebuild. We will endure."

The ghosts that lie within our shared food history can guide us to the future. Let the water flow. The water will come back, has come back. In the 1930s, persistent floods allowed nesting pelicans to return briefly to the lake; such is but a glimpse of the reanimation that can unfold in erstwhile ghost acres. Part of that restoration must include the Yokuts people and their traditional foodways. The reanimation of ghost acres does not only call for nature preserves or wildlife parks; if our food history played a role in arresting complex ecosystems like the Tulare Basin, so too must our eating patterns help reanimate them. Breathing new life into our food system should revolve around restoring Indigenous stewardship and decision-making over their food landscapes. As ethnobotanist Kat Anderson notes, "the conservation of endangered species and the restoration of historic ecosystems might require the reintroduction of careful human stewardship rather than simple hands-off preservation." An Indigenous management model can not only restore vibrant cultural food landscapes, it can be productive as well. Modern studies are beginning to appreciate that Indigenous land management was significantly more productive than originally believed by Western science. It is time to use past models and current held knowledge to replace food systems built on genocide and land mining.

The reanimation of ghost acres of Tulare Lake will require policy that acknowledges Indigenous claims to land and water, and the academic expertise of ethnobotanists, food historians, agronomists, ecologists—but it should be led by the Yokuts people. Only they have proven adequate to the task of feeding large numbers of people while at the same time storing nutrients for future use. Food is an excellent venue to begin and see through these public–university–community collaborations.

Due to the traumatic history of so many ghost acres, only hard-earned trust and embedded relationships can restore food landscapes that acknowledge past trauma and use Indigenous and academic knowledge to reanimate ghost acres into verdant landscapes that will feed us in the future. Truly restorative food justice will use history and dialogue with people like the Yokuts, who still live next to ghost acres held back by irrigation canals, herbicides, and plows. Let the deep wisdom held in place by Yokuts past and present seep into small networks of irrigation canals that water a patchwork landscape of local plants and agricultural plots tended by scientific knowledge. History, restorative ecology, and food culture studies can work together to create just food systems that work within the patterns of place. Only then will the ghost of Tulare Lake truly come alive.

JOSH DZIEZA

Revolt of the Delivery Workers

FROM *New York Magazine*

THE WILLIS AVENUE Bridge, a three-thousand-foot stretch of asphalt and beige-painted steel connecting Manhattan and the Bronx, is the perfect place for an ambush. The narrow bike path along its west side is poorly lit; darkened trash-strewn alcoves on either end are useful for lying in wait. All summer, food-delivery workers returning home after their shifts have been violently attacked there for their bikes: by gunmen pulling up on motorcycles, by knife-wielding thieves leaping from the recesses, by muggers blocking the path with Citi Bikes and brandishing broken bottles.

"Once you go onto that bridge, it's another world," one frequent crosser said. "You ever see wildlife with the wildebeest trying to cross with the crocodiles? That's the crocodiles over there. We're the wildebeests just trying to get by."

Lately, delivery workers have found safety in numbers. On a humid July night, his last dinner orders complete, Cesar Solano, a lanky and serious nineteen-year-old from Guerrero, Mexico, rode his heavy electric bike onto the sidewalk at 125th Street and First Avenue and dismounted beneath an overpass. Across the street, through a lattice of on-ramps and off-ramps, was the entrance to the Willis, which threads under the exit of the RFK Bridge and over the Harlem River Drive before shooting out across the Harlem River. Whatever happens on the bridge is blocked from view by the highway.

Several other workers had already arrived. The headlights of their parked bikes provided the only illumination. Cesar watched,

his arms crossed, as his older cousin Sergio Solano and another
worker strung a banner between the traffic light and a signpost on
the corner. It read WE ARE ON GUARD TO PROTECT OUR DELIVERY
WORKERS.

Sergio walked back beneath the overpass, took up his mega-
phone, and whooped the siren, signaling to workers riding up
First Avenue to wait and form a group before crossing. When five
assembled, he announced the next departure for the Bronx.

Cesar, Sergio, and three other members of their family, all of
whom work delivering food, had been standing watch each night
for nearly a month. They live together nearby and heard about
the attacks through the Facebook page they cofounded called El
Diario de los Deliveryboys en la Gran Manzana, or "The Deliveryboys in the Big Apple Daily." They started it in part to chronicle
the bike thefts that have been plaguing workers on the bridge
and elsewhere across the city. Sergio himself lost two bikes in two
months. He reported both to the police, but the cases went nowhere, an experience common enough that many workers have
concluded calling 911 is a waste of time.

Losing a bike is devastating for a delivery worker, obliterating
several weeks' worth of wages as well as the tool they need to earn
those wages. "It's my colleague," Cesar said in Spanish through an
interpreter. "It's what takes me to work; it's who I work with and
what takes me home." He's customized his with dark blue tape covering its frame, blue spokes, and color-changing LED light strips
on its rear rack. Two Mexican flags fly from his front fork. He
also attached a second battery since the main one lasts only seven
hours, and he rides fast and for every app he can, typically working
from breakfast to dinner. He maintains his bike with the help of
a traveling mechanic known only as Su, who broadcasts his GPS
location as he roams upper Manhattan. Recently, Cesar added a
holster to his top bar for his five-pound steel U-lock so he can
quickly draw it to defend himself in case of attack.

Even before the thefts started, the city's sixty-five thousand
delivery workers had tolerated so much: the fluctuating pay, the
lengthening routes, the relentless time pressure enforced by mer-
curial software, the deadly carelessness of drivers, the pouring rain
and brutal heat, and the indignity of pissing behind a dumpster
because the restaurant that depends on you refuses to let you use
its restroom. And every day there were the trivially small items peo-

ple ordered and the paltry tips they gave—all while calling you a hero and avoiding eye contact. Cesar recently biked from 77th on the Upper East Side eighteen blocks south and over the Ed Koch Queensboro Bridge, then up through Long Island City and over another bridge to Roosevelt Island, all to deliver a single slice of cake for no tip at all. And now he had to worry about losing his bike, purchased with savings on his birthday.

For Cesar and many other delivery workers, the thefts broke something loose. Some started protesting and lobbying, partnering with nonprofits and city officials to propose legislation. Cesar and the Deliveryboys took another tack, forming a civil guard reminiscent of the one that patrolled San Juan Puerto Montaña, the small, mostly Indigenous Me'phaa village where they are from.

That night, the space under the RFK overpass was a makeshift but welcoming way station. Aluminum catering trays of tacos and beans were arrayed beneath the trusses of the bridge. Arrivals never went long before being offered a plate and a Fanta. The parked bikes flashed festively. Some workers lingered only long enough for a quick fist bump before forming a convoy and departing. But a rotating crew of around a dozen stayed and chatted—sharing stories about who got in an accident and how they're doing, how orders had slowed lately. Cesar, who hopes to be a video editor, livestreamed his nightly broadcast to the Deliveryboys page. It was something between a news bulletin and a pledge drive, with Cesar interviewing workers, thanking people for donating food, and shouting out to his viewers, who number in the thousands and tune in from Staten Island to their hometown in Mexico.

Just before 1:00 a.m., a delivery worker rode up, his right arm bleeding. People rushed to him. The worker had been waiting, he explained, at a red light on 110th when someone leaped in front of him with a knife and demanded his bike. The worker accelerated but was slashed on the arm as he fled. Soon, a police cruiser arrived and later an ambulance.

The worker, his blood pooling on the street, at first refused to be taken to the hospital. But the Deliveryboys convinced him to go. Sergio and Cesar shared their phone numbers and took his bike home when they left around 2:00 a.m. He retrieved it the next day before the Deliveryboys began their watch again.

*

For years, delivery workers in New York have improvised solutions like the bridge patrol to make their jobs feasible. These methods have been remarkably successful, undergirding the illusion of limitless and frictionless delivery. But every hack that made their working conditions tolerable only encouraged the apps and restaurants to ask more of them, until the job evolved into something uniquely intense, dangerous, and precarious.

Take the electric bike. When e-bikes first arrived in the city in the late 2000s, they were ridden mostly by older Chinese immigrants who used them to stay in the job as they aged, according to Do Lee, a Queens College professor who wrote his dissertation on delivery workers. But once restaurant owners and executives at companies like Uber, DoorDash, and Grubhub–Seamless figured out it was possible to do more and faster deliveries, they adjusted their expectations, and e-bikes became a de facto job requirement.

Today, delivery workers have an overwhelmingly preferred brand: the Arrow, essentially a rugged battery-powered mountain bike that tops out at around twenty-eight miles per hour. A new Arrow runs $1,800 and can easily exceed $2,500 once it's equipped with phone-charging mounts, lights, second batteries, air horns, racks, mud flaps, and other essential upgrades. What began as a technological assist has become a major start-up investment.

Delivery workers now move faster than just about anything else in the city. They keep pace with cars and weave between them when traffic slows, ever vigilant for opening taxi doors and merging trucks. They know they go too fast, any worker will say, but it's a calculated risk. Slowing down means being punished by the apps.

A few days after the Deliveryboys began their Willis guard, I met Anthony Chavez in front of a sleek glass apartment building near Lincoln Center. Chavez is something of an influencer among delivery workers, though his fame was inadvertent and the twenty-six-year-old is too reserved to fully embrace the role. Wanting to share the tricks and texture of New York delivery, he started filming his work in late 2019 and posting the videos to a Facebook page he started called Chapín en Dos Ruedas, meaning "Guatemalan on Two Wheels." Later, his posts about bike thefts would expand his audience to more than twelve thousand, but at first it was mostly just the six other Guatemalan delivery workers he lives with in the Bronx. Long stretches of his videos pass with little dialogue, just the background whine of his bike and the Dopplering traffic punctuated occasionally by his advice: always wear a helmet, only listen to music with one earbud, avoid running red lights, and, if you must, really look both ways.

For about half his week, Chavez works at a rotisserie chicken spot in Midtown. He likes it there; the delivery radius is a bit over a mile, and the kitchen is good at batching orders. The restaurant pays him even when an accident takes him out of commission. He doesn't even need his Arrow. Instead, he rides his pedal-powered Cannondale. An enthusiastic cyclist who rode BMXs back home and wears a small gold bike on his necklace, he likes cycling best about the job.

This used to be how delivery worked across the city. A restaurant that made delivery-friendly food like pizza or Chinese employed people to take it to customers in the neighborhood. Managers could be cruel, and owners frequently exploited a worker's immigration status with illegally low wages, but the restaurant also provided shelter, restrooms, and often free meals and a place to eat them alongside coworkers. Unfortunately for Chavez, the chicken spot never has enough hours, so the rest of the time, he works for the apps.

Before the apps, sites like Seamless and Grubhub simply listed restaurants that already offered delivery. But DoorDash, Postmates, and the other apps that arrived in the mid-2010s had their own delivery workers, armies of contractors directed by software on their phones. If a restaurant didn't offer delivery or was too far away, the app just sent a gig worker to order takeout and bring it to you.

The main reason restaurants weren't already letting you order a single bacon, egg, and cheese from fifty blocks away for almost no charge is that it's a terrible business model. Expensive, wasteful, labor intensive—you would lose money on every order. The apps promised to solve this problem through algorithmic optimization and scale. This has yet to happen—none of the companies are consistently profitable—but for a while they solved the problem with money. Armed with billions in venture capital, the apps subsidized what had been a low-margin side gig of the restaurant industry until it resembled any other Silicon Valley consumer-gratification machine. Seamless, which merged with Grubhub and added its own gig platform to compete, was particularly direct in its pitch, running cutesy subway ads about ordering delivery with zero human contact and requesting miniature entrées for your hamster.

The apps failed and bought each other, and now three giants remain: DoorDash, Uber Eats, and Grubhub–Seamless. Each divides the New York market more or less equally, and each uses the piecework model pioneered by Uber itself. Workers get paid when they accept and complete a delivery, and a gamelike system of rewards and penalties keeps them moving: high scores for being on time, low scores and fewer orders for tardiness, and so on. Chavez and others call it the *patrón fantasma,* the phantom boss—always watching and quick to punish you for being late but nowhere to be found when you need $10 to fix your bike or when you get doored and have to go to the hospital.

Then there is a fourth app, which Chavez and thousands of others work for but few customers have heard of, called Relay Delivery. It's a privately held company founded in 2014 and mostly limited to New York. The best way to understand Relay is to think of most delivery apps as two different businesses: the lucrative digital one that customers order from and that charges restaurants commission and advertising fees, and the labor-intensive, logistically complicated—"crummy," in the words of Grubhub's founder—business of getting the food to the customer. Relay handles just the second one.

Restaurants can outsource all their delivery to Relay, no matter if the customer ordered on Seamless or DoorDash or called direct. When the food is ready, the restaurant uses the Relay app to summon a worker who is supposed to appear in under five minutes. It's often cheaper for restaurants than the other apps, and it's extremely reliable.

This is in part because the rewards Relay offers workers are greater and its penalties more severe. Rather than piecework, it pays $12.50 per hour plus tips. But unlike Uber and DoorDash, workers can deliver food only if they're scheduled, and the schedule is designed through daily zero-sum competition, with the best-rated workers getting first dibs. If you get an early enough sign-up time to grab the Upper West Side from 5:00 to 9:00 p.m., you can rest easy knowing you'll have a decently paying job tomorrow. But if you rejected a delivery, or went too slow, or weren't in your designated zone the second your shift started (even if that was because you were delivering a Relay order from your prior shift), or committed any other mysterious infraction, your sign-up time moves back twenty minutes. Maybe all that's left is Hoboken from 2:00 to 4:00 p.m. Worse, maybe there's nothing and you're relegated to *picoteo,* or "pecking."

You see them around the city, sitting on benches jabbing their screens, refreshing the schedule on the off chance some unlucky colleague had to cancel. It's a fate terrifying enough that when one worker hit a storm drain, flew from his bike, and suffered a concussion so severe he was passing in and out of consciousness and had to be taken to the hospital, he still made sure to have a friend message the company explaining why he wasn't accepting orders. Later, trying to get his score up, he volunteered to work during Hurricane Ida, wrecked his bike, and got bumped from the schedule entirely.

So while DoorDash and Uber workers have some leeway to pick which deliveries they take, as a practical matter, Relay workers accept every order assigned to them. They obey the bespoke instructions that pop up on their screens: don't wait outside Benny's Burritos, don't ask to use the restroom, be "super nice!" to Dig Inn because it is a "VIP client"—or have your account suspended. Above all, they try to maintain the ideal pace of a delivery every fifteen minutes, no matter the delivery distance.

If these sound more like the demands placed on an actual employee as opposed to an ostensibly free independent contractor, many class-action plaintiffs have agreed. The company has been sued multiple times for worker misclassification, tip theft, and other infractions. It settled three times, avoiding a ruling that could torpedo its business model, and another case is currently in arbitration.

A spokesperson said the company has implemented a fix to prevent restaurants from unilaterally expanding their delivery zones, but it currently only works for new entrants to the platform. The tip theft that workers often complain of occurs when restaurants receive an order, then enter the wrong tip information into the Relay app, the spokesperson said, and the company has added a way for workers to dispute this. As for the intense pressure, the company said that it matches the number of riders each day with anticipated demand but that there is a large backlog of people who want to work.

That's true. Many would rather work for a restaurant, but when forced to pick among the apps, Chavez, Cesar, and others choose Relay, which they say pays better and more consistently than its piecework peers. It is, after all, the closest among them to a traditional job. But all the apps have this in common: the physical practicalities of maintaining the modern buffet of speedy delivery options fall to the workers.

I followed Chavez down the ramp of the glass tower's parking garage and around the corner to where delivery workers have set up a subterranean base. Electric bikes were parked in front of plywood shelving crammed with charging batteries, their lights blinking red and green. Under the garage ramp, five workers sat on a pipe eating lunch beneath a harsh fluorescent light, clothes hung to dry on another pipe above their heads. About a dozen people sat on folding chairs around a long table, eating from Styrofoam takeout trays and playing with their phones. Others napped in the carriages of bike rickshaws draped with plastic flowers.

Garages like these are scattered across the city, a solution worked out to replace some of the necessities once supplied by restaurants. Another option for shelter, particularly in the winter, is to get a Chase debit card and take refuge in the lobbies of the bank's ubiquitous branches, warming yourself with a coffee before you're told to move on. But the coffee raises another pressing question: where to find a restroom. The garage solves both problems and others, like bike storage and battery charging. Now, instead of shift meals during the predinner lull, workers take turns ordering delivery and eat underground. (They always tip well.) Chavez pays $120 a month for his spot.

Every adaptation has a cost, the Arrow being by far the largest. The appeal of the Arrow is the network of shops that sell it. They sell only Arrows, and if you have one, they will do simple repairs for cheap or free. The shops also charge second batteries for a monthly fee. The city's pocked streets are rough on the bikes, and each evening just before the dinner rush, delivery workers wait outside Arrow stores as mechanics strip and rewire water-damaged controllers and replace bald tires with the fluid focus of a NASCAR pit crew.

Bikes, cold-weather gear, garages, maintenance: the costs add up. Workers even pay for their own app-branded cooler bags. So while DoorDash claims Manhattan workers make $33 per hour, including tips, when you factor in expenses, delivery workers have a base pay of $7.87 per hour, according to a recent study of app-based workers conducted by the Cornell Worker Institute and the Worker's Justice Project. Neither estimate includes time spent waiting between deliveries.

Workers developed the whole system—the bikes, repair networks, shelters, charging stations—because they had to. To the apps, they are independent contractors; to restaurants, they are emissaries of the apps; to customers, they represent the restaurants. In reality, the workers are on their own, often without even the minimum in government support. As contractors and, often, undocumented immigrants, they have few protections and virtually no safety net. The few times city authorities noted the delivery worker's changing role, it was typically with confused hostility. Until recently, throttle-powered electric bikes like the Arrow were illegal to ride, though not to own. Mayor de Blasio heightened enforcement in 2017, calling the bikes "a real danger" after an Upper West Side investment banker clocked workers with a speed gun and complained to him on the *Brian Lehrer Show*.

The NYPD set up checkpoints, fining riders $500, seizing their bikes, and posting photos of the busts on Twitter. The police would then return the bikes because, again, they were legal to own. It was a costly and bewildering ritual. For years, bike activists and workers pushed for legalization, though the apps that benefited from them were largely silent. It was only when another group of tech companies—hoping to make scooter sharing legal—joined the fight that a bill moved forward in Albany. Then the pandemic hit, restaurants were restricted to takeout, and the mayor had to acknowledge that the bikes were an essential part of the city's delivery infrastructure. He halted enforcement. The bikes were officially legalized three months later.

Maybe it was legalization that triggered the robberies. Maybe it was the pandemic-emptied streets. Maybe it was all the people out of work who needed money, or all the other people out of work who were enlisting to serve the newly formed Zoom class and suddenly needed e-bikes. Everyone has a theory. But what happened next is a familiar story. The workers turned to the city for help, got none, and started figuring out a solution themselves.

Chavez has no history of activism and no interest in being a leader. Those things take time, and he came to the city with a plan: work

hard for five years and save enough money to buy a house in Guatemala City. Many workers treat the job like a dangerous but temporary trial they hope will give them a shot at pulling themselves
out of poverty back home. Cesar has a plan, too: work until he
can buy a house for his parents and himself, then return. Things
don't always go according to plan. You meet someone here and
start a family. You discover that all the money you thought you
were saving has gone to bikes and food and rent. The city becomes
familiar. Years go by.

That was the case for Eliseo Tohom, Chavez's thirty-six-year-old
roommate. He's been working delivery for fourteen years. Chavez
teases him on his livestreams. "That Eliseo is well known around
these streets," he said when Tohom chimed in on the chat. "Single
ladies, delivery worker Eliseo is looking for a girl to take back to
Guatemala."

Last October, the two were eating pizza in Central Park and
talking about the robberies. A fellow garage member, seventeen
years old, had been unlocking his bike after depositing a dinner
on Riverside Drive when two men tackled him from behind. A
third grabbed his bike and rode off as the other assailants leaped
into a waiting car.

It was the second such attack to befall a garage member and
one of countless they had heard about. According to NYPD data,
robberies and attempted robberies of delivery workers increased
65 percent in 2020, to 332, and are on track to exceed that number this year. But those are only the small fraction of cases that
are reported to the police. Workers say officers often discouraged
them from filing reports and showed so little progress solving the
thefts they did report that many stopped bothering to do so. In
contrast to the NYPD's numbers, the Worker's Justice Project's survey found that 54 percent of the city's delivery workers have had
their bikes stolen. About 30 percent of those thefts were violent.
The group said it receives approximately fifty reports of thefts and
robberies a day.

Tohom had put together a pool to buy the kid a new bike, but
he wanted to do more. He proposed going to the local precinct,
maybe with a dozen or so people from their garage and another
group in Midtown, and asking the police to do something. Chavez
posted the announcement on Chapín.

About thirty people showed up to the park at 72nd and Amsterdam and rode honking to the precinct. There, they blocked the street, shouting "No more robberies!" to nonplussed cops. Eventually, a Spanish-speaking officer came out. Tohom stepped forward and listed robbery after robbery—Monday at 150 Central Park, yesterday at 100th, another at 67th; knives, guns, machetes; thefts they reported months ago and received no response about; bikes stolen with GPS that police refused to pursue—as the crowd yelled, "Help us."

Chavez posted a video of the scene, and it ricocheted through New York's delivery community. Overnight, he gained a thousand followers. The next day, a representative got in touch from the Worker's Justice Project, which had previously supported construction workers and domestic laborers and had started organizing delivery workers during the pandemic. WJP helped file the paperwork for a more formal rally the following week. Again, Chavez announced it on his Facebook page. This time, hundreds showed up. Chavez livestreamed as the armada rode honking down Broadway, flags waving from their bikes, to City Hall.

It was the first time so many delivery workers had gathered in one place, and it sparked an explosion of new groups. It was there that Cesar met Chavez. Soon after, he and his cousins and uncles launched the Deliveryboys page. Like Chavez's page, it soon became a hub for theft alerts, but it was also a place to memorialize slain and injured workers. When the DoorDash worker Francisco Villalva Vitinio was shot and killed for his bike in March, the Deliveryboys posted videos of vigils in New York and of Villalva Vitinio's casket being carried down the streets of his hometown in Guerrero, Mexico. Later, they broadcast live from the precinct on the day the suspect was arrested.

Small cadres of workers had already begun forming groups on WhatsApp and Telegram to share information and protect one another. But now they built more formal and larger versions with names like Delivery Worker Alerts, Emergency Group, and Robbery Alerts in the Big Apple. At the protest, workers scanned QR codes on one another's phones to join. Approximate territories took shape, with groups for the Upper West Side, Astoria, and lower Manhattan.

"There are thousands of delivery workers on the streets, and if we are all connected, we can see the thieves and act ourselves," Chavez later told his viewers as he rode. Join a group, he said.

Buy a GPS and hide it on your bike; that way, when it gets stolen, you can track it down and call on your fellow workers for help. If the police wouldn't get their bikes back, maybe they could do it themselves.

It was Gustavo Ajche, a thirty-eight-year-old construction worker and part-time DoorDasher, who contacted Chavez's group after the impromptu precinct rally and helped get permits for the larger one. Even then, he was pushing the group to think bigger. Chavez and Tohom wanted to march to Columbus Circle; Ajche said the thefts were affecting everyone, so they should march all the way to City Hall. He also wanted them to think beyond the robberies, to regulations and durable improvements to working conditions.

I met Ajche at 60 Wall Street, a gaudy '80s atrium decorated with palm trees and columns that is a frequent hangout for delivery workers in the Financial District. The nearby parking garage where Ajche stores his bike isn't as nice as Chavez's, he explained, on account of leaks and rats.

There were about a dozen Arrows parked outside, all with stickers bearing the red-and-black fist-raised deliveryman logo of Los Deliveristas Unidos, an arm of the Worker's Justice Project that Ajche helped start. An animated speaker with an open face, Ajche is an effective organizer, and he's eager to grow the movement. Taking out his phone, he showed me a new Deliveristas logo written in Bengali—part of the group's effort to expand beyond Spanish-speaking workers. He would soon make versions in Mandarin and French. I noted the green gear-eyed skull logo on the back of his phone case, the symbol of Aztecas en dos Ruedas ("Aztecs on Two Wheels"), a fixie-riding, alley-cat-racing club of delivery workers. "They are my friends; they are with us," he said by way of explanation. A worker, still helmeted, pushed through the turnstile door and waved to Ajche before joining a group seated on the other side of the hall—Ajche's friends too.

After the success of the October march, the Deliveristas planned an even larger rally for April. This time, thousands gathered and rode honking to City Hall, where they were joined by representatives from SEIU 32BJ, the powerful union that backed the Fight for $15. City Council member Brad Lander, then running for city comptroller, and State Senator Jessica Ramos spoke. Later, the City Council introduced a package of bills crafted in discussion with

the Deliveristas that would establish minimum pay and give workers more control over their routes, among other changes (it will
likely be voted on this month). In June, the Deliveristas helped
kill a bill pushed by Uber and Lyft that would have allowed gig
workers to unionize while falling short of offering them full em-
ployment rights.

Some of the apps also began discussions with the Deliveristas.
DoorDash announced that nearly two hundred (out of eighteen
thousand) of its restaurants would let delivery workers use their
restrooms and that the company is working on an emergency-
assistance button for its app.

Ajche is far from appeased. He recalled a Zoom meeting in
which DoorDash put forward a "top Dasher" to tell them how great
working for DoorDash was. Ajche silenced him by saying that he
can bring five hundred people with complaints. "They are afraid
of us," he said. "They think we are trying to unionize."

Later in June, around the time when Cesar and the Deliveryboys
were beginning their watch at the Willis Avenue Bridge, Ajche and
other Deliveristas met with the NYPD chief of department, Rodney
Harrison, who agreed to appoint an officer to act as a liaison with
the workers and to increase security on the bridges.

Progress is slow. The NYPD said it encourages people to register their bikes with the department and to call 911 if their bike is
stolen. But the department is a sprawling organization with tremendous inertia and little understanding of what modern delivery work entails. "What we've been doing is conquering precinct
by precinct," said Hildalyn Colón Hernández, whom the WJP
brought on to handle police relations and policy. Colón Hernández, who previously worked on a construction-fraud task force in
the Manhattan DA's office, recalled a recent exchange in which
she was pushing an officer to investigate a stolen bike and he said,
essentially, "What's the big deal? It's just a bike." Colón Hernández
launched into an explanation: First off, it's their tool; they lose that
tool, they don't work tomorrow. Second, it probably cost around
$3,000. "That patrol officer looked at me very differently," she
said. "They were like, 'Wait a minute. This is a grand larceny?' "

She has been having conversations like that across the city's bureaucracy. Take the Willis Avenue Bridge. First, she had to talk to
the precincts on either side of the bridge because the city splits
jurisdiction down the middle. Then came the cameras, which

workers complained were broken, because despite the NYPD sign
saying the bridge was under twenty-four-hour surveillance, whenever they went to the police asking for footage of their assaults,
they were told none existed. But the cameras worked just fine;
it's just that they were pointed at the cars, not the bike path. To
change that, Colón Hernández will need to track down someone
in the Department of Transportation and explain why it's urgently
important that they shift the traffic cameras on a bridge.

Chavez and the Deliveryboys rarely attend these meetings. They
stress their independence and express skepticism that anyone—
police, city officials, sometimes even the Deliveristas—will ever
help them. Chavez sees himself as just a guy with a Facebook
page. Juan Solano, Cesar's uncle and the most outspoken of the
Deliveryboys, sees a distinction between "politics," which is futile,
and what they are doing, which is "organizing our people" to help
themselves.

Ajche understands the wariness. "In our countries, organizations show up, promise to do stuff, and never deliver," he said. It's
not like they've gotten much help from institutions here, either.
Yet he is palpably frustrated at the resistance. "A change of mind
would be good for them. They have potential; they've done things.
But they reached a point where they can't do much more since
they're not in touch with politicians."

Ajche pointed out that earlier this year, the Deliveryboys told
their followers to barrage the Relay app with a cut-and-paste in-
dictment of the company's rating system, long routes, and vanish-
ing tips. "Us delivery workers are tired of so much injustice," they
wrote, threatening to "stop working without prior notice."

"It's the same thing that we are trying to do!" Ajche said.

Not long after the walkout threat, Relay added a dispute-tip button. It was a victory, but a partial one. Making use of the feature
requires workers to know the actual amount a customer tipped,
and many lack the language skills to ask. Juan is thinking about
making cards in English so they can show customers why they need
to know.

Compared to the grinding progress of New York's bureaucracy,
when it comes to thefts, self-defense yields immediate results: a
bike recovered, a thief apprehended, a bridge defended.

Chavez advises workers to keep a photo of their bike on their phone. If it's stolen, send the photo to the group, and often another worker will soon spot someone selling it on the street. The spotter sends the location, then pretends to be an interested buyer—"Hey, buddy, how much you want for that?"—until reinforcements arrive and unobtrusively encircle the two hagglers before closing in. Ideally, surrounded by a dozen delivery workers, the suspect gives up peacefully and returns the bike to its rightful owner.

But not always. In June, a Lower East Side group saw someone selling a stolen bike on Lafayette, but the suspect hopped on the bike and fled. The group gave chase for several blocks before tackling him on Delancey. At that point, the police took notice and detained the suspect. When the bike's owner arrived, he ceremoniously inserted his key into the lock, dangling from the frame, and opened it to cheers.

Two weeks later, a Relay worker named Angel Lopez was cruising up Amsterdam with a dinner from Celeste when he noticed someone sawing through a bike lock with a power grinder, throwing up sparks. He stopped, shocked. While he was debating what to do, workers from a nearby Chinese takeout place rushed out, grabbed chairs from their outdoor-dining setup, and started hitting the thief, who responded by brandishing his buzz saw. A standoff ensued until the thief, deterred, jogged off. Lopez sent an alert to his group, Upper Furious, and followed from a distance.

If I let him go, he's just gonna get away, just like every other guy, he thought. Lopez crossed paths with two other workers and told them what was happening. They joined in cautious pursuit. Periodically, the thief looked back and yelled, "Keep following me. I got something for you," Lopez said, and they wondered what that could mean, whether he could have a gun in his backpack and be luring them to a less crowded part of town.

The man stopped at another locked bike and began again with the buzz saw, threatening the workers whenever they got close. "That thing will cut your face off," Lopez recalled. The bike freed, the thief started to pedal away.

There were now about ten workers, and they chased the thief, trying to shove him off his bike as he attempted to strike them with his saw. Lopez said they passed a cop car and shouted for help, to no avail.

They hit the downward slope toward Riverside Park, and a few workers gunned their bikes forward to head off the thief. Surrounded, he got off the bike and swung the saw, then hurled the cut lock at the gathered crowd. But in throwing the lock, he lost his grip on the saw, and it fell to the ground. It was at that moment that police arrived, pushed through the workers, and pinned the suspect to the ground with, Lopez said, a degree of force he felt ambivalent about. "It got to the point where he said, 'I can't breathe'—you know those famous lines," he recalled. A few workers shouted that he deserved it. "You could feel the anger in the air," Lopez said.

He couldn't stay to talk to the cops. He was thirty minutes late with his order and worried Relay would deactivate him. "You're no superhero," he imagined the company telling him. "Just deliver the food." The suspect was charged with attempted robbery, possession of a weapon, petit larceny, and resisting arrest.

These ad hoc sting operations worry Colón Hernández. She believes that some of the thieves are organized, possibly transporting the bikes out of state. They are often armed. Workers have been stabbed and attacked with fireworks when they tried to recover their bikes themselves. Chasing down and apprehending every thief in the city is both unsustainable and dangerous.

"The first time works. The second time may work. What happens when the third time, somebody gets killed? Or you hurt somebody because you're chasing people at a very fast pace?" she said. "I've been saying this to the NYPD: one day I'm going to get a call that I don't want to get."

On a Friday night in July, Nicolas was coming back outside after dropping off a pizza near Madison Square Park when he saw that his bike had vanished. *What am I going to do?* he thought. *How am I going to work?*

Originally from Puebla, Mexico, Nicolas, forty-two (who, fearing retaliation from the thief, requested a pseudonym), worked to send money home to his four children, whom he hadn't seen since he crossed the border twelve years ago. The more he worked, the sooner he could return, and he worked a lot: a 5:00 a.m. cleaning shift at a pizza place, then delivering either for the restaurant or for DoorDash.

He called his brother, another delivery worker, and asked him to post a photo of his bike to the Deliveryboys' WhatsApp. An hour later, he got a hit: someone had spotted his bike, a teal-taped Arrow, being wheeled into an apartment building in the Bronx. The tipster had followed the man, filmed him, and noted the address. Nicolas got on the train and headed there.

He was met by five other workers from the WhatsApp group who'd come to help. Standing in front of the building, Nicolas called 911 and was told to wait for a patrol car, so they waited. And waited. After midnight, he thanked the others for standing by him and told them to go home.

Three days later, after he'd given the bike up for lost, one of the workers who had stood with him Friday flagged him down. Another bike had been stolen and traced to the same building. A group was gathering to get it back.

When the two arrived, they encountered fifteen or so workers standing in front of the building. Cesar was there, along with a contingent that had caravanned from the Willis Avenue Bridge. Chavez was there too. Nicolas introduced himself.

Cesar and Chavez had been called there by the owner of the other bike, Margaro Solano. Unlike Nicolas's bike, Margaro's had a GPS. Seeing his bike had been taken to the Bronx, he and his wife—who left her restaurant job to help—had immediately headed there. They confirmed they had the right place by obtaining building surveillance footage of a man—the same one filmed carrying Nicolas's bike—lugging Margaro's up the stairs and into his apartment. They could hear Margaro's bike alarm blaring through the door.

After Margaro was unable to get help from the nearby precinct, he called Chavez, who texted Cesar, who put out a call on WhatsApp. By the time Nicolas arrived, the group had gone back to the precinct, failed to get help, and settled in for a stakeout.

Rather than risk a confrontation inside the building, Chavez and the others decided the safest approach would be to wait for the thief to emerge and ask for the bikes back. Two workers stood just outside the building entrance, while another loitered in the lobby. The rest gathered on the sidewalk outside, chatting. The stakeout was the first time most of them had met in person.

Around midnight, conversation began to shift to how late it was and when they should decide to call it a night. Many had come directly from work, skipping dinner. Then he emerged, the man from the videos. The workers on the street watched as he opened the lobby door and stepped outside.

The group followed him for a block, tailing him as stealthily as a dozen deliverymen on electric bikes could manage. After a second block, they descended, surrounding him on the sidewalk.

For vigilante justice, it was a restrained confrontation. No one touched anyone else. The workers, masked, stood back in a circle and asked for their bikes to be returned; the man towered over them by at least two heads. Chavez was filming, Cesar broadcasting live. Nicolas stood at the margins, watching.

To Cesar's surprise, the man asked how many bikes they had come for.

Two, he answered.

When the thief asked for $1,000 to give them back, the workers started shouting. "Show him! Let him see!" they yelled in Spanish. "The camera was watching you!" in English. Chavez said they didn't want trouble and wouldn't call the police if the man just gave back the bikes—a bluff. Chavez knew the police wouldn't come. The man didn't budge.

A worker held out his phone to the suspect, showing him the surveillance video. He watched footage of himself carrying the bike up the stairs. Then he watched it again. He paused, thought it over, and agreed to return the bikes. The group formed an escort down Grand Concourse, the suspect surrounded by workers on foot who were circled by bikers cruising slowly.

Chaos ensued once they entered the building. An acquaintance of the man blocked the workers in the entryway while attempting to assure them he would bring their bikes down. Unconvinced, they pushed forward until everyone—the two men, followed by Cesar, Chavez, Nicolas, Margaro, and several others—started running up the stairs. As they neared the fifth floor, they could hear the bike's shrill alarm. Nicolas was too thrilled at the prospect of being reunited with his bike to be scared. One man held the workers at bay while the other brought out Margaro's bike, lights flashing, and then Nicolas's. Cesar glimpsed two other bikes inside before the men shut the door.

"Thank you!" a worker shouted in English as the group shuffled the bikes down the stairs. "Let's go! Two bikes—we came to get one, left with two," he continued in Spanish. "Let's go tell the precinct we actually could get it. Police don't know how to do their job."

Cesar was bringing up the rear and still streaming when someone grabbed him from behind. In the video, the suspect's acquaintance can be heard shouting that he should be rewarded for helping them. Cesar elbowed his assailant and broke free, dashing down the stairs to join the others in front of the building. They mounted their bikes and sped away, riding down the bike lane together.

The next day, Chavez would tell Colón Hernández what had happened and send her the evidence they'd gathered. She'd watch the video of the raid with dismay—reckless, dangerous, no plan at all—and then work the system her way. She'd finish the process of filing Nicolas's police report and stay on the detectives. She'd involve the new delivery liaison. Three weeks after the bikes were recovered, the suspect would be arrested and charged with petit larceny and criminal possession of stolen property.

But the workers didn't know any of that that night. In fact, they wouldn't hear about the arrest until I told them. The night they got the bikes back, they had little reason to believe justice would be served. It was their own detective work that had succeeded when the system failed them.

After they rode some distance from the building, Chavez filmed a news broadcast outside a bodega. It was a mix of anger and triumph.

"The police did nothing," Chavez narrated as Nicolas held up the paperwork he'd been given by a precinct days before. "We had agreed with them that they would be there for us whenever a bike got stolen, and they weren't. Don't commit then. We organize. We recover our bicycles."

They didn't linger to celebrate their victory. It was late, and they had work in the morning. Nicolas's predawn shift would begin in just four hours. He hopped back on his bike and sped home to get some rest.

ADESH THAPLIYAL

How Vietnamese Americans Made San Jose America's Tofu Capital

FROM KQED

SAN JOSE IS America's tofu capital, and nowhere else comes close. Soy milk curds have been strained and pressed in the South Bay since the early twentieth century, but it's not San Jose's long history with tofu that earns it the title: it's the diversity, freshness, and convenience of the tofu on offer throughout the area in restaurants, supermarkets, and an uncommonly large number of dedicated tofu storefronts.

To put San Jose's embarrassment of bean curd riches in perspective, San Francisco has only one dedicated tofu storefront to its name—Chinatown's reliably inexpensive Wo Chong. Megacities like Los Angeles or New York might eke out a technical numerical victory, but San Jose comes out on top when calculating tofu wealth on a per capita basis: with its population of a little over one million, the city still manages to sustain a diverse and lucrative soybean scene that can go toe to toe with any place in America. By my count, San Jose is home to at least ten outlets specializing in fresh tofu, catering to a dedicated clientele of workers looking for a hot snack, home cooks picking up tonight's dinner, and local restaurateurs stocking up on their supply.

The tofu in the Bay's U-bend covers a wide swath of traditions and cultures: At US SoyPresso, Japanese-style tofu pudding is topped with soy milk and sweet beans. At Taiwanese Sogo Tofu, it is deep fried in "biandang" lunchbox-sized pieces. And at Vietnamese Thanh Son Tofu, it can be ordered tucked inside a bành mi.

Today, the dominant style of tofu in San Jose is Vietnamese, with a half dozen strip-mall tofu delicatessens like Thanh Son clustered in a small stretch of San Jose's heavily Vietnamese East Side, with additional outposts spread out across the city.

This wasn't always the case, though. As documented in William Shurtleff and Akiko Aoyagi's exhaustive history of tofu making, the first tofu shops in San Jose came with the earliest Japanese American immigrants, who settled in the Santa Clara Valley to work as farm laborers. Okumura Tofu-ya, founded in 1906, was the first recorded tofu business in the city. It was located on 6th Street, smack-dab in the middle of Japantown, and the neighborhood would have at least one tofu maker or another for more than a hundred years, until the last one closed in 2017. Tofu shops like Okumura spread wherever there were Japanese immigrants in the US; by 1950, at least 425 Japanese tofu businesses had been established throughout the country.

The Japanese American community's grip on tofu started loosening in the late twentieth century as the population aged and shrank relative to other Asian American groups. By then, the growth of tofu shops had slowed if not regressed; they had become redundant after the invention of packaged tofu in Los Angeles in the '50s, which enabled the ingredient to be sold in supermarkets instead of specialty stores. In some cities, these developments spelled the end of the tofu shop—but in San Jose, they would live on in the hands of a new population that arrived in the city after 1975 in large numbers: Vietnamese immigrants.

In the subsequent decades, Vietnamese Americans would create their own kind of tofu shop, one that sells bean curd alongside a wide variety of snacks and drinks in a deli-like format, and usher in a new tofu renaissance in the South Bay. Vietnamese tofu delis now make up the majority of tofu businesses in San Jose. But despite the delis' omnipresence—it feels like no Vietnamese grocery store in San Jose is complete without a fresh-tofu maker nearby—they rarely get the same level of mainstream recognition as other neighborhood institutions like pho restaurants and bành mi takeout joints. Nevertheless, they play just as essential a role in the community and are just as valuable a part of San Jose's culinary landscape.

For the loyal customers these delis serve, the prepackaged stuff sold in grocery stores is no substitute for what their local tofu store can offer. Andrea Nguyen, an authority on Vietnamese cooking and the author of an entire book on tofu, is a longtime customer of tofu delis. "Americans want tofu to be sturdy," she says about Safeway refrigerator-aisle tofu, "whereas the tofu that you buy at an Asian tofu shop, whether that's Japanese, Chinese, or Vietnamese, tends to be more tender because we love that tenderness. That tenderness means that the curds are not as compressed and they suck up flavor."

It's a difference that customers can feel—literally. Nguyen claims it is a Vietnamese American habit to poke at the Saran-wrapped tofu on display to check for quality, "like you're poking the belly of the Pillsbury Doughboy." Good Vietnamese tofu should, like a soft cheese, threaten to fall apart into airy curls with the slightest pressure.

The texture is one that many Americans might not be familiar with, as Japanese- and Chinese-style firm tofu dominates the grocery aisle. Aside from the creamy kind that's only used for pudding, Vietnamese bean curd comes in one, ricotta-esque consistency. Vietnamese tofu makers play up this textural quality by using a different process than Japanese and Chinese artisans. Instead of using nigari or gypsum, they use the leftover whey from straining the last batch to thicken the soy milk into curds. While it cools, they leave it to set loosely in a bread-pan-sized trough instead of, say, subjecting it to the wooden press of Japanese tofu making.

This process produces a softer, wispier tofu than rival methods, highlighting the supple mouthfeel that makes the ingredient a desirable addition to Vietnamese soups, stir-fries, and noodles. It also doesn't turn tofu into anything resembling ersatz meat— intentionally so, because Vietnamese cuisine, like most Asian food cultures, doesn't treat tofu only as a meat substitute. Sometimes tofu can be a velvety complement to the savoriness of meat.

But it's not just the culinary superiority of the fresh stuff that draws Vietnamese Americans to their tofu delis, says Nguyen. "People like fresh tofu because it's part of the food traditions. We're a relatively new immigrant refugee community to America, and there has been so much foodcraft, transported and translated to American soil from Vietnam. We value freshness. We also value the community that forms around that freshness—you feel in touch with your people and your soul when you go to these delis."

Thanh Son Tofu, a prominent Vietnamese tofu deli located near Lee's Supermarket on Senter Road, is a good example of how these stores can be an anchor for the community. The shop has been around for three decades now, according to Anh Nguyen, a member of the family who owns the store. The Thanh Son Nguyens were a traditional tofu-making family in Vietnam until the fall of Saigon, after which they fled their country. Reaching America without anything to their name, they resumed making and selling tofu to their new neighbors in Southern California's Orange County through the '70s and '80s. Eventually, they saved enough capital to open their first storefront in Westminster's Little Saigon in the '90s—and that operation was successful enough that a cousin who lived in San Jose wanted to open a Northern California location with the same name.

Today, Thanh Son is one of the busiest tofu delis in the neighborhood. The storefront, spacious and buzzing with commotion, sports stainless-steel counters and see-through refrigerators packed with green-tinted pandan soy milk, golden fried tofu, yuba sheets rolled up in an imitation of chả lụa hàm, and soy pudding with bright noodles of fruit jelly. A long line of customers wraps around the counters. They point at their preferred soybean product behind the glass, the staff bags it up, and then they head to the register to pay and receive their gelatinous treats.

It's no accident that Thanh Son does brisk business. Tofu this fresh doesn't last more than a few days in a refrigerator, so customers need to come back regularly for their fix. That also means the store needs to refresh its stock regularly, so the staff makes most of its inventory from scratch every morning—all of which will be gone by the afternoon.

The store also sells a wide variety of packaged snacks and goodies like bánh bèo (shrimp-dusted rice cakes), nem chua (tangy rolls of raw fermented pork), and Bánh bò nướng (pandan-flavored "honeycomb" cakes)—some made by Thanh Son staff, some sourced from smaller local producers, but all very addictive. These snacks are piled up on every available inch of counter and shelf space, giving the deli a lively, market-hall feel.

It's the kind of store that can be found all over Vietnamese

American enclaves, from Houston to Los Angeles, but, crucially, not in Vietnam. These delis are uniquely a diaspora phenomenon. "When I have seen tofu vendors in Vietnam, they're just selling tofu, sometimes soy milk too. But the whole thing about these delis serving other dishes and having a menu, that's the next level of Vietnamese Americanness," says Andrea Nguyen, the cookbook author. The fusion of the Vietnamese tofu market stall with the German-Jewish-American delicatessen is an adaptation of one shopping culture to another, a synthesis encouraged along by the generous real estate of the California strip mall.

Thanh Son isn't the only kind of Vietnamese tofu deli that's out there. Some, like Binh Minh (1180 Tully Road) or Hung Vuong (1741 Berryessa Road), serve only vegetarian food, in accordance with a Buddhist monk's diet. Not all Vietnamese Buddhists are vegetarian, but many do observe a vegetarian diet on occasion as an act of religious piety. These Buddhist delis have a slightly different format than their nonvegetarian peers, with a greater focus on hot prepared meals and, of course, the presence of lots of Buddhist tchotchkes on sale.

Dong Phuong Tofu is a long-standing example of this alternative format; it has stood across from Lion Market in the heart of San Jose's Little Saigon for almost two decades. There are meditation CDs and Buddhist scripture posters for sale at the doorway, and a small selection of specialty groceries like vegetarian fish sauce and pork floss displayed on a wooden island in the middle of the store. At the front, hungry patrons dawdle, trying to decide between the two dozen dishes in the hot-food counter tubs as well as everything else on the large menu of made-to-order food tacked up on the wall.

The star attractions are the meatless stir-fries, rice noodles, and other mealtime staples at the hot-food counter. The staff at Dong Phuong make the tofu for these dishes on site, which gives its lemongrass tofu, for example, a springy chew that other restaurants can't pull off.

While some vegetarian diets, like those of brahminical Hindus or white American hippies, shy away from the close imitation of meat, East Asian vegetarianism doesn't have such scruples. Some of the double-take-inducing dishes on display at the hot counter include seitan "fish," battered, deep-fried, and coated in a brown sauce; as well as a pork-belly clay pot where the "belly" has convincing stripes of konjac jelly "fat." Some of the seitan is made in the kitchen, but the most convincing meat substitutes are sourced from specialized Asian fake-meat producers, who have been operating on the continent long before the Impossible Burger was an idea in a Stanford biochemist's head.

The quick-service counters at delis such as Dong Phuong plug an important hole in the market, providing convenient and tasty meals at a price better than sit-down vegetarian places like Green Lotus, which is just across the street. Plus, the quality of the food doesn't suffer despite sitting out for most of the day: tofu and seitan dishes only suck up more flavor during a long marination time.

On a recent Saturday, I visited both Thanh Son and Dong Phuong to assemble a three-course, under $20, all-tofu lunch, with the former providing an appetizer (fried tofu) and dessert (ginger tofu pudding), and the latter providing the entree (lemongrass tofu with rice noodles). Afterwards, I sat on the lip of the Grand Century Mall fountain, set out my assorted tofu, and thought about how lucky the neighborhood is to have this abundance. In a lopsided American food system that gives artisanal food to the rich and the processed scraps to the poor, fresh tofu is the rare luxury that remains stubbornly affordable, able to be enjoyed by all.

As I ate, I couldn't stop thinking of the melancholy note on which my conversation with Nguyen ended: "I think that we take for granted what is available in these enclaves," she mused. "Because I think, my God, how lucky are we to be in America and be standing here, waiting in line to buy this tofu that's been freshly made. It's not the same as going to buy it on a wet market in Vietnam, but, gosh darn it, it's a very similar experience. I think about the many depths of these experiences. And I said to myself: how fucking lucky am I? How long is that going to last?"

Nguyen points out that young Vietnamese Americans usually aren't the ones behind the register at these tofu shops, but an older generation of first-wave immigrants. She's worried that the graying of the community might spell an end for the tofu. There's some precedent for this in San Jose: The last tofu maker in Japantown, San Jose Tofu Company, closed three years ago after the retirement of its owners.

But perhaps tofu will survive in San Jose like it always has. Hodo

Soy, the buzzy, high-end tofu factory now based in Oakland, got its start in the South Bay. The company is owned by Minh Tsai, whose parents would bring him to traditional tofu stands in Vietnam when he was a child. Tsai started making the product for his new brand at Sogo Tofu, San Jose's only Taiwanese tofu makers, and his dense style of tofu still betrays a strong Chinese influence. And when it came time to introduce his line to a wider audience, he opted for Japanese terminology, like "yuba" for tofu skins.

Maybe the next generation of South Bay tofu entrepreneurs will be more like Tsai: multicultural in emphasis, reflecting the diverse history of tofu making in San Jose itself. Still, what's lost in the hype is that companies like Hodo stand on the shoulders of the humble strip-mall tofu shops, which have been making fresh bean curd with care and sophistication, and with little fanfare, long before mainstream America deemed the product worthy of fine-dining menus. Let's keep their memory alive, too.

I Ate Like a Boy to Avoid Being a Queer Man

FROM *Bon Appétit*

ON MY TWENTY-FIFTH birthday, I declared a second adolescence. I ate to be a boy again: half a banana for breakfast, a mini bag of Doritos for lunch, one slice of American cheese for dinner. Whenever I felt faint, I'd chew a piece of candy-flavored gum. I went through packs of Juicy Fruit Starburst and Stride Sour Patch Kids like a chain-smoker. All morning and night, in my adult onesie, I'd maniacally blow sweet magenta bubbles while watching reality shows about middle-aged beauty pageant contestants and Mormon sister wives, counting down the hours to my next slice of American cheese.

When I'd moved to Michigan three years prior for grad school, I'd hoped for a different kind of transformation. I came out of the closet at nineteen but had been too timid back home on Long Island for a full queer self-awakening. In Ann Arbor, where I knew no one, I should've been ready to finally cultivate relationships with other queer people and possibly even find love. Instead, unformed, lost, and in need of comfort and familiarity, I went wildly back in time.

I grew up facilitating other kids' dreams. At recess, I helped girls spin convoluted love plots and basked in their princess fantasies under the monkey bars. My pleasure wasn't vicarious. I didn't want the happily-ever-after for myself. I cherished my role as the matchmaker, the mingler, the fun-loving gay sidekick.

Back then, when I was an actual boy, I didn't enjoy eating. The only foods that excited me were grilled cheese sandwiches and french fries dipped in Russian dressing from the diner around the corner from my house, but I'd never finish my plate. More than the typical pickiness of a tween coddled by, and addicted to, the bland cuisine of white American suburbia, I found a twisted pleasure in consuming as little as I could.

Always the smallest kid in my grade and determined not to feel inadequate for my size, I'd learned early on to embrace my tininess. I let boys pick me up and throw me around. I let girls marvel at how much taller they were than me. My smallness became so tied to my identity, I eventually feared growing up.

So I decided I'd need to stay the smallest, cutest kid in my class for eternity. Becoming a vegetarian at nineteen, incidentally the same year I came out of the closet, made it even easier to limit my consumption. I lived off Tofurky slices, pretzels, chocolate soy milk, and Tofutti-slathered mini bagels.

I kept my prepubescent physique throughout most of grad school, vowing never to go above a certain number on the scale. Still vegetarian, I began using kiddie treats for meat replacements. The food from my childhood was a balm, a reassuring indulgence I turned to instead of seeking new connection. The nights I could've attended the "homo potlucks" hosted by a queer classmate, I opted out and lost myself in Teddy Grahams and Kraft singles. I kept my social circle small and normative, going to Thursday happy hours in straight spaces, where I returned to the sidekick role I knew and loved. With mac 'n' cheese and infinite variations on nachos at every bar, Ann Arbor was the ideal place to subsist on orange-colored snacks. I was Peter Pan, only my pixie dust was Cheez Doodle powder, my Neverland suburban Michigan.

Prolonging boyhood allowed me to exist comfortably stunted, just as I had as a child, on the margins of straight life. But there was actually a place for my scrawny body in the gay imagination. On Grindr, the twink is a sought-after commodity—an eighteen- to twenty-two-year-old, slim boy-man who will let you do to him whatever you want. I'd unwittingly become my own almost-celibate twist on the twink. I wasn't actively dating. I lived alone in a tiny apartment that resembled a Gymboree more than a bachelor pad. I ate with the irresistible puckishness of an eight-year-old at a never-ending slumber party—pink and red Starbursts and frozen mozzarella sticks. I was grooming myself to be a boy-man who no one else was allowed to enjoy.

Meanwhile, the subject of my own joy was too daunting to even broach. It scared me to think of the vulnerability I'd have to confront to achieve pleasure. Remaining small and boyish wasn't just easy: it seemed like my only option. As long as I could remember, I'd never been able to envision a future as an adult gay man. I couldn't think beyond the present, because I had no models for long-term queer happiness.

For all my time in the fratty bars of Ann Arbor, I'd managed to build a profound connection with a queer classmate. K felt more like me than anyone I'd ever met. Over my first few years in Michigan, we bonded over our shared pasts as band nerds and our unironic love for the musical *Cats*. We spoke the same language of withering sarcasm and quiet but unwavering warmth.

After turning twenty-six, I moved in with K. We spent a magical year sitting around finishing our dissertations on weird women writers, watching *Barefoot Contessa* on glorious loops. Far from a sidekick, I was her sister and she was my confidante. I cried to her when my dad had open-heart surgery, told her how lost I felt in navigating my future. I watched her develop a mature romantic relationship with a woman she loved deeply. K cooked for us: lasagna and vodka sauce and brownies and chocolate pudding and cheddar-dill scones. And I let myself eat well. Before leaving Michigan, I'd caught a glimpse of what my life could be.

At thirty-three, I live in Brooklyn now, with a generous, nurturing, queer surrogate family. They share with me heavenly lentil soups and cheddar-onion-potato pizzas and vegetable pot pies. Though I don't cook much myself, I do assemble a hummus sandwich every day for lunch, which I eat with snack-size bags of Cheez-Its. Sometimes I observe the swirls of orange cheddar dust on my still-boyish hands, like a palm reader. I see zigzag paths of intimate friendship. I see cackling parties. I see risks I don't yet know.

LIGAYA MISHAN

The Humble Beginnings of Today's Culinary Delicacies

FROM *The New York Times Style Magazine*

IN THE NEWLY moneyed Beijing of the early 1990s, a curious type of restaurant started to appear. Limousines idled in the street while, inside, diners hunched on logs or camp-style chairs strung with rope and feasted on the likes of crackly locusts, ants boiled into soup, damp weeds and wotou (a steamed bread of coarse cornmeal)—a subsistence menu that evoked the scant rations served at rural work-unit canteens during the Cultural Revolution, less than twenty years before.

A number of patrons were former *zhiqing*, among the more than sixteen million urban and educated young people who, between 1956 and the official termination of the Up to the Mountains and Down to the Countryside movement in 1981, were forcibly resettled in undeveloped areas and assigned hard farm labor to purge them of bourgeois thinking. (China's current leader, President Xi Jinping, was himself sent to work in the northern province of Shaanxi at age fifteen after his father, a party official and revolutionary hero, fell from grace and was imprisoned; he spent seven years in Shaanxi, living in caves, building dams, and cleaning out latrines.) Why would they wish to relive their difficult pasts—and pay a premium for the pleasure? For pleasure is what these restaurants promised: not a sober history lesson but feel-good theme park nostalgia, re-creating in denatured form a time of atrocities when, historians estimate, between five hundred thousand and eight million people died because of political upheaval, and tens of millions more were subject to persecution.

As the anthropologist Jennifer Hubbert argues in her 2005 essay "Revolution *Is* a Dinner Party: Cultural Revolution Restaurants in Contemporary China," such spaces memorialized the zhiqing era, with dining rooms decked out in farm tools and attended by waitstaff wearing the army-green uniforms of the feared Red Guard, but also exoticized it and turned it into a kind of perverse luxury commodity, "linking leisure to dispossession." These restaurants, with names like Remembering Bitterness (from *yiku sitian*, a political campaign of the 1960s and 1970s in which citizens testified to past miseries to underscore the sweetness of life under communism), were private enterprises, after all, implicitly committed to capitalism, in repudiation of the Maoist ideology celebrated by their decor. And the people who could afford to eat at such places—where a meal might cost ten times the average working-class lunch, as Rone Tempest reported in the *Los Angeles Times* in 1993—were far removed from their onetime suffering on the black-earth plains of Heilongjiang, China's most northeastern province, or the steppes of Inner Mongolia.

But it was precisely this distance, in space, time, and above all class (even in a supposedly classless society), that made the food— once the barest minimum, eaten and endured only in order to survive—suddenly palatable. Because that distance meant it was no longer a necessity but a choice. The diners were eating out of a peculiar calculus of desire that had little to do with what the ingredients on their plates actually tasted like or how much nourishment they offered. They were displaying their power, to eat as much as they wanted, to crowd the table with plates, then leave them unfinished; to defy the austerity of old; to dare to waste.

The phenomenon is hardly unique to China. Throughout history, foods that were once a marker of precarity and a lack of resources—dishes eked from scraps, tough cuts of meat, seafood too abundant to be of value to those who treasure rarity, wild roots scraped out of the earth with hardened hands—have gradually been co-opted by the upper classes, sometimes to the point that they're no longer accessible to the people who once relied on them. For deliciousness has never been a fixed quality, wholly measurable by sensors on the tongue; it's an invocation and reflection of memory, history, and prevailing hierarchies. To *have* taste, in the cultural sense of showing discernment and an awareness of higher aesthetics, is to *defeat* taste in the physical sense: the animal instinct to simply eat what pleases us.

Caviar originally came from the Caspian Sea, where roe was extracted from giant prehistoric sturgeon (to make the harvest more efficient, they were killed first) and cured in salt. The Cossacks sent it as a yearly tribute to the Russian czars from the sixteenth century until the imperial house's brutal end in the early twentieth—at first just one symbolic bowl and eventually eleven tons. Since 2005, the most coveted variety, from the Caspian's wild beluga, a sturgeon species that's listed as critically endangered by the Switzerland-based International Union for Conservation of Nature, has been banned from sale in the United States; only last year did American-bred beluga caviar, from fish farmed in Florida, become available, at $830 an ounce.

Today, those who can afford this treat often approach it with ritualistic reverence, scooping out the inky orbs with mother-of-pearl spoons, so no hint of metal will intrude upon the delicacy of the flavor. But in medieval Russia, caviar was a peasant staple, less expensive than fish itself, and a sanctioned fasting food on holy days: an emblem of deprivation, dolloped on porridge for a burst of brine. There was more than enough to go around: peasants fed it to their pigs to fatten them up. In Persia (now Iran), which borders the Caspian Sea, khaviyar (the root of the English "caviar") was considered "a cheap seasonal seaside snack, not worth exporting into the hot interior of the country, although mountain folk would eat it on bread with a glass of milk," the Scottish writer Nichola Fletcher writes in *Caviar: A Global History* (2010). Had it continued thus, seventeen species of sturgeon might not now be at risk of extinction.

So much seafood was once dismissed as the debris of the sea: eels, snared from the Thames River in sixteenth-century England and tucked into pies in lieu of meat; clams, eaten by New England colonists only in times of desperation; oysters, offered all-you-can-eat for 6 cents at bars in nineteenth-century New York City; whelks, pickled and trundled by wheelbarrow through London streets, which in the mid-nineteenth century the British social reformer Henry Mayhew tallied "among the delicacies of the poor" and which housemaids wouldn't eat in public, lest they be judged unladylike. Even lowlier were lobsters, scorned as indiscriminate bottom feeders, fobbed off on servants and put on prison menus, or else consigned to fertilizer. (Their flesh and shells are still used in this way, as their high concentration of nitrogen and calcium helps plants grow.)

Such was the abundance of the American lobster in the North Atlantic that coastal peoples didn't need to set traps to catch them. Instead, they plucked them straight from the shallows and raked them up by the hundreds off the beach after storms—a gift from the ocean that went largely unappreciated. "Their plenty makes them little esteemed and seldom eaten," the Massachusetts Bay colonist William Wood wrote in 1634, observing that Native Americans speared them on hooks as bait for fish, the true prize. In an 1876 report on life among British settlers in Nova Scotia, John J. Rowan noted that people were "ashamed" to be seen eating lobsters, and that lobster shells strewn around a house were "looked upon as signs of poverty and degradation."

Even into the twentieth century, schoolchildren living in New England and the Canadian Maritimes were mortified to find lobster sandwiches in their lunchboxes, proof of their poverty. In World War II, American GIs ate tins of lobster in the trenches. Yet this past summer, lobster rolls, heavy with sweet claw and knuckle meat and dripping butter, sold for as much as $34 each in Maine. Like caviar, the American lobster has risen in status as its stocks have declined. Although populations are currently stable, as the ocean grows warmer, lobsters seek colder waters farther offshore and to the north, leaving fewer specimens to be found along the southern New England coast.

Still, the price is high due not to scarcity but to demand. For the rich have claimed both lobster and caviar, in seeming disregard for their humble origins—because those origins are now essentially invisible. The lobster on a silver platter, the caviar in a lustrous spoon: these foods only became extravagances once deracinated, taken out of context, and presented as novelties for people who neither lived where they were harvested nor had any role in procuring them, beyond waging war, like the czar, or handing over a fistful of cash; who didn't have to depend on proximity to furnish their feasts; who could pay the price to have anything shipped from anywhere, in any season, and make the world (mad phrase) their oyster.

*

Historically, cheap ingredients have required effort to be coaxed into edibility. Before Auguste Escoffier codified the recipe for boeuf bourguignon in his magisterial 1903 cookbook, *Le Guide Culinaire,* it was a peasant's trick: subdue a tough slab of beef by leaving it to wallow in wine—not the fancy stuff—for hours, until the connective tissue breaks down into gelatin and makes the meat melty and ready to give. (In fact, the more coveted, leaner cuts, lacking as much collagen, are not just wasted in such a dish but yield less satisfying results.) So, too, with haggard old roosters, slotted for the pot in coq au vin. These dishes are now prized beyond rustic tables precisely because they attest to the skill and patience of the chef.

In the American South, barbecue likewise emerged as a way to doll up inferior meat, by first anointing it—be it with vinegar and sugar, a tincture of tomato and molasses, a pat-down of garlic and cumin, or just straight-up salt and pepper—then letting it unknot over a low, vigilantly monitored fire for close to a day as it takes in smoke and learns to yield. As the culinary historian Adrian Miller has chronicled, in the antebellum era, enslaved people did the hard labor of barbecue—"someone had to . . . chop and burn the wood for cooking, dig the pit, butcher, process, cook and season the animals, serve the food, entertain the guests and clean up afterward"—and after Emancipation, white diners sought out Black pitmasters and cooks, although their talent was often subsumed into white-fronted businesses.

For much of the twentieth century, barbecue remained a "folk art," as Miller describes it, enshrined at tumbledown roadside stands, which languished in the 1960s as customers turned to fastfood chains. But in the 1980s, this plainspoken art gained new admirers, perhaps because of the rise in national prosperity and a society-wide embrace of wealth as a virtue—eating meat has always been a way to telegraph riches, since the breeding of livestock is an expensive proposition, consuming enormous resources of land and water—or because the rapid pace of globalization inspired a longing for the steadying anchor of regional traditions: something to call our own.

Then, in the early 2000s, Americans took barbecue further, into the realm of fetish, an obsession for tinkerers equipped with the latest technology in home grills, who descend on barbecue competitions armed with pistol-grip injectors, headlamps, and bungee cords, and for pilgrims who wait in line in the beating sun, sometimes for as long as five hours, then post pictures online of their trophy meals. Is the luxury the stack of meat, or having that much time to spare in pursuit of lunch? It's notable that, despite the long history of Black barbecue, today's celebrity pitmasters, those singled out by the media for fame, are mostly white men.

And while in many places the no-fuss trappings haven't changed—crumply butcher paper, squeeze bottles of sweet-smoky sauce, pallid white bread or saltines still in the wrapper—an aura of fine dining now surrounds the pit. Brisket, long a budget cut, today commands $34 a pound at Franklin Barbecue in Austin, Texas, because the pitmaster buys USDA Prime Black Angus beef. This is in keeping with the notion, also of recent vintage, of "elevating" what are, by that verb, implicitly "lesser" foods, like the $28 mozzarella sticks that come bearing caviar at Carne Mare in Manhattan or the $120 cheesesteak accented with foie gras mousse and truffles (elsewhere it's more commonly sluiced with Cheez Whiz) at Barclay Prime in Philadelphia. The toppings are intentionally outrageous, part of the joke, although it's not clear if it's the original dish and the people who eat it that are being mocked, or the suckers who pony up the big bucks for a simulacrum.

For some people who are, if not rich, then comfortable (or at least secure enough not to fear a wolf at the door), it's become a badge of honor to eat as if they lived in want, or like their working-class counterparts of old: sticking to what's in season, tending a kitchen garden, foraging in the hills, making their own bread from scratch, laying away preserves for the winter. This is labor, but freely given, and a choice to accept restrictions on pleasure for the greater good, be that a closer attunement to nature, a shunning of the corporate world of supermarkets and processed goods, or a sense of connection to the ways of their ancestors.

In the 1979 study *Distinction: A Social Critique of the Judgment of Taste,* the French sociologist Pierre Bourdieu argues that, whereas the working class tend to crave meals of straightforward nourishment ("hence the emphasis on heavy, fatty, strong food"), the bourgeoisie approach eating more daintily, as a matter of style, as if they were above such petty concerns as physical survival: "It is a way of denying the meaning and primary function of consumption, which are essentially common, by making the meal a social

ceremony, an affirmation of ethical tone and aesthetic refinement." Thus the triumph of kale in the past decade, a hardy and
nutritious if not particularly lovable vegetable. The horticulturist
Matt Mattus notes in *Mastering the Art of Vegetable Gardening* (2018)
that as late as the nineteenth century, French gardening texts referred to the winter green as "more curious than useful." People
ate it because they had to—until it started showing up on high-end
menus that trumpeted local ingredients from small farms, and as-
ceticism became a kind of indulgence.

Eating, or rather being able to eat whatever you like, whether
sumptuous or spartan, can be a means of exerting control. Sometimes this manifests as culinary tourism, dabbling in the foods of
other cultures or classes, with the assurance of knowing you can always retreat to the safety of your own. I've never forgotten a restaurant that opened briefly in Brooklyn about a decade ago, dedicated
to the Baltimore working-class specialty of lake trout, the name a
euphemism for silvery little whiting, sheathed in cracker meal and
deep-fried. The dining room was dismal, with graffiti bubble letters on the walls and a vulgar word emblazoned on the bathroom
door, as if trying to conjure some imagined shattered inner city—
the urban decay of predominantly Black neighborhoods that were
long neglected as a legacy of segregation—as atmosphere for the
mostly white hipsters who wandered in.

Perhaps this was meant as homage. But I was conscious of the
food only as a souvenir from another life: someone else's struggle,
reduced to a commodity, with a backdrop of distress as window
dressing. A few years later, there was an outcry in New York City
when the chopped cheese—a sandwich immortalized in rap lyrics, of ground beef, onions, and melted cheese, whose invention
is credited to a bodega in East Harlem—was "discovered" by out-
siders, remade, and sold at a markup. Was this a crime? Foods
travel; recipes aren't static. And yet, a certain carelessness seems
to take hold when people borrow (or simply take) from those of
lesser means. "Poverty becomes wealth, despair becomes fun," the
American sociologist Karen Bettez Halnon writes in *Poor Chic: The
Rational Consumption of Poverty* (2002). To play at being poor is to
pretend real poverty doesn't exist.

People aren't static either, of course. Some of us have traced our
own trajectory from childhoods of limited resources, of clipped
coupons, parents pulling overtime, and the splendor of lunch

at McDonald's. And no matter how refined our palates become, however much we believe we've freed ourselves of that taint of cheapness, there are certain foods, certain shames, that will always be ours. For me, it's Spam, a canned meat of ground pork and ham, bound by potato starch and seasoned with salt and sugar—a terrine of sorts, albeit in highly processed form. (Terrines themselves were once exemplars of peasant ingenuity, a way to use up scraps.) Spam came to the Philippines and South Korea via American military bases, and is still beloved in those countries, submerged in stew with hot dogs and kimchi or crisped for breakfast alongside garlic rice and a lace-edged fried egg. It has come to high-end restaurants, too, although typically with a heavy helping of irony.

Don't fuss with it, I say. I grew up in Hawaii, where a slab of Spam is given a quick burnish of soy sauce and sugar in a pan, then tied to a mound of rice with nori to make musubi. We all eat it there, rich and poor alike, without pride. Caviar may have its mother-of-pearl spoons and rooms aflame with chandeliers; Spam musubi has 7-Eleven and a peel of plastic wrap. Salty-sweet, it makes you thirstier with each bite. I could eat kale all day, I could denounce globalization and the inequities of the capitalist food system with a pure heart—and still that blue tin from Hormel would remain.

TOM PHILPOTT

After a Century of Dispossession, Black Farmers Are Fighting to Get Back to the Land

FROM *Mother Jones*

IN THE DECADES before the Civil War, one of the South's largest slave enterprises held sway on the northern outskirts of Durham, North Carolina. At its peak, about nine hundred enslaved people were compelled to grow tobacco, corn, and other crops on the Stagville Plantation, thirty thousand acres of rolling Piedmont that had been taken from the Occaneechi Band of the Saponi Nation. Today, the area has a transitional feel: old farmhouses, open fields, and pine forests cede ground to subdivisions, as one of America's hottest real estate markets sprawls outward.

On a sunny winter afternoon, farmer and food justice activist Tahz Walker greets me on a forty-eight-acre patch of former Stagville property called the Earthseed Land Collective. Walker and a few friends pooled their resources and bought this parcel, he says, to experiment with collective living and inspire "people of color to reimagine their relationship to land." He leads me through the gate of the property's Tierra Negra Farm, a two-acre plot of vegetable rows, hoop houses, and a grassy patch teeming with busy hens. It's one of several enterprises housed within the land collective, which also features a commercial worm-compost operation, a capoeira studio, and homes for several members, including the 1930s farmhouse where Walker lives with his wife and co-farmer, Cristina Rivera-Chapman, and their two kids. Tierra

Negra markets its produce through a subscription veggie-box service that goes to twenty nearby families—including descendants of Stagville's enslaved population—and supplies Communities in Partnership, a local nonprofit that brings affordable fresh food to historically Black, fast-gentrifying East Durham.

As it's January, most of the rows are fallow. Walker points to a patch of bare ground that grew sweet potatoes the previous season. "It's a variety that was grown by a Black farmer in Virginia for, like, forty years," he says. "He stopped growing them, and I started growing them from slips," referring to the green shoots used to propagate sweet potatoes. "It's a cool variety—instead of running, it kind of bushes up, so it's really great for cultivation with the tractor." And "it still makes great pies and fries."

Like many Black Americans born in the second half of the twentieth century, Walker has ancestral ties to agriculture, but he grew up alienated from it. His father had spent summers working on his family's farm operation in rural Kentucky, where they sharecropped on land owned by white people. Walker's dad fled as soon as he could and ultimately set up an IT services business in Atlanta, raising Walker and his sister in the city's then semirural far northern suburbs. Stories about life in the Kentucky fields were scarce. To his father, farming represented "trauma [that] gets passed down," something to escape. When Walker began to devote his life to agriculture as a young adult in the late 1990s, "my dad would always say, 'Everybody's trying to get off the farm. Why are you trying to get *on* the farm?' "

Walker is part of a growing movement of young Black Americans striving to reclaim the legacy of agrarianism. Acquiring land isn't easy, as he knows all too well: a century of land loss has been compounded by escalating real estate prices. Yet the quest to reclaim farmland is gaining momentum as part of the broader reparations movement, which seeks redress for the unpaid debts owed to many Black Americans.

After a traumatic history marked by enslavement and then sharecropping, followed by a century of racist federal farm policy that largely stripped Black farmers of the ability to hold land, "I never in my wildest dreams thought that there would be young people wanting to become farmers," says Karen Washington, a pioneering community gardener in the Bronx who now co-owns a farm in the Hudson Valley. While the wounds of the Black agricultural experience can't be forgotten, Washington says, "a different narrative has started to surface: power behind owning land and controlling what you eat."

In January 1865, Major General William Tecumseh Sherman met with a group of Black ministers in Savannah, Georgia, to discuss the path forward for 3.9 million recently freed Black people. "The way we can best take care of ourselves is to have land and turn it and till it by our own labor," a Baptist minister and former slave named Garrison Frazier told Sherman. The general proposed to expropriate 400,000 acres owned by white plantation owners and grant it to freed slaves in allotments not to exceed forty acres. The region would be politically autonomous, with the "sole and exclusive management of affairs . . . left to the freed people themselves." Sherman's Special Field Orders, No. 15, popularly known as "forty acres and a mule," were soon approved by President Abraham Lincoln, but died with him; his successor, the Southern white supremacist Andrew Johnson, hastily canceled the orders.

As the land remained in the hands of white plantation owners, millions of Black people had little choice but to work as sharecroppers—tenants who rented a patch of farmland in exchange for an often-meager share of the harvest. This arrangement quickly morphed into a form of debt peonage. Sharecroppers had to rely on high-interest loans from their landlords and merchants to run their operations, leaving scant profit. The ruling white gentry, in turn, used credit as a tool to ramp up production, which "forced sharecroppers to grow ever more cotton, the only crop that could always be made into money," Harvard historian Sven Beckert writes in his book *Empire of Cotton: A Global History*. As cotton output rose, prices fell, putting sharecroppers on a debt treadmill, enabling the Southern ruling class to continue extracting monumental wealth from the labor of Black people long after abolition.

And yet, despite violent backlash from Southern planters, Black growers managed to gain a toehold. The key was collective action, University of Wisconsin sociologist Monica White explains in her book *Freedom Farmers: Agricultural Resistance and the Black Freedom Movement, 1880–2010*. Launched in 1886 to organize landless Black farmers and to pool money to buy land and tools, the Colored Farmers' National Alliance and Cooperative Union boasted

1.2 million members at its peak. At the Tuskegee Institute, the Alabama land-grant college founded by Booker T. Washington and other formerly enslaved people, agricultural scientist George Washington Carver pushed crop diversification, composting, and other proto-organic methods to help sharecroppers "make enough profit to purchase their land, feed their families, and achieve economic autonomy," White writes. Carver toured Alabama in an "agricultural wagon," delivering lectures and demonstrations of his techniques.

These efforts helped Black farmers acquire land against long odds at a time when ownership was the surest path to a measure of economic security within a highly stratified, racist society. By 1910, although sharecropping remained dominant, the US census reported, about 219,000 Black farmers owned land. Together, the Land Loss and Reparations Project found, they held an estimated twenty million acres. According to Thomas Mitchell, codirector of Texas A&M's Real Estate and Community Development Law program and an expert on Black land tenure, as much as 80 percent of the Black middle or upper-middle class at that time were farm owners.

Those Black landowners would soon come under severe attack. As historian Pete Daniel shows in his 2013 book *Dispossession: Discrimination Against African American Farmers in the Age of Civil Rights,* the loss of Black farmland accelerated after the Great Depression, driven by two factors. One was the industrial revolution that had transformed farming: farmers had to scramble to pay for expensive new fertilizers and machines, while the resulting boom in crop yields triggered a steady fall in prices. The total number of farms plunged from 6.8 million in 1935 to fewer than 3 million in 1974. The Department of Agriculture, Daniel shows, promoted the modernization push, plying rural areas with loans and aid to encourage the adoption of new technologies. While millions of farms failed even with a gusher of post–World War II USDA support, few could survive without it.

But all that government support flowed through the far-flung county offices of various Department of Agriculture agencies, which were often dominated by local white landholders. As the revolt against Jim Crow gained force, "USDA programs were sharpened into weapons to punish civil rights activity," Daniel notes. Black farmers found themselves increasingly cut off from the aid they needed to survive, resulting in defaults, bankruptcies, and forced sales on a grand scale. To make matters worse, "planters evicted tenants and sharecroppers who attempted to register to vote and replaced them with machines and chemicals," Daniel writes. Poverty and hunger within rural communities spiked, driving the Great Migration of Black people fleeing the agrarian South for factory jobs in the urban North and West, which in turn reinforced white political power back home.

Some Black farmers who stayed responded once again by forming cooperatives. Fannie Lou Hamer, born in 1917, grew up picking cotton on her family's sharecropping operation in Mississippi. After being evicted from the plantation for her voting rights activism in 1962, Hamer quickly seized on land tenure as key to Black liberation. In 1969, she launched the Freedom Farm Cooperative in Sunflower County, Mississippi, one of the poorest, most agriculture-intensive regions in the country, using what we would now call crowdfunding, cobbling together fees from speaking tours with donations from a nationwide campaign led by Harry Belafonte. At its peak in 1972, the Freedom Farm Cooperative housed seventy families who grew commodity crops like cotton and wheat as well as fresh vegetables that fed another sixteen hundred families in the surrounding community.

Then a series of floods and droughts struck, and Hamer became seriously ill. In 1976, the Freedom Farm Cooperative had to sell its land to pay back taxes. "The dream of a self-sufficient agrarian community was over," recounts White. Yet today Hamer's model is inspiring the next generation of Black agrarians to create "an oasis of self-reliance and self-determination in a landscape of oppression maintained in part by deprivation," White adds.

White farmers, too, felt the brunt of the postwar rise of industrial agriculture, which drove millions of them out of business. But when they sold out, their land was largely bought by other white people, meaning overall white land ownership held steady. Lost Black farmland, however, also largely accrued to white people. The result is that the number of Black farmers has dropped by 98 percent from its high in 1920, and the total amount of Black-owned farmland has withered to 10 percent of its peak.

This change amounted to an enormous transfer of wealth from Black to white people. When a family is forced to sell off its land at fire-sale prices, the loss cascades through generations. Land was wealth—an asset that could be used to borrow money. "You could use the land as collateral to get a loan to send your kids to college or university and improve their economic outcomes," Mitchell says. Along with Harvard scholar Nathan Rosenberg and journalist Bryce Stucki, Mitchell is part of a research team called the Land Loss and Reparations Project, which is analyzing the economic impact of the great dispossession. According to its preliminary analysis, the total economic hit to Black wealth from land loss could be in excess of $300 billion—a significant contributor to the persistent racial wealth gap that hangs over US society. Today the median white family is nearly ten times wealthier than its Black counterpart.

The consequences continue to reverberate. George Floyd, whose murder last year by now-convicted Minneapolis police officer Derek Chauvin sparked global protests, grew up in a public housing project in a "predominantly Black Houston neighborhood where white flight, underinvestment and mass incarceration fostered a crucible of inequality," reported the *Washington Post*'s Toluse Olorunnipa and Griff Witte. One reason Floyd's family lacked resources: his great-great-grandfather, Hillery Thomas Stewart Sr., had five hundred acres of North Carolina farmland stolen from him in the late nineteenth century, the *Post* reports. Instead of inheriting property that would have ballooned in value over the twentieth century, his children worked as sharecroppers.

Agriculture, the backbone of the Black middle class just a century ago, has largely vanished as a force in Black American life. According to the latest US Census of Agriculture, only 1.7 percent of farms were run by Black people in 2017. Meanwhile, the value of farm real estate has exploded: during the twentieth century, its price rose dramatically and has continued its ascent since, representing both a devastating loss of Black wealth and a major obstacle for would-be farmers trying to break into agriculture.

Despite these odds, there are signs of a resurgence of interest in farming among young Black people. In Virginia's Northern Neck region near Chesapeake Bay, Chris Newman, the son of a Black mother and a Native American father, left a tech career in 2013 to launch Sylvanaqua Farms, where he raises chickens, cattle, and hogs on pasture along with vegetables. From his Instagram and Medium accounts, Newman has emerged as one of the most influential voices in the movement, laying out a vision of agriculture quite different from the Jeffersonian family farmer model that, he argues, thrived on stolen land and labor and now functions as a bulwark for maintaining white dominance.

Then there's Leah Penniman, who uses her farm in upstate New York as a training ground for farmers of color, and whose book *Farming While Black: Soul Fire Farm's Practical Guide to Liberation on the Land* is, she writes, a "reverently compiled manual for African-heritage people to reclaim our rightful place of dignified agency in the food system." From eighty acres of land surrounded by forest, Soul Fire markets its fruit, vegetables, meat, and eggs through a sliding-scale subscription vegetable-box service, using the principle of *ujamaa,* a form of cooperative economics developed in Tanzania. The group's impact goes well beyond its efforts to deliver fresh food to low-income neighborhoods in Albany, near where Penniman once worked as a public school teacher. Its weeklong immersion courses have provided more than a hundred aspiring growers of Black, Indigenous, and Latino heritage on-the-ground training to "heal from inherited trauma rooted in oppression on land, and take steps toward [their] personal food sovereignty," as the group's website states.

As children in the 1980s, Penniman and her siblings split time between rural Massachusetts, where they lived most of the year with their father in a trailer, and Boston, where they spent summers with their mother. Out in the country, she and her sister would "go out into the woods and propitiate the trees and the soil and the rocks and bring offerings," she recalls. "When we were very little, maybe were six, seven years old, we thought we invented this new religion called Mother Nature."

Ironically, it was in the city where she experienced an agrarian awakening. In 1996, at the age of sixteen, she got a summer job at the Food Project, a Boston-based program that taught teenagers to grow food for soup kitchens at a community garden and a forty-acre farm in the suburbs. "I just fell in love with that elegant simplicity of seed-to-harvest," she says. "It was just undeniably good."

The experience led her to seriously consider a career in farming: "I went to all the conferences, I read all the books." But in college, she almost gave up on agriculture: "I was disillusioned by the fact that everybody was white at these conferences."

At the 2010 Northeast Organic Farming Association conference in Amherst, Massachusetts, Penniman had a fateful encounter with Karen Washington, the community-garden activist. "She
said to me, 'Don't give up; one day we will have our books, we'll
have our conferences, we'll have our community, because this is
our heritage.' "

Not long after, Washington launched the inaugural Black Farmers & Urban Gardeners (BUGS) conference in Brooklyn. The annual conference has emerged as a space where Black agrarians
of many kinds—young, old, city, country, Southern, Northern—
meet, compare notes, and collaborate on a future that centers
food and land justice. Penniman says the urban-rural connections
highlighted by BUGS are a driving force of the new Black agrarian movement. "Almost everybody who comes to our trainings at
Soul Fire and is interested in commercial farming or larger-scale
farming started out in these [urban] community gardens, like the
Garden of Happiness in the Bronx that Mama Karen started," she
says. "The folks who've held on to that little bit of earth, that little
corner of soil, are the folks who are going to be feeding us in the
future."

And collaboration remains key. Working with a network of
new and aspiring farmers, Penniman helped launch the Northeast Farmers of Color Land Trust in 2019. The trust came about
through the realization among young farmers of color that land in
the region is "really hard to access; it's expensive; it gets scooped
up by wealthy investors," says Stephanie Morningstar, the group's
director and a member of the Mohawk Nation. The group hopes
to acquire at least two thousand acres of farmland over the next
five years, and to make it available to Black, Indigenous, and
Latino farmers through long-term leases.

The May 2020 murder of George Floyd and the subsequent
wave of Black Lives Matter protests "just broke open a dam," leading to "tons" of offers to donate parcels of land to the trust, she
says. At the same time, the trust is taking it slow, acknowledging
that the region is essentially the "unceded territory" of "dozens
of sovereign nations" with whom it must build relations before it
can accept and manage the land in good conscience. Currently,
Morningstar says, "we're a land trust without land, because we're
building trust."

*

For most young Black farmers, land is out of reach. To launch their operation, Walker and Rivera-Chapman did what a lot of aspiring farmers do: they rented. Their vision was to grow top-quality food for underserved communities within the Raleigh–Durham–Chapel Hill "Triangle," a region marked by rapid economic growth and massive racial and economic inequality. Open land within easy range of the Triangle is pricey. So, for several years, Tierra Negra was an itinerant operation, hopping from rented patch to rented patch held by owners always on the lookout for more lucrative tenants.

But that approach was in direct opposition to the organic agriculture Walker and Rivera-Chapman are devoted to. Growing food that doesn't rely on chemical pesticides and fertilizers requires years of patient investment in the soil. "The last straw" came in 2017, when the couple rented an acre-and-a-half plot in downtown Durham. The price was reasonable—around $500 per month— but the landlord, a New York investor, could void the lease at any time with a thirty-day notice. "We saw the writing on the wall with the land there. We're just like, it's a vacant lot in the middle of the city—it's probably not gonna be there long," Walker says. "There's a high-rise there now."

For years, Walker and Rivera-Chapman had been plotting to pool their resources with friends, including Courtney Woods, an assistant professor of environmental engineering at the University of North Carolina, Chapel Hill, and Justin Robinson, a musician and scholar of Southern foodways who was a fiddler for the Grammy-winning Black old-time group the Carolina Chocolate Drops. (In his own off-farm job, Walker works at RAFI-USA, a North Carolina-based rural-justice advocacy group, managing the Farmers of Color Network.) Together they formed the Earthseed Land Collective (the name pays homage to a series of books by the Afrofuturist novelist Octavia Butler) and bought the twelve-acre property that houses Tierra Negra. More recently, with a community bank loan and support from a local land trust, they bought an additional thirty-eight acres of adjoining land. Such prime real estate, Walker says, would not have been affordable "if we weren't able to work through a collective model."

People pooling resources and buying land for multiple uses "presents one of the most viable options" for young farmers to access land right now, says Noah McDonald, a former Soul Fire apprentice who now works as a researcher at the Southeastern African American Farmers Organic Network. Sharing resources was "functionally how our ancestors were able to acquire so much land in the Southeast in the first place," he says. Yet efforts like Earthseed take time, and high prices mean that it's hard for anyone besides midcareer professionals like Walker's crew to break in.

A Senate bill introduced last year could shake things up dramatically. Introduced in November, the Justice for Black Farmers Act would reverse the "destructive forces that were unleashed upon Black farmers over the past century," says Senator Cory Booker (D-NJ), who sponsored the bill along with Senators Elizabeth Warren (D-MA) and Kirsten Gillibrand (D-NY). The legislation would devote $8 billion annually to buying farmland and granting it to Black farmers. The goal: twenty thousand grants per year through 2030, with maximum allotments of 160 acres. The bill would also fund agriculture-focused historically Black colleges and universities, provide farmer training, and support the development of farmer cooperatives.

The bill grew out of a letter that Black farmers and advocates had sent to Warren during her presidential campaign in 2019, urging her to directly address racism at the USDA and the loss of Black farmland. One of the signatories was Lawrence Lucas, president emeritus of the USDA Coalition of Minority Employees, who calls the bill "a quantum leap for justice" that confronts the "racism embedded in the USDA since its founding and that has been allowed to control the destiny of Black farmers' lives." Penniman, who also played a role in shaping the bill, says, "I never dared to imagine that such an elegant, fair, and courageous piece of legislation as the Justice for Black Farmers Act could be introduced."

The bill will likely draw opposition from budget hawks and senators opposed to any form of reparations, but it has also been criticized by some food-justice activists. In a widely shared Medium post, Chris Newman, who's enrolled in the Choptico Band of Piscataway Indians, denounced it as a "bill so loaded with oversights, anti-solidarity, and implied acceptance of settler-colonial agricultural ethics that it can't even be viewed as incremental progress or a step in the right direction." Not only is the bill modeled on nineteenth-century Homestead Acts that handed Native territory to white settlers in allotments of 160 acres, he notes, it also doesn't address or even mention the epic theft of land.

To be clear, any land that changes hands under the act would be bought by the federal government at market price from a willing seller. But Newman's critique still resonated with several Black farmer advocates I spoke with. In Black agrarianism, McDonald says, "we grapple with that tension because we come from an Indigenous spiritual home in the deep past." Black Americans are also "displaced Indigenous people" who should act in solidarity with Native Americans. Yet the bill's "greatest contribution," he adds, "is that it's ignited this conversation around Native land sovereignty, homesteading land reform, and land redistribution."

Jessica A. Shoemaker, a professor at the University of Nebraska College of Law and a scholar of Native American land issues, offers a similar view. The bill "is one step in a longer and desperately overdue reconciliation process in this country, and at least it is a start where there has been nothing for far too long," she says. "Even having this conversation at the federal level seemed impossible until a few months ago."

As the bill sat in limbo, another piece of legislation made its way into the $1.9 trillion COVID relief bill after a push from senators including Booker and Raphael Warnock (D-GA): $4 billion in payments to help farmers of color "pay off outstanding USDA farm loan debts and related taxes" and another $1 billion to fund training and support for them, as well as to confront racism within the USDA.

Standing under the winter sun, Tahz Walker contemplates the future of Tierra Negra Farm. For the past four years, he and Rivera-Chapman have focused on building infrastructure like covered growing spaces that extend the season into the cold months, and a greenhouse that will free them from relying on a commercial nursery and provide "more control over varieties that we grow."

That has them contemplating growing special crops just to harvest and sell the seeds, opening another income stream while providing the region's farmers and gardeners with traditional varieties like cabbage collards, a light green North Carolina heirloom that Walker grew for the first time last year. "Doing the math, it looks like we could grow out cool varieties, have food and eat it, and still sell it," he says. He's still figuring out the details. Like the Black agrarian movement, Tierra Negra remains a work in progress, seeding a brighter future in the fertile soil of a complicated past.

CYNTHIA R. GREENLEE

Innovation and the Incinerated Tongue: Notes on Hot Chicken, Race, and Culinary Crossover

FROM *The Counter*

HISTORIAN RACHEL MARTIN grew up in Nashville, Tennessee, without ever learning about—or eating—her city's iconic dish, hot chicken.

It's a deceptively minor point in her book, *Hot, Hot Chicken: A Nashville Story,* which explores Music City history through this dish and the undeniably racist "urban renewal" policies that gutted her hometown's Black neighborhoods. Still, it's a point to which I kept returning. I wondered: *How could she not have known this delicacy created within miles of her home, or its roots in a legendary lovers' spat?* Suffice it to say the answer lies in persistent racial, spatial, and culinary segregation, which kept hot chicken in Black Nashville for years—and the author and her family in white Nashville until her adulthood.

As the hot-chicken origin story goes, infidelity is the mother of invention. Sometime, probably around the 1930s, pretty-man Thornton Prince III's wandering eye led indirectly to this gastronomic breakthrough. Thornton incensed his lover after staying out all night. The woman-at-home suspected he'd been gallivanting with another woman and prepared a hearty breakfast of blistering-peppery fried chicken, designed to punish his palate and make a point. Thornton was apparently oblivious to her heartache and heartburn, but loved the chicken. He saw a marquee menu item for his "chicken shack." And so that act of he-won't-do-right cooking planted the seeds for his family's modern business, now known as Prince's Hot Chicken.

What began as local love-hate on a plate has become a national phenomenon. The family-owned restaurant won a coveted James Beard Foundation America's Classic award in 2013. This hyperlocal specialty has spawned countless imitators, from fast-food chains—KFC came to Nashville for "inspiration"—to food trucks and restaurants nationwide. A particularly bourgeois version is currently enticing New Yorkers to wait up to eight weeks for a $35 three-piece (laced with peppercorns and accompanied by almond-pesto sweet potatoes). You can even buy hot-chicken pizza, heavy on the pickles and drizzled with sriracha.

How did Prince's hot chicken become a trendsetter? And, more generally, how do Black culinary novelties leap into white consciousness? Of course, there's no one-size-fits-all answer; region, mode of creation, historical period, market trends, and access to capital all factor in. And goals do, too. Not every Black food innovator starts in the same place or aims to serve the same population (and may not indeed aim to specifically serve Black audiences). And access to white markets doesn't ensure commercial success.

Martin's account is equal parts mystery, policy explainer, and entertaining business and food history. But hot chicken, as told through Martin's book, pushed me to think about how Black food migrates into white communities, a larger cultural process that the book leaves too implicit until its later chapters. That process includes multiple ways a food is racialized, consumed, commercialized, and rendered fashionable and ultimately co-optable. Black food innovations spread first inside African American communities, before gradually penetrating layers of racial segregation—past or present—to register with successive generations of white diners.

Their changing palates can be a boon or burden for the Black culinary creative. After all, white America has an insatiable appetite for Black "cool," the seemingly effortless capacity of Black people to create distinctive aesthetics and the ineffable, be it in fashion, music, hairstyles, or food. Yes, white appreciation can translate into respectful consumption, the kind that self-consciously references Black originators. But that admiration and emulation can quickly devolve into something much more extractive.

I ask myself, and this is no trivial question: is it possible to have

Black culinary crossover without appropriation, in a country built on stolen Black labor? Because, in America, Black innovations are too often translated into crass or soulless reproductions (think Kardashiana), monetized by white culture for white culture. It's an established pattern, one that hot chicken exemplifies: there's a slide toward deracialization and the erasure of the dish's Black roots, until the average eater has little idea that their hot-chicken tenders came from anywhere other than the joint that sells them.

Take, for example, Dave's Hot Chicken, which has sold three hundred franchises since it opened in East Hollywood, Los Angeles, in 2017. As Dave's—cofounded by a chef trained in Thomas Keller's "Bouchon organization," according to the company's website—describes its origin story, "four childhood friends came up with a simple concept—take Nashville Hot Chicken and make it better than anyone else in America."

What a poor yet revealing choice of words. "Take" hot chicken and improve its soul-food insufficiency with "chefly" know-how. The website mentions its "proprietary brine," but not the Prince family, which now owns two locations.

The Princes have something else as well: a legion of non-Black business descendants who rarely acknowledge their pioneering and ongoing work. Some shout-out the Princes in homages that cost newbie hot-chicken entrepreneurs nothing and imply a sort of creative kinship that's utterly lacking in this wholesale hijacking of hot chicken.

Chicken; a spicy, savory rub (wet or dry); pickles; and that tabula rasa of carbohydrates, white bread: one can argue that's too general to constitute intellectual property. What makes a concept—not a recipe with defined quantities of ingredients and delineated cooking methods—ownable?

I'm not sure—and I'm not sure I'll ever be sure. But culinary authorship—and who's responsible for a dish's popularization—counts.

Long before hot chicken set anyone's lips afire, the domesticated chicken was linked to Black Americans. As scholar Psyche Williams-Forson wrote in *Building Houses Out of Chicken Legs: Black Women, Food, and Power,* free and enslaved people were often the "primary chicken vendors" of their antebellum communities, despite laws that prohibited trading by and with slaves. Hocking poultry gave enslaved women a measure of economic autonomy, if not freedom. That preponderance of Black chicken sellers before the Civil War likely influenced much nastier associations, the enduring stereotypes that Black people would do anything—steal, tap dance, or abandon all common sense—for chicken, preferably fried.

So, decades before Thornton got that wee-hours tongue burn, hot chicken's saga had already begun. Hot chicken had a historical head start in its designation as Black food, simply because it was chicken. The spicy, peppery delight made by the original angry woman became triply Black: created in a Black home in a segregated neighborhood; prepared in a growing number of Black restaurants in Nashville; and consumed in Black homes for decades.

Hot chicken started as many innovations do: in a burst of domestic creation—and, as often happens in Black history, by a person who can't be fully credited. On one hand, the Princes' hot chicken can be traced with remarkable precision (unlike other soul food dishes with fuzzier and disputed origins, such as chicken and waffles). On the other hand, the name of the angry woman behind that first incinerating batch has been lost to time. In *Hot, Hot Chicken*, Martin gamely tries to identify her, using all the archival materials and historian's tricks at her disposal. But because Thornton Prince III was a serial groom with an itinerant phallus and outside children, he left a cortege of pissed-off contenders for the crown. Was it first wife Gertrude, or Mattie, with whom he had a child during his marriage to Gertrude?

Though this woman's namelessness seems to be a function of time and a shattered relationship (if we believe the narrative), that's not the only explanation for her absence.

Chasing historical leads and dead ends, Martin helps readers see invisible hands at work: the urban planning that made today's Nashville into a booming, still segregated metropolis, and the Black women and men who established an enduring food tradition. The American food economy has long hidden or pooh-poohed the contributions of important laborers, even as it's relied on them for profit: the enslaved cook, the Black domestic in freedom, the unnamed Black chef behind Bisquick mix, the immigrant, the mother who makes meals, the woman whose home-based work isn't separate from wage-earning activities. It's largely erased countless figures like John Young, the man whose mumbo or mambo chicken sauce paved the way for another hot, saucy chicken dish: buffalo wings.

At some point, Nashville's hot and saucy chicken ceased to be a family meal or a secret. Maybe Thornton Prince, apparently once a hog farmer, decided to raise more chickens. Maybe he started selling takeout hot chicken from his back porch. But someone decided this chicken was salable, and many other someones agreed it was worth buying. Hot chicken became *intraculturally* popular in Black Nashville. That community sustained Prince's and also birthed local Black competitors who recognized a hot thing and business model when they ate it or made it (because a few former Prince's employees have started businesses with their own versions of hot chicken).

The originators of hot chicken and their customers were what communications scholar Everett Rogers called "innovators" and "early adopters" in his 1962 book *Diffusion of Innovations*. He categorized people by how fast they embrace new ideas or products. In his much revised and debated theory, 2.5 percent of people are "innovators," the risk takers. They're followed by "early adopters," who catch on quickly, thrive on novelty, and ply their influence. The masses—estimated to be nearly 70 percent of a given network—are the "early and late majorities" who wait to embrace newfangled thingamajigs. The "laggards" bring up the rear, resistant or slow to change. A person can innovate in one sphere and lag in another part of their life, and many factors influence an individual's engagement with an unfamiliar concept: whether the idea or product seems advantageous, is easy to learn, can be tried before adopting it, and whether it fits into an existing belief system.

All that sounds neutral and perfectly reasonable—and absolutely raceless. In Rogers's theory-speak, Thornton Prince III and his great-niece, André Prince Jeffries (who runs the business today), would be the innovators. Those who've recently discovered the Princes' fabled hot chicken—much of white and middle America—are laggards. But Rogers's original research, which investigated why farmers hesitate to use new technology that could boost their yields and bottom lines, didn't explore the way racial dynamics can complicate habits of adoption. "Existing belief systems" also include racism, Jim Crow, and lasting disparities in access to material and social capital—and those factors help to ex-

plain both hot chicken's deep community roots and its seemingly
sudden, mass-market virality.

Given this country's rapacious harnessing of Black cultural production, Rogers's theory needs a significant tweak. When it comes
to hot chicken and other Black innovations, some white laggards
eventually see opportunity. And not only do they accelerate adoption of something that is foreign to them, they claim it as their own
in an act of material and narrative gentrification. The way they tell
it, they were the innovators all along.

Let's pause for a moment here: there can be a beautiful inaccessibility to Black culture, things that white and non-Black people do
not know or cannot fully grasp even if they're momentarily invited
to the cookout. That inaccessibility—and segregation past and
present—helps the laggard convince himself he's an innovator.

Nashville hot chicken was created in an environment where racial cultural divisions were made all the more stark by physical and
structural barriers such as Black people's unequal access to desirable real estate or bank loans. Martin exhaustively recounts how its
genesis dovetails with the rise of a Jim Crow innovation in her city:
urban renewal policies that declared Black areas to be unlivable
"D" zones in need of "redevelopment." Among many changes, the
"beautification" of Nashville cleared the mostly Black area near
the Capitol and made way for not one but three highways that bi-
sected Black neighborhoods. Streets were dead-ended, businesses
closed, children and families cut off from their playgrounds and
walking routes.

Nashville's spatial and cultural segregation contained hot
chicken to Black neighborhoods where upper-crust whites rarely
tread. Segregation had its unintended benefits, giving Black communities the freedom to create and Black businesses a stream of
culturally consonant consumers barred from boundless shopping
in white retail spaces. It could also inhibit growth, though, limiting
access to the white market or forcing Black businesses to relocate
according to the whims of white urban planners.

But communities aren't hermetically sealed, even and especially
in the segregated South. Black and white Southerners have always
lived together or near one another, regardless of segregationists'
Herculean efforts to craft a divided world. Their own laws proved
how futile their efforts were, and that Jim Crow was powerful but
not omnipotent. The era's obsessively detailed lawmaking reveals

just how often racial boundaries were breached; in 1930, Birmingham, Alabama, banned whites and Blacks from playing cards, dice, or checkers with each other—a frantic attempt at legislating against interracial interaction that was already occurring.

It was only a matter of time before a greater share of white Nashville got wind of the chicken. Everett Rogers's diffusion theory would have seen the late-night eaters, those country music stars hungry after a gig, as the early majority. They preceded "proper" white tastemakers, another stage in my theory of Black food diffusion. Late to the game, these conventional influencers are few enough and sometimes powerful enough that no restaurant is going to serve them side-eye.

In the case of hot chicken, former Nashville mayor Bill Purcell started patronizing Prince's and became an evangelist. According to Martin, he often conducted political lunches over its plates, telling André Prince Jeffries (who invented Prince's spice scale of mild to will-almost-take-you-out) to serve his lunch dates the most scorching—no matter what spice level they ordered. That element of palate surprise meant he'd always have a laugh and the upper hand. A journalist who endured this nonconsensual trial by chicken said, "After three bites I figured out he didn't ask reporters to lunch because he liked them. He was trying to kill us off, one by one." Like that woman who gave Prince's its famous recipe, Purcell believed in the sneak attack.

Prince's Hot Chicken carved out a territory of its own: generations of faithful Black customers and competitors; a new privileged class of eaters, admirers, and usurpers; national awards; hot chicken festivals; and pop-ups sprouting willy nilly. Chalk that down to hard work, creativity, the Southern jones for chicken, and, as André Prince Jeffries told Martin, "This chicken is not boring. You're gonna talk about this chicken." Not every edible product regularly provokes a response, much less sweat, nose drippings, and tears of joy or pain.

External factors—such as Americans' foray into spicier foods—also helped propel hot chicken to its Moment. Heat-heads have flocked to the Fiery Foods Festival since 1987. Salsa has long surpassed ketchup in our national favor. Even salsa seems, well, milquetoast compared to the potent and piquant condiments making frequent appearances in previously blah food-mag recipes. The pendulum of spice preference and fashion has swung to the point that a March *New York Times* article presumed that spice love is approaching cultural norm status, and deviance from it may prompt shaming and taunts; it advised readers who "can't take the heat" that a "taste for spicy foods can be learned" or at least tolerated if you want to fit in.

That flavor recalibration—as Americans get hip to foods that have always been here but are often associated with our immigrant neighbors—is close cousin to an important "flava" transformation vis-à-vis Blackness. To eat hot chicken isn't merely an act of consumption. It can refute the reputation for white blandness, prove that the white eater is in the know, and provide some superficial entrée into Black culture.

The acquisition of Black cool, perhaps the most critical stage for this humble yardbird's spread, fuels American popular culture. From there, it can be a rush toward enhanced profitability or expansion. Maybe that arrives in the offer to franchise or to package that spice blend. It almost inevitably comes with another cycle of friendly and hostile competitors.

That success—where everybody knows your name and everybody wants your secret sauce—comes with increasingly loud whispers of appropriation. But in a country based on Black stolen labor, it's on message to demur that a particular preparation of chicken, pepper, salt, pickles, and white bread is a pleasing combination of ingredients. And that it belongs to no one.

In fact, this insistence may be the final stage of appropriation—and it's the American way. African American food is always up for grabs. I think of it as the worst form of takeout, really. And few people want a side of history with their meal.

ERIC KIM

A Year of Cooking
with My Mother

FROM *The New York Times*

LET THE RECORD show that I make a terrible roommate. I can
still hear my mother's voice as she encountered the sink full of
dishes, the counter spilling over with spices and syrups: "I can't
live like this!"

About nine months ago, I moved back home to Atlanta to write
a cookbook with my mother, Jean. A couch-surfing freeloader, I
was only supposed to be there for a couple of months to work on
the kimchi chapter, a selection of heirloom recipes I would never
have been able to develop over the phone from New York, where
I live now. But as each month passed, I found more and more
excuses to stay.

By cooking with Jean in such a structured, quotidian way, I was
able to stop time, a compelling state for an anxious mind like
mine. I could finally slow down and ask her questions about the
foods we ate when I was growing up. What I didn't know was that I
was entering a master class in Korean home cooking.

All my life, I thought I knew how my mother cooked, because
she had done it for my brother and me every day, breakfast, lunch,
and dinner. And I had watched. But there were so many details I
missed, like how, when making her signature kimchi jjigae, she
blanches the pork ribs first with fresh ginger to remove any gam-
iness. Or how she always blooms gochugaru in a little fat before
starting red pepper–based stews. Or how she adds a small handful
of pine nuts to her baechu kimchi, because that's what her mother

did. (I wish I could interview my grandmother and ask her why she did that.)

In 2004, in this very newspaper, the columnist and cookbook author Nigella Lawson wrote, "Quite often you cook something the way your mother did before you." Describing an allegory that has since been dubbed the Pot Roast Principle—in which a cook cuts the ends off a roast because her mother does it, who does it because *her* mother does it (the punch line being that the grandmother only does it because, depending on the telling, her pot or her oven is too small)—Ms. Lawson discussed the way children of cooks straddle wanting to honor tradition and, as sentient beings, wanting to carefully tinker.

"So we credit recipes with much more authority than they necessarily deserve," she wrote. "It might be better to regard them really as more of an account of a way of cooking a dish rather than a do-this-or-die barrage of instructions."

At first, I treated some of Jean's culinary quirks as accounts rather than barrages. I gave her a hard time about cooking with maesil cheong, a Korean green plum syrup (often labeled an extract), to lend sweetness to her savory dishes. I told her that if more readily available sweeteners can be used, we should use them. But maesil cheong is a main ingredient in her kimchi recipe and not infrequently finds its way into her jjigaes as well. When we tried certain recipes with, say, granulated sugar in place of the idiosyncratically tart, fruity syrup, she'd take a bite and say, "It's not the same." And she was right. It wasn't the same.

As I watched my mother cook and move and breathe in her own kitchen, I realized that maesil cheong is an essential ingredient to her in the same way maple syrup and dark brown sugar are to me. So I started to bend.

But even then, I had questions. I wanted to tinker.

Growing up in Georgia, after long days at the swimming pool, my brother and I often came home to Jean's kimchi jjigae, a bubbling, cauldron-hot stew of extra-fermented kimchi and other bits and bobs from the refrigerator. We usually had it with Spam, pork belly, or tofu, but my favorite was when she stewed ribs in that gochugaru-flecked lagoon. But I wouldn't, for instance, inherently think to blanch those ribs. Wouldn't you lose some of the pork flavor, not to mention the glorious fat, that would be better pooled in the stew instead of in the sink?

Sure, she explained. But the resultant broth will taste much less clean, and the kimchi will be overcooked by the time you get the pork tender enough. "Anyway," she told me, "the point of kimchi jjigae is the kimchi."

Unsatisfied, I pressed her again. "So why *do* you add pine nuts to your kimchi?" She thought hard and finally came up with her own response, one that wasn't, "Because that's how my mother did it."

"The pine nuts are surprises for future you," she said. "When you bite into one, it releases a Sprite-like freshness." According to Jean, it's the little things that find you later.

During my time in Atlanta, I was in charge of dinner. One night after work, I only had a few minutes to get food on the table, so I opened the fridge: sad vegetables, all languishing in the crisper drawer. Bibimbap, or mixed rice, came to mind. So I took a sheet pan and arranged the sad vegetables on it to roast in a hot oven. The sad vegetables were no longer sad. I realized I could also re-heat leftover white rice and bake a handful of eggs on a second sheet pan, the way my editor Genevieve Ko does.

As dinner took care of itself in the oven, I poured myself a cold beer and waited patiently with empty bowls to be filled with the rice, eggs, and roasted vegetables, each portion dabbed with gochujang for savory heat and dribbled with toasted sesame oil for nuttiness.

When Jean took a bite of my sheet-pan bibimbap, she said, "I'm never doing it the other way again."

On the last day, the morning before I drove back to New York, I noticed that my mother had left on my bed a tray of gyeranbap, or egg rice, with kimchi and a mug of burdock-root tea. I would miss these little deliveries we made each other, two introverted room-mates leaving behind treats like anonymous neighbors. I usually left her late-night recipe tests with a note: TASTE. Or toasted slices of milk bread. Once, she left me a mojito at three in the afternoon.

When I brought the empty tray downstairs, I saw that she had finally cleared the counters of all my spices, equipment, and sheet pans. "Oh, this is what the kitchen looks like," I joked.

"You were here a long time," she said. "Now I can live in peace."

For weeks, I dreaded this moment, the leave-taking. But it came and went, as things do. I packed the car, hugged my mom good-bye, and drove off, promising to visit again in a few months.

Back in my New York apartment, I made a batch of her kimchi.

I sprinkled in some pine nuts, thinking of what she had said, how the little things are what find you later. When the jar of kimchi fermented, weeks later, I turned it into kimchi jjigae, first blanching the ribs like she did and blooming the gochugaru in butter. That first bite was clean, the disparate parts alloying like copper and tin, and I had totally forgotten about the pine nuts until I bit into one. It surprised me with its Sprite-like freshness.

I picked up the phone and called her.

Other People's Kitchens

FROM *The Cut*

FOR THE PAST year or so, I've cooked in other people's kitchens. Washing their dishes and the rest of it. Pays more than you'd expect but it's still not very fucking much.

The first time in someone else's home is the hardest. The scents are always different. I never know where to step. And of course the bathroom's hardly ever in the same place, but if this virus has shown us nothing else it's that people can get used to anything. The first few months, I didn't know to ask for head counts. Or masks. Or any of the other things I check in on now. Didn't even prod about test results, and of course we were months away from a vaccine—I just assumed that my customers weren't sick because they always made sure I wasn't either. And these were the money zip codes: River Oaks, West U, Montrose.

Then other cooks at the company I work for started popping positives. After the first few died, our boss started poking us about signing liability waivers. But even if our gig wasn't exactly public, it was just another risk: in the end, you were still behind four walls. You still worked with people. The biggest fucking hazards of all.

And of course I had to take the jobs I could get. Gas isn't cheap anymore. You can't live in Houston without it. Before this gig, I took shifts at the tech store that's hoarding all of our data, down by the Galleria, and I'd worked at this family doughnut shop in Alief a few years before that—but that family went bankrupt. And the Apple store started cutting my hours. My boyfriend told me not to worry about it, because he said jobs come and go, and his company had only made *gains* since the beginning of the pandemic, but then his gig promoted him, and said promotion took him out to the Bay which left me broken up with and horny *and* broke, with a new half of the rent to account for.

So a friend put me onto the cooking gig. At first, I was only sub-bing in for someone else. I'm not a pro or anything like that. But, a little absurdly, it wasn't long before they moved me onto their roster full time.

A tiny capitalist blessing.

I've been saving for an electric car or a few weeks in Hokkaido—if the borders ever reopen to idiot Americans—but cooking six nights a week means it'll still be a few years before that happens. Even with my rates, as overpriced as they are.

I ask my customers for everything up front, before they make their reservations. If they give me problems, I cancel quicker than anything. Sometimes the extra cash isn't even worth it.

Lately, I've been working the same set of houses. My regulars. Some folks ask for a week's worth of food, but most just want enough for the night—they're paying for the *experience*.

One family off of Kirby only eats kale salads with poached shrimp and broiled chicken. Another couple with this kid, living right down Shepherd, prefers Thai-ish menus with like half the spice. Some folks won't touch egg yolks for anything, and others have hang-ups about fish, and plenty of people are lactose intoler-ant but quick to tell you they aren't. If there's an accommodation that someone's looking for, I just add it to their tab. The check clears either way.

There was one family that asked for a temaki party. I brought the crab and the tuna and the nori and the rest of it, but they insisted I use their rice, brown and whole-grain, which still makes no fucking sense to me but it also meant I could pocket the bag that I'd bought. Another couple I cooked for wanted chicken and waffles, but after I'd set down their plates and said Bon appétit, the husband took off his mask right in front of me and said it didn't smell the way his mother's did.

I'd have to make it again. Or he'd refuse to pay past the deposit. His wife looked mortified, but she didn't say shit about it—and I get it. Who wants to find another partner in this mess, let alone some fucking man.

So I picked up his plate and said Aye-aye, and I made it again, tripling every spice into indiscernibility.

My rates are simple: you can pay for one meal for two people. Or I can cook for three. Or I can cook for a family, or a gathering, but I cut it off at six—too many bodies, and I can't tell who was around when I arrived. You get folks wandering in and out of the kitchen, around the house, dancing offbeat to the music and breathing up all of the air. It's more trouble than it's worth. There's a singles package too, where I cook for one person, and even though that's the most expensive by far it's also the most popular. For a minute, I added a little bit to the rate every week, but my bookings only ever increased. Loneliness is a pandemic of its own.

One time there was a lady whose place I showed up at, and before I could unpack my knives or anything else she told me that she'd already picked up dinner. There was a massive box of take-out noodles in black bean sauce on her coffee table. Good stuff, from out in Bellaire. She asked if I could just sit with her, and that was all she was looking for, because she hadn't sat and eaten with someone in months, and I was spooked a bit at first because that's how all of those murder podcasts start; but then this lady started eating, and I joined her, and eventually she turned on a movie and we watched it over beers.

This woman ended up tipping me the most I've ever gotten. It all went to the travel fund. And it was nice to think that things like that could still happen, even now.

Then the next house I went to was this straight couple who seemed nice enough, laughing and smiling and complimenting every little thing I did. But eventually I noticed that they weren't really eating. And that's when the guy told me that the food was nice, but what they really needed was a third. Then he started coughing, and I bailed. Wasted an entire week's worth of food on the counter. You really never know.

The last house I passed through was another singles package, for a guy about my age. I was already booked for the week, but he wanted a late-late reservation. Most people don't send their photos, but he did. And he was cute. And a little chubby, which was a plus. And maybe he looked a little sad in the picture, but I figured why not. We live in a sad fucking time.

When he opened the door, he was scruffier than in the photo, and I told him that and he laughed. His place was pretty sparse, all plants and wood tones and an overstuffed bookshelf. But I didn't spot a statement piece. His television sat on the floor. He stood beside me the whole time I prepped, watching. And then, once I'd started slicing the beef, he asked if he could help.

Usually my thinking is: go fuck yourself. It's a safety hazard. A client cuts their nose off and says you're the one who passed them the knife. They trip and bounce their heads across the counter because you distracted them. They stick their hand in the drain. A mystery allergy surfaces from the ether and you're the one who should've warned them.

But before I could say anything, this guy goes ahead and grabs a peeler from his counter and starts skinning potatoes. He made it through three by the time I looked up.

You're a chef, I said.

No, he said, smiling. I just live alone.

Doesn't mean you're not a cook.

Well. I'm not getting paid for it.

That doesn't mean as much as you'd think, I said, slipping the beef into some broth, simmering it on the stove.

While the stew bubbled beside us, the guy asked if I wanted to smoke outside. I don't usually accept things from clients, but again—he was cute. And I've learned to never turn down pot. You could see the entire park from his balcony, over the bayou, and into the backyards of the neighborhoods I worked in, where the houses probably had someone just like me dicing cucumbers and pulling spinach stems.

If you had a telescope, looking past the horizon, you could probably see my place, too. It was foggy and humid, with a muddy Houston skyline. But we'd only just entered August. The worst was yet to come.

The guy beside me puffed, looking out at the view. And then he turned to me, grinning.

No offense, I said. But you seem pretty normal.

Like not a creep?

Like financially.

Oh, said this guy, and then he laughed.

I just mean that what I'm doing isn't cheap, I said. And most of my clients are rich. Or they've got rich parents.

Sounds about white.

Exactly.

Not me, said this guy. Just thought this would be a nice way to spend the evening.

With a meal?

With someone else. It's hard, you know?

I do.

The two of us smoked, passing his vape pen back and forth, leaning over the railing. And then a funny thing happened: the guy asked if I thought things would always be this way.

I looked at him, blinking. Then I told him I didn't know.

But this is life too, said the guy, smiling.

Yeah?

Yeah. It's different. But it's still happening.

I looked at his face for a moment. He really did mean it. When he finally caught my stare, he grinned.

Then I heard the oven go off, and neither of us moved, and he said we really should go back inside, since he was paying me and all—and I laughed. But it felt funny. Because I'd forgotten, just for a second. And why would I have been there otherwise.

JAYA SAXENA

Margaritaville and the Myth of American Leisure

FROM *Eater*

THE 5 O'CLOCK Somewhere Bar does not open until 5 o' Clock, which puts a crimp in trying to live out the metaphor of its name. The whole point of the phrase is a justification to start drinking early, before the workday is done, because somebody, somewhere, is off work. But no, for the 5 o'Clock Somewhere Bar, one of four restaurants and bars at Manhattan's new Margaritaville Resort Times Square, you must wait until the workday is over. I am furious about this. Sure, the License to Chill Bar opens at two, but it's the principle of the thing. Jimmy Buffett would not wait until the boss says you can go home.

The Margaritaville Resort Times Square sounds like an oxymoron. "Resort" conjures pristine beaches with reservable cabanas, room service delivered with an orchid, spas, and restaurants that will just charge your room, so you needn't worry about even carrying a wallet on the grounds. To me at least, it does not mean a thirty-two-floor hotel in Times Square. Like, I have been to a Times Square hotel bar before, and while I've enjoyed myself, it has never been a transformatively relaxing experience.

I'm biased though; being from here makes it hard to view the city through a tourist's eyes. But while I can picture wanting to visit New York for many things—the museums, the theater, the history, the chance to meet a pigeon who's eaten a whole slice of pizza—I can't imagine coming here to engage in leisure. The kind of leisure where you get on a plane and check into a resort just to not leave for a week, to see no other sights besides the novelty tiki drink cups lining the hotel's bars.

But this is the kind of leisure Margaritaville is built on. Almost all the Margaritaville restaurants and resorts—a vaguely tropics-themed hospitality empire inspired by one of Jimmy Buffett's most popular songs—exist within massive tourist destinations like Cozumel, Mexico, or Atlantic City, New Jersey. On the surface, Times Square feels like a natural addition. But while other locales can at least offer some seclusion from the world in the form of a beach or an island, Times Square is in the middle of everything. It is hectic, crowded, overpriced, and blatantly capitalistic, a place where no one actually lives and few New Yorkers hang out unless they're seeing a show or bringing their out-of-town niece to the Disney Store. It has no chill. But maybe the point is, it's not unsalvageable. Amid the stress and the noise, if you delude yourself enough, you can turn off your brain and have fun. So for twenty-four hours, I tried.

Walking into the resort on the lower border of Times Square, at the corner of West 40th Street and Seventh Avenue, I am first greeted by a statue of a gigantic blue flip-flop, with one of the straps busted, and a gigantic discarded pop-top just in front of it.

If you are a Jimmy Buffett fan, you probably already get the reference (if not, look up the lyrics to "Margaritaville"). The entire resort is like if *Ready Player One* was only Jimmy Buffett references. There is a painting of a naked woman made to look like a parrot, asking, "Can you spot the 'woman to blame'?" There is live-laugh-love-esque wall art of lyrics and sayings as generic as "strummin' on my six-string," "thank God the tiki bar is open," and a pillow in my room that reads "changes in attitude, changes in latitude." The surfboards on the wall of the LandShark Bar & Grill ask you to put your "fins up," and the televisions on the walls play footage of Parrothead (Jimmy Buffett fan) tailgates. Oddly, I did not actually hear a Jimmy Buffett song for many hours.

I wore a tropical-print shirt and sandals to get in the mood, but when the concierge complimented my choice during check-in, I felt like I had worn the band's shirt to the concert. I dropped my stuff in my room—which was all white and teal faux-clapboard, evoking breezy porches that none of the rooms seemed to have—and headed out for my first meal.

When I was a teenager, my mom and I spent a spring break

driving around the Florida Keys, and I ate coconut shrimp every single day. This, to me, was luxury, and also what I assume retirement is like. So I figured that should be my order at the Land-Shark Bar & Grill on the building's sixth floor. The restaurant opens out onto an actual patio covered in sky-blue lounge chairs and yellow umbrellas, which surround a pool that was torturously not open (they were waiting on a last inspection). Lying in a chaise by the pool with my Pink Cadillac margarita would have really been resort life, but instead I settled for eating my coconut shrimp with coconut ranch (??) at a table next to it. My partner got a lobster roll and some drink that came with a full wedge of pineapple in it. We ate everything, but decided it all tasted lightly of sunscreen.

Still, eating at a table next to the pool was relaxing in its own right; something about having water nearby did distract from the Midtown of it all. I felt the sun and the breeze, and saw a woman with daiquiris embroidered on her lime green T-shirt. *I'm doing it,* I thought; *I'm relaxing.* I made a mental note to return to LandShark once the pool opened, and we headed one floor up, to the License to Chill Bar.

Margaritaville does an incredible job of catering to every type of person who might be in Times Square. While LandShark may have been for Parrothead tourists or *New York Times* employees on an ironic lunch break, License to Chill is more like an outdoor wine bar, with cushioned bucket seats that looked like the baskets I learned to weave in Girl Scouts, and a fireplace that was thankfully not lit in July. Also, for some reason, there was a screen showing a live feed of the traffic at the intersection right outside the hotel, in case you wanted to keep tabs on the WEED WORLD truck parked on Seventh Avenue.

I ordered an $18 drink with "botanicals" and ginger syrup, and my partner got what was basically a $20 gin and tonic. We nestled into our bucket chairs and took out our books, and for two hours, decided to lounge and read while our drinks slowly sweated. To my shock, I could barely hear any traffic, and as I snuggled into the pile of pillows, some emblazoned with a compass to let you pretend this was an exercise in great-world adventuring, I did feel distant from home. Then again, I reminded myself, that was probably because this was all going to be on Vox Media's dime. I'm technically here for "work" and not spending any of my own money. So of course I'm not worried about anything, except how to properly waste away.

The song "Margaritaville," which forever solidified Jimmy Buffett's persona as the king of the beach bums, was off his eighth album, and it only took seven years between the release of "Margaritaville" the song (1977) and the opening of Margaritaville the restaurant (1984). The first location was in Alabama, as Buffett couldn't get the trademark rights in Florida for the name "Margaritaville" because "there are so many using the name around the country," he told the press at the time. Eventually, he won.

Margaritaville, the one Buffett sang about, is actually an awful place. He allegedly wrote it after ordering a margarita in Austin, Texas, and was also inspired by an influx of tourists to Key West, Florida, where he was living at the time. It's about a man "wastin' away" in a touristy beach town, whose only solace from hinted-about heartbreak and foot injuries is tequila. This is not a song about someone who rejects the pressures of workaday life in order to pursue radical pleasure. This is about a man who is depressed and perhaps on the run from the law, for whom shrimp and sea and tattoos provide no peace, and who needs blended beach drinks to "hang on" to whatever semblance of a life he has left. It is not escaping. It's fleeing. And it's sort of pathetic.

But fans have instead turned it into a "national anthem for generations of college kids on spring break, burnt-out stockbrokers, and wishful thinkers who long to leave careers behind and let their biggest worry be which beach to sleep on that night," wrote Dan Daley for *Mix*. The song has been completely recontextualized so that not even Jimmy Buffett himself can declare this man's life an unsalvageable mess. Instead of a song about despair, it's a song about defiance, insisting despite all evidence to the contrary that you are *having a good time*.

It's a specific type of fun, though. Jimmy Buffett made his name with "gulf and western music," a style that combines American country and rock with instruments and tonalities more commonly found in the Caribbean. But while his songs are full of steel drums, lyrically they are mostly about being a white American man dreaming of a Bahamas without Bahamians. It's an overworked man in a bar, imagining moving to an island paradise, without all the pesky stuff that's already on the island. There are now more than sixty

Margaritaville bars and restaurants across the US, Mexico, Canada, and the Caribbean, selling this fantasy of "island" drinks and American foods with coconut or pineapple added to them, sometimes on top of the very places those flavors were taken from. It's a shame, but not a surprise, how popular a sell that is.

I called another friend to join in the festivities, and he arrived just as I was about to doze off in my bucket seat. By then, it was 5:30, and we were finally allowed to head up to the two-story 5 o'Clock Somewhere Bar, on the hotel's top floors with views of nearly the whole island. There was barely a smack of Jimmy Buffett there. Inside there were smooth midcentury modern chairs and tasteful patterned wallpaper. A woman with a guitar was singing mellow pop covers. On the outside deck, aqua booths were separated by fabric ferns, and the bar was lined with brushed-brass cocktail shakers. The altitude also seemed to have a filtering effect on the clientele. Except for a group of clearly teenagers, who I assume were served mocktails, trying to live out some joke of an adult night (Why does every group of teens trying to go out on the town consist of five girls in cocktail dresses and sparkling chokers, and one gangly boy in jeans who never talks?), the patrons all looked like they were meeting for a ten-year business school reunion. I stared as they ordered LandSharks and drinks named All Right, All Right, All Right with straight faces. They knew they could go to any other rooftop bar in Midtown, right? The place is lousy with them! And they all look like this! Was it a joke that they were here or did they all also love Jimmy Buffett? Finally, a man in a Phillies "Margaritaville Night" giveaway shirt sat at the booth next to us, and I felt some sense of normalcy again.

I could see why the business bros wanted to be here, though. Despite all having names like Jamaica Mistaca, the drinks at the rooftop bar were of the upscale kind that perhaps warranted the $20 price tag, or at least the aura of wealth. Instead of the juicy, sweet frozen daiquiris of twenty-five floors down, these were made with things like allspice dram, pineberry, and yuzu puree. Drinking a W. 40th St & Agave, a margarita made with Earl Grey agave, and looking out over the Manhattan skyline, I felt . . . sophisticated? Rich? If not like Shiv Roy, then at least like Cousin Greg? This is *my* city. This is *my* time!

At this point, I had not had anything to eat since the coconut shrimp. Neither bar's kitchen was open yet, which once again reminded me that while it may be 5 o'clock literally here, the spiritual essence of 5 o'clock evaded me. My plan of having a snack of ceviche or wagyu sliders to tide me over was foiled. I switched to wine, but I was still many strong drinks in. I kept referring to being in Manhattan as "being on island time." I felt far away from all my problems, most likely because I was drunk, but also because my surroundings were so different. I had, in the parlance of the resort, escaped. Finally, it was time to descend to the main event.

The Margaritaville restaurant within the Margaritaville resort takes up two floors. The walls are lined with the same TVs playing the same footage of Parrotheads; the floor-to-ceiling windows give you a great view of the Lot-Less discount store across the street; and in an atrium-like space in the middle, there is a massive Statue of Liberty bust, holding a margarita instead of a torch, that takes up both stories, big enough that it can be seen from the street. The giant Statue of Liberty rules. It just rules. It's so cool. I'm drunk and I'm screaming and I am ready to fight the people who get to eat at the lone table inside the giant Statue of Liberty because I want to sit in there so badly.

After the pseudosophistication of the upper floors, the Margaritaville restaurant smashes vacation resort vibes with the madness of Times Square tourism. It is LOUD. There are novelty glasses everywhere. My friend Dan and I order various takes on punch, while my spouse gets a Lime In D'Coconut, and we ponder how much Jimmy Buffett wishes he had written that song, which is actually good. It comes with an extra can of coconut Red Bull, a flavor I didn't even know existed.

As we shared our Caribbean chicken egg roll appetizer, I was reminded of a time my spouse chatted up a tourist on his way back to LaGuardia Airport while they were both on the bus. The tourist said he loved the city, but complained of the food being too expensive. My spouse said that's quite possible, but that there was plenty of amazing, affordable food to be found, and asked where he had eaten. The tourist said he and his daughter went to the Times Square Red Lobster. I know these large chain restaurants exist because they are popular, because they are fun or family-friendly or because in a trip probably full of decisions and risks, ordering a burger at a restaurant with name recognition is at least one thing you don't have to worry about. Here at Margaritaville, I frankly didn't care what I put in my body, I was just having fun and taking in the fact that on one TV they were playing footage of Parrotheads, and on another was Nancy Pelosi talking about the January 6 riots.

But the mediocrity of my fish tacos almost pulled me out of it. They were grilled and dry and slightly mealy, served with plain rice and black beans that tasted like they had just been dumped out of the can. I was suddenly too aware that I was not actually on vacation, and that all the pressures I desperately needed a break from were going to need my attention tomorrow, and that some might be filling up my text messages at that very moment. There were CSA vegetables in the fridge that needed to be cooked before they turned, and invoices to send, and family to check in on, and a job that I was *technically at* that I hadn't gone on an actual vacation from in a year and a half because of a global pandemic, because oh God I need my job, I need health insurance, everything hinges on this. And I was too aware that there were other restaurants in this city, other things I could be doing that would make me happier, but instead I was here. I was working. I was not escaping. There was no escape.

Then, suddenly, the lights went out. From behind me, music started blaring even louder than it already had been. Something was happening with the giant Statue of Liberty. Dan and I jumped out of our seats and ran to see a light show projecting onto her majestic margarita, choreographed in time to the music. There were neon dolphins, erupting coral reefs, flames giving way to ice cubes fading into a shimmering mirror ball. It was overwhelming like Times Square is overwhelming, and for the first time I understood how this level of light and noise could be awe-inspiring rather than just annoying. It forced all other concerns and worries out of my head and replaced them with the phrase DISCO MARGARITA. It was aggressive, it sent me to the edge of my joy and had me teetering on panic, but I couldn't think of anything else—the taco-induced, work-is-killing-me crisis of moments before was gone. No thoughts, just Buffett. I became aware that, for the first time that day, "Margaritaville" was playing.

The 5 o'Clock Somewhere Bar wouldn't exist if work didn't end at 5 o'clock. The UN Universal Declaration of Human Rights, adopted in 1948, states in Article 24 that "everyone has the right to rest and leisure, including reasonable limitation of working hours and periodic holidays with pay." This article came after, and seems likely to have been influenced by, labor movements around the world at the turn of the twentieth century, as activists campaigned and died for things like a weekend, or the eight-hour workday. The concept of leisure, what economist Thorstein Veblen defined as the "non-productive consumption of time," for anyone but the richest classes, was still new in the twentieth century. But by 1948 more people had time for it.

In *The Theory of the Leisure Class,* Veblen outlines the concept of conspicuous leisure—essentially being nonproductive in order to brag about it, rather than for your own rest and self-betterment. At the time he wrote it, he said it was a behavior of the idle rich, who would rather risk whittling away their fortune by devoting their days to obscure hobbies than work a factory floor. But as the middle class grew and labor protections were enshrined, especially in America, leisure time began to be more available, and began to resemble the activities that previously belonged to only the wealthiest. In 1950, the French Club Med pioneered the all-inclusive resort, which seemingly overnight existed everywhere. You could drive to Florida or California, or fly to Hawaii. You could do nothing, but do it somewhere exotic, and bring a souvenir back to show everyone. Tans, bikinis, and a drink in hand. A beach at the end of the world.

People of all classes can now engage in conspicuous leisure, or at least emulate it. Not to be all "everyone be on their phones," but leisure increasingly exists to be simultaneously documented and publicly acknowledged. A resort like Margaritaville is, foremost, designed to be looked at: the novelty of sitting by a pool in Midtown, the overwhelming Statue of Liberty light show, the view from the rooftop bar. However, conspicuous leisure has taken on a different flavor as it has spread. The rich who spent their days breeding dogs did not have a job to return to at the end of the week. The rest of us do. So when we engage in conspicuous leisure, there is a tinge of anxiety. Staying at Margaritaville may not result in anyone's rest or self-betterment, but we need to convince ourselves it does. And we do that by trying to convince others it has.

In America leisure only exists in relation to work, and we are a culture that fetishizes work. Even leisure, that nonproductive time, is spoken of through its value to production, how we all need time off so we can be better workers when we return. And our

leisure time is being eroded. "In a number of developed countries, steady jobs—with benefits, holiday pay, a measure of security
and possible union representation—are increasingly giving way to
contracts," warns the UN's Office of the High Commissioner for
Human Rights. Workers in the US take relatively few vacation days
compared to workers in other countries, maybe because we aren't
afforded any paid time off on a federal level, and often work far
longer than eight-hour days. Dolly Parton bastardized her own ode
to the working woman by releasing "5 to 9" as part of a Super Bowl
ad, an uncritical appreciation of working more in one's free time.
People aren't even guaranteed paid time off to get the COVID-19
vaccine.

That culture of hustle and greed disguised as effortless relax-
ation created Jimmy Buffett and Margaritaville. Many of his songs,
and now his resorts and restaurants, and the entire aura he projects, are about escape from your life, which assumes your life is
something you want to escape. If the inspiration for Margaritaville
is a song about a man who has left it all behind to do nothing, the
resort may as well be a theme park for conspicuous leisure—you
too can leave it all behind, and then come back and brag about
how you left it all behind to assure yourself you indeed did that.
Leisure becomes an exercise in labor. The "eight hours for what
we will" the Wobblies fought for is increasingly slipping away. You
have this rare opportunity for nonproductive time, something to
be scrimped and saved for, so you *must* chill out. You cannot waste
this.

In short, the whole ethos behind the resort is acknowledging
that work sucks and no one wants to do it, but that ethos can only
thrive in relation to work. If work didn't suck, no one would be
there. Though the executives behind the Big Flip-Flop may not
have intended it, there is a desperation in the song "Margaritaville" that permeates the Times Square resort. Entering the building was like signing a contract, that everyone here is agreeing to
buy into the facade so as not to kill the vibe. Everyone here needs
this, on some level, and while I'm also aware of the organized fun
of it all, I also need it.

As I returned to the 5 o'Clock Somewhere Bar for a final drink
before collapsing in my room, I thought of what Margaritaville
might look like if we acknowledged we had enough resources to
go around, that no one has to work as hard as they do for as little

as they get. What would a vacation, a nice meal, or a rooftop cocktail look like if it didn't have to carry so much weight? I don't think it would involve a two-story light-up Statue of Liberty. For a second, that makes me sad.

The next morning I realized my mission to not leave the resort would be nearly impossible when it came to breakfast. The room came equipped with two bottles of water and a Keurig machine with four coffee pods (one of which was, surprise surprise, coconut coffee). However, there was no cream or sugar, and the mini fridge was empty. I scrounged the drawers for a room service menu and found there was none, and when I attempted to call the front desk, there was no dial tone. The restaurants didn't open until eleven.

Still, there was the Joe Merchant's Coffee & Provisions stall in the lobby, and I thought there might be at least something to eat there. I took a shower with St. Somewhere Spa–branded body wash that smelled mostly of teenage-boy cologne, and went downstairs, hoping to find a Calypso Breakfast Sandwich or Parrothead Parfait or whatever weird beach-branded meal they offered. Instead, I found a mediocre bodega, with plastic-wrapped bagels and tuna sandwiches and granola bars. I could find this, and better, outside. I wanted to go back outside.

My partner and I packed up and left. We got bacon, egg, and cheese sandwiches and iced coffee on the way home, and since we had already budgeted having that afternoon off, we enjoyed them on our real-life balcony in the sun. I took a midday nap on the couch, content in the knowledge that there was nowhere I had to be and nothing I had to do at that moment. It could be like this all the time. It's always 5 o'clock somewhere.

"It's Hospital Soigné"

FROM *Grub Street*

COURTNEY KENNEDY REMEMBERS the relief she felt when she lost her job. She was working in the kitchen at Flora Bar, the high-end, and highly acclaimed, restaurant located inside an iconic brutalist museum on the Upper East Side. Standouts on the restaurant's dinner menu included flat omelets topped with multiple quenelles of caviar and plump dumplings filled with lobster meat, floating in yuzu-scented broth. Kennedy had only worked there for a few months, but she had already grown frustrated with her role as a cook—which meant shucking a lot of oysters—and was dreading the conversation she'd have to have when she resigned. "I hate putting in my notice. I thought, *This is going to be so awkward and so weird*," she recalls. This was in March 2020, just as the pandemic arrived in New York City. "Then they were like, *Oh, everyone's fired*. I was like, *Great!*"

She tells me this story while sipping on a glass of cold-brewed coffee, sitting in the mocha-hued outdoor dining shed at Nolita's Thai Diner. A recent heat wave has just broken, and it's the kind of breezy day that makes you want to drop everything and head for the park, or at least grab brunch on Kenmare Street. We order ribs that have been crusted in shrimp paste and a green-papaya salad with more dried shrimp, and I push for a salad of chicken and banana blossoms. "I love big chunks of herbs," Kennedy says.

Even though Kennedy has spent the better part of the last decade working in some of New York City's most acclaimed professional kitchens, this meal is one of the only times she's been to a restaurant since leaving Flora Bar. That's because instead of looking for another restaurant job—at the height of the pandemic in the city, a time when many New Yorkers had either fled the city or were quarantined inside their apartments—Kennedy started cooking for patients at the Memorial Sloan Kettering Cancer Center on York Avenue.

"It's still serving people food," Kennedy says. "It's just way more gloves than I've ever worn." Before COVID, the Culinary Institute of America graduate spent six years working in New York restaurants. Her first job was at Torrisi Italian Specialties, the tiny but luxurious Italian American dining room named after Rich Torrisi, one of the chef partners of the Major Food Group, which had just twenty seats and served made-to-order balls of fresh mozzarella to begin its multicourse tasting menus. When that restaurant closed eight months after Kennedy began, she went to Dirty French, MFG's glitzy hotel restaurant on Ludlow Street, followed by a front-of-house stint at the Lobster Club, a sister restaurant to the company's revamped Four Seasons space. Between that restaurant and Flora Bar, Kennedy also spent an "intense" year at Momofuku Ssäm Bar in the East Village. "Working at Ssäm Bar, I used to work my butt off until 2:00 a.m., and I'm like, for what?" she says. "I think I did a good job," she continues, before saying that she's reconsidered the sense of pride she took in the work. "Like, *Look at me, I am the meat cook*—did anyone know?"

At the hospital, she works as a cook in a kitchen staffed by about fifty people at any given time, with thirty of those involved in preparing the food. They're responsible for providing room service, three times a day, to the hospital's 498 patients, who can choose from any of the menu's sixty dishes in addition to daily specials. In the kitchen, there are employees whose only job is to work the tray line, ensuring the food matches the right ticket. Cooks, meanwhile, are assigned to different stations—not unlike a restaurant line—such as eggs, grilling, and saucing. "The first shift I worked was 6:30 a.m. to 2:30 p.m., and I was just like, *Oh wow, I have never seen this many eggs in my life,*" Kennedy laughs.

There are plenty of other differences. To start, she's now making $25 an hour, compared to the $15 to $17 she made toward the end of her time in restaurants. She has health insurance (something that many in the hospitality industry can't afford), and she's felt less anxious since starting the new job. She is also adjusting to the idea of a set schedule—she usually works a 12:30 p.m. to

8:30 p.m. shift—and paid time off. "People take lots of vacation," she says. "I don't because I literally don't know how."

Early on, Kennedy was also surprised to find she wasn't constantly being asked to stay late or come in early. "I was like, *Are they going to come in and say, 'Can you stay until 3?'"* she says. "Once in a while we'll have to stay later, but they'll pay us, and it's not like they'll sneak it up on us or something." For Kennedy, it's a big change. "In restaurants, they'd say you should come in at one o'clock, but if you came in at one o'clock, you're going to be so far behind." Instead, cooks jump right into service when they arrive at the hospital, and anyone who works the 9 a.m. to 5 p.m. shift helps prep for other cooks.

All of this stability is one reason that staff tends to stay with the hospital—something Kennedy realized when she began to meet her new coworkers. "I'm like, *Wow, you've worked here for fourteen years,*" she says. "I've never met anyone who has worked somewhere for fourteen years. If it's a restaurant, it's like, *Oh, you worked here for a year—that's a long time.*"

The new job also required more abstract adjustments, and Kennedy had to shift her thinking in terms of whom she was cooking for and why. "When you work in a restaurant, it's always *you*"—the cook—"versus *them*"—the customers, Kennedy explains. The mentality is, "They're out to get you." What Kennedy has come to realize is that this is not the case at *all* restaurants, but it was absolutely the case at the restaurants where she worked, where the chefs' names and distinct styles were ostensibly the draw for customers. (Momofuku became famous in the company's early days for its restaurants' strict no-substitutions menu policies.) "We were very *our way or the highway,*" Kennedy says. "The chef is right—that's it."

Now, Kennedy's day-to-day concerns go far beyond proper char on a steak; for example, like assembling a proper low-microbial diet for recipients of bone-marrow transplants, or making something for esophageal cancer patients who cannot swallow. "Getting people nutrition is the hard part," Kennedy explains. (Loss of appetite is also an issue, and a patient suffering from malnutrition can't fight cancer as well.) "I'm not a dietitian, but to get someone something worth eating when they can only eat purée—we need to get fat in there—or if they want just a little bit of food, it's hard."

This isn't to say comfort or pleasure aren't factored into the food. The kitchen is always looking for ways to add slivers of enjoyment to patients' days, and they do indulge the occasional plating flourish, like shingles of strawberries crowning a cup of cottage cheese. Kennedy says this has become especially crucial as COVID limited visitation guidelines, meaning those same patients can't depend as much on company. Kennedy knows the potential that food has to make someone feel less alone, which was impressed upon by her father's own enthusiasm for the food after undergoing quadruple bypass surgery. Even now, he sends her photos of the food he ate during his stay. "This is two years ago, and we're still talking about it," she says. "It really did change his day because he got something and thought it was amazing."

Mostly, she just wants to make patients happy, which is different from impressing hard-to-please customers inside rarefied Manhattan dining rooms. "We have a million things in the hospital," Kennedy says. "If someone asks for something—you want to have it, to say, 'We'll go get it, sure, not a problem.'" There is no ego, in other words, only a desire to make patients feel cared for. "We're not doing it for finesse," she says, before explaining that it's a different approach to VIP treatment than what you'd find at even the most exclusive New York restaurants. "It's soigné," Kennedy says, "but it's a different kind of soigné—it's hospital soigné."

When dessert arrives at Thai Diner, Kennedy pulls out her phone to take some pictures for Instagram. She loves a banana-rum pudding's decorative sesame tuile and the desserts' flowery "grandma" plates. "I started an Instagram that's just the ice cream that I get," she says. "We're ice cream snobs, I guess you could say."

I ask her if she ever misses working in restaurants. "No," she says, before using her spoon to break off a bit of the tuile.

MAYUKH SEN

The Wild and Irresistibly Saucy Tale of the Curry Con Man

FROM VOX

IN THE FALL of 1901, a false prince was turning heads in New York high society. Blessed with an aquiline nose and teeth as white as caster sugar, he cut a striking figure. He coiled his mustache into tight curls and often costumed himself in shimmering silk robes and turbans. He told people his name was Prince Ranjit of Baluchistan. Media reports even identified him that way—at least initially.

More discerning folks recognized him immediately. He was no prince at all, but a chef—and quite an accomplished one at that. Two years prior, he had grabbed headlines as Joe Ranji Smile, sometimes shortening the Joe to "J." He was a cook at Sherry's, a tony Manhattan establishment, and he hailed from what was then colonial India but is today Pakistan. As an 1899 article syndicated in papers across the country surmised, this colorful man who dazzled diners with his "curry of chicken Madras" and "Bombay Duck" was "the first India [sic] chef America has ever seen."

Smile spoke about the dishes he made as if they possessed the potency of superfoods. "If the women of America will but eat the food I prepare, they will be more beautiful than they as yet imagine," he promised in that same article. "The eye will grow lustrous, the complexion will be yet so lovely and the figure like unto those of our beautiful India women."

Such pieces on Smile highlighted the novelty of his "trendy" Indian cooking to white Americans, sure, but also elements that had nothing to do with food at all. Smile's position at Sherry's made him the subject of splashy profiles in fashion magazines such as *Harper's Bazaar,* yet he was dubbed a "chef who makes a strong appeal to the eye as well as to the palate." His actual food—the "snowy mound" of white rice, per the *Bazaar* piece, drowned in "the golden brown of the sauce of the curry of chicken, or lobster, or veal"—was often secondary to the glamorous way he looked and carried himself.

The media penchant for tying a male chef's talent to his sexuality—the kind that built and bolstered the machismo and rakish public personas of figures like Bobby Flay or the late Anthony Bourdain—may seem like a rather recent phenomenon. But the story of Smile and his remarkable ruse shows that fawning over male chefs, and the ache to anoint them celebrities, is a very old American pastime. In fact, it's a practice that predates the advent of food television, stretching back over a century. Smile actively courted journalists' attention, using his notoriety to advance both his native land's cooking and his own name. Members of the press were content with the arrangement, too, for a time.

Smile's decline was as precipitous as his ascent. After spending a few months abroad in 1901 and returning to America with the curious new moniker of "Prince," he toured America giving cooking demonstrations for housewives, working in restaurants, and even trying to mount some ventures of his own. But legal skirmishes tainted him in the eyes of the press: he found himself entangled in immigration law while also being accused of exploiting workers he'd smuggled into America from his native country. He also had a habit of taking a series of young, white brides.

In the early twentieth century, white Americans began to view immigrants from India as "racially unassimilable laborers who competed unfairly with white workers and sent their money home," Erika Lee and Judy Yung wrote in the 2010 book, *Angel Island: Immigrant Gateway to America.* Though the country took to Smile's food, America was growing less friendly to people of his kind, which also may have informed the newly hostile tone that journalists took in reporting on him. Members of the media who had once pampered the chef with attention suddenly found glee in poking holes in his narrative.

In spite of these prejudices, Smile's preternatural ability to make headlines is partially why numerous scholars, among them

the authors Colleen Taylor Sen of *Curry: A Global History* and Sarah
Lohman of *Eight Flavors: The Untold Story of American Cuisine,* have
called him America's first celebrity chef.

It's risky to definitively classify any person as the "first" to ac-
complish a major feat because it often erases prior figures in history. But if you buy the assertions about Smile, it may help make
sense of this current moment in American dining, when stories of
worker exploitation and abuse in restaurant kitchens are finally
demolishing the fragile myth of the lone genius (often male, often
white) celebrity chef. During the heat of the MeToo movement in
late 2017, accusations of sexual assault leveled against the once
renowned chef Mario Batali expedited his exit from the public
eye; the past year alone has seen greater scrutiny of chefs who were
once media darlings, including Jean-Georges Vongerichten, Abe
Conlon, and David Chang.

Smile's story might lead you to believe that the phenomenon of
the celebrity chef in America has, from its onset, been predicated
on an individual's skill to manipulate the masses—a talent that
Smile had in spades. But it is only with an assist from the media
that many keep the grift going.

That Smile could climb to such summits of stardom is remarkable considering that he was brown, Muslim, illiterate, and what
many would now refer to as an undocumented immigrant. Given
the scandals that trailed him and his series of seemingly calculated
deceptions, it might be easy for some to just write off Smile as one
would a man selling snake oil. But thinking of Smile as a con man
tells only half the story.

The narrative around Smile's origins changed depending on the
source. He was, according to Lohman's book, likely born to a Muslim family on May 11, 1879, in the city of Karachi. Scholars like
Lohman have suspected his original surname was Ismaili.

But the story gets murky when it comes to his parentage. A
1901 *Boston Daily Globe* article wrote that his father had been a
merchant. But in 1904, the *Philadelphia Inquirer* said his father
"once reigned in Marochi, India," while in 1907, the *Washington
Post* identified Smile as "fifth son of the late Ameer of Beluchistan." In 1910, the *Detroit Free Press* had his father's name as Haji,
his mother's as Princess Zora; a 1912 *New York Herald Tribune* article repeated this claim, naming him as the "son of Princess Zora

Kahlekt and the Ameer Haji Narbeboky of Beluchistan, British East India."

Smile's whimsical tales found a willing audience in journalists who reported his words with little pushback. A 1919 profile in *Variety* would paint a fanciful picture, placing him in a royal family in Punjab before "[h]e left his home when he was a boy, wandering into the hills, becoming lost and finally picked up by bandits, who held him for a ransom approximating $100,000 in American money, when learning who he was." The bandits eventually stranded him in the mountains, the *Variety* piece said. He wandered the jungle in those years and even forgot his real name until an English colonel rescued him at sixteen, taking him to Burma. The elaborate story strains credibility, and the American media's willingness to print it was evidence of its exoticizing attitude toward people with roots in what was then called India.

As for where and when his zeal for cooking developed, the *Variety* account said that "the instinct to prepare Indian dishes was inherent with him," as if he'd been blessed with a gift awaiting a proper platform.

What few accounts dispute, however, is that he found that stage in London in the 1890s. There, he cooked professionally at the Hotel Cecil and the Savoy, establishments where he reportedly served upper-crust clientele like England's aristocracy and members of the royal family. Maybe that's where he got the name Ranji Smile. In a 1901 article in the *Philadelphia Inquirer*, a columnist would claim he christened the chef as Ranji upon meeting Smile at the Hotel Cecil in 1897, naming the chef after a famous cricketer of the same name who bore a passing resemblance to Smile. The Smile surname may have come a bit later, from the British food journalist Nathaniel Newnham-Davis, who, in his book *Dinners and Diners: Where and How to Dine in London,* called him "Smiler."

Both writers agreed on his prodigious culinary gifts (Smile would have been in or around his twenties when he was cooking in London). The *Inquirer* writer observed that "this graceful and Chesterfieldian young Oriental" was "an undoubted artist at the game of curry building." Newnham-Davis wrote that Smile "thinks that I should not go to the Savoy for any other purpose than to eat his curries."

Most articles on Smile were scant on any details about his food. "It is a mistake to boil curries," he'd say in that widely syndicated

1899 article trumpeting his arrival in New York. "They should simmer gently and not lose their flavor." Description of his curry's
makeup was minimal; the story simply stated that Smile would take
a diner's plate and plant a circle of "the whitest, flakiest curried
rice, in the center of which he places a bit of chicken."

His other dishes bore names like "Muskee Sindh," "Bombay
Duck," and "Lettuce Ceylon," leaving food historians today to
parse what they really were. Lohman wrote in her book *Eight Flavors* that she believed Muskee Sindh was a dish of whitefish that
Smile poached in a storm of onions, tomatoes, ginger, chilies, cilantro, and turmeric. As Sen wrote in a 2006 article for the magazine *Food Arts,* Bombay duck was usually a "dried, pungent salted
fish" that got fried, but Sen theorized that Smile more likely made
it into a "curried duck" to appeal to British and American palates.
"Lettuce Ceylon," both Lohman and Sen seem to agree, may have
just been a salad.

In any case, the gushing reviews that Smile received in London
caught the eye of the American restaurateur Louis Sherry. After
a visit to London, he lured Smile to his eponymous Manhattan
restaurant in the autumn of 1899. American outlets treated Smile
as a creature of curiosity, seizing on his looks. "This foreign cook
is a very handsome representative of his country—clear, dark skin,
brilliant black eyes, smooth black hair and the whitest of teeth,"
read one article. Smile arrived at patrons' tables "immaculately arrayed in a heavy white linen India costume, with a gorgeous turban
of white all outlined in gold braid."

In that early account, it was evident that Smile saw himself as
far more than a chef. He was a personality, keenly aware of how
to market himself. "I must think out each day something new and
very novel, because, dear me, the American public must be enter-
tained as well as fed," he said.

Making a living as a chef in America wasn't just a job, Smile
understood; it was a performance.

Smile dropped off the radar of the American press until late 1901,
when he reemerged in New York under the name Prince Ranjit of
Baluchistan.

Smile had just returned from London, where he and a mighty
entourage of more than twenty of his fellow countrymen apparently rented out twenty-three hotel rooms under that princely

name. But he reportedly dodged questions about who he really was. "The India Office has issued an official announcement that there is no such Indian chief as Prince Ranjit of Baluchistan," a *New York Times* report on his arrival in New York read. The paper still made sure to note that he was "a man of fine physique, dark-skinned and handsome."

That article made no mention of Smile being a chef, which feels fitting. In keeping with the modern archetype of the celebrity chef, he was growing a cult of personality that extended far beyond his food. And when he spoke about his royal ancestry, unsuspecting onlookers took him at his word.

Until they didn't.

"Ex-Waiter, Not a Prince," a later headline in the *Times* blared. There was a tinge of nastiness to the piece, which downplayed Smile's talents as a chef, diminishing him to "a former servant in a Fifth Avenue restaurant" who had the wild dream of opening his own place. Smile explained that he'd left America that May to go back home to collect some money he'd inherited—though, in actuality, he may have been recruiting cooks for that new restaurant.

Over the next few years, legal trouble brewed for Smile. Just months after his rearrival, a *New York Tribune* article identified him as the proprietor of a Fifth Avenue restaurant (other reports suggest it was called the Omar Khayyam, funded by two wealthy brothers, Roland and Stanley Conklin), where, among other purported offenses, seven men from Smile's native country alleged that "they had been inveigled . . . by Smile under false representations." Smile had apparently met the men in Bombay and told them he was a prince.

A few months later in 1902, he and the Conklins faced a fine of $15,000 for importing fifteen contract laborers from India. Smile, along with the men whom he'd hired as waiters, faced deportation on suspicion of violating the Alien Contract Labor Law, a restrictive 1885 mandate that forbade any individual or entity from bringing immigrants to America with the promise of contract work.

A year later, he was once again under investigation for breaching that same law. His restaurant, according to a *Times* article, had failed, thus leaving fifteen "stranded Hindus" scrounging for work in America.

Many in Smile's circle were allegedly deported following that case. Smile, though, was spared, and he seemed determined to make America his home. In 1904, he'd apply for citizenship. His bid wasn't successful, likely because he wasn't white. (Less than twenty years later, in 1923, a landmark Supreme Court decision would also strip Bhagat Singh Thind, a Sikh immigrant, of citizenship on the grounds that he wasn't white, barring future attempts of people from India to become American citizens.) But that didn't deter him. Smile embarked on a tour of the country, his presence at department stores and hotels marked by a series of ads.

His mythology swelled in the years that followed. A 1907 *Washington Post* article said that King Edward VII himself dubbed Smile "King of the Chafing Dish." And Smile himself spoke of his cooking talents as if they were God-given. "When I was a baby I used to cry," he said while touring St. Louis that year. "They wouldn't know what I was crying for. Then they would give me something to mix and cook, and I would be happy and keep quiet." A 1910 piece in the *Post* even named him as a graduate of Cambridge University.

No aspect of Smile's romantic exploits went unexamined by the papers, either. They named a couple of would-be brides: an American woman named Rose Schlacter (sometimes spelled Schlueter) in 1905, a Welsh woman named Anna Maria Washington Davies in 1910. Both were in their early twenties. According to later reports, though, neither marriage materialized; instead, he found love in 1912 with Violet Ethel Rochlitz, an up-and-coming Broadway performer. Per a *Times* article documenting the wedding, he was thirty at that time, and she twenty.

But more legal commotions awaited him. In 1915, he found himself arraigned in a New York City court for being unable to pay a $6.50 bill at a restaurant in Manhattan. The *Times* took delight in reporting on this incident: "Self-Styled Prince Arrested When He Refused to Pay Dinner Check," laughed a headline. Smile said that he'd been dining innocently enough until a clan of admirers rushed to his side upon learning they were in the presence of a supposed prince. They took advantage of him by eating and drinking on his dime, he insisted, deserting him to pay the bill.

The magistrate dismissed him, but the incident left him humiliated. He was determined, however, not to become a laughingstock. "I'm good for $6.50," he announced to the magistrate, "but I'm hanged if I'll let them make a fool of me."

Records of Smile in the American press are spotty following that case. There were more ads over the next few years showing that he was cooking at hotels across the country. There was even another marriage, in 1918, to a nineteen-year-old named May (sometimes spelled Mae) Walter, when Smile was well into his thirties. (Rochlitz had died.) Months after the marriage, though, his young wife slapped him with a warrant for disorderly conduct.

America, meanwhile, was becoming even more inhospitable for people of Indian origin. The Immigration Act of 1917 effectively barred immigration from what was then India to the United States. Smile seemed to do anything he could to stay in America, filling out a draft card in 1917 at the start of World War I. There's no indication, however, that he fought in the war.

Smile was occasionally still catnip for prurient gossip. In 1920, the New York–based columnist O. O. McIntyre wrote that Smile was "[g]arbed in oriental robes and turbans. Goes from one cafe to another making Indian dishes. Married three white women."

Mentions of him in the media petered out throughout the 1920s. The *Times of India* listed him as a passenger on a ship due to arrive in Bombay at the end of July 1929, implying that he went home.

No news followed until spring 1937, when a series of notices in the *Brooklyn Daily Eagle* indicated that his wife, May, was requesting an annulment of their marriage. And that was the last time the American press made mention of J. Ranji Smile—at least by that name—in the early twentieth century.

There are certain things you can glean about Smile's life if you take these archival texts at face value: That he was a charismatic figure who bewitched white America. That he was a phony who swindled gullible Americans to further his own name. That he was a Lothario, seducing young women as if it were a sport.

But a skeptical reading of these records might guide you to a more complex truth: Smile became an object of mockery for his primarily white, well-off American audience. He faced enormous challenges as a man who was brown, Muslim, and unable to gain citizenship. Smile lived in America during an era of great turmoil for people who looked like him.

As a figure of history, Smile is beguilingly difficult to categorize, both a pioneer and a prevaricator. "He must have been incredibly charismatic—he truly, truly was a star," Lohman says of Smile in a phone conversation. "And he was also such a mess."

She hesitates to label Smile as a crook, speculating on the traumas he may have endured trying to assimilate in America. Lohman, who has compared Smile to "a Food Network star," argues that there's symbolic power in designating him as America's first celebrity chef. "His whole spirit and identity challenges the contemporary notion of who an American is and what American history is," she says. "His story says that immigrants and people of color have been in this country all along, and have been part of this story all along, too."

The modern avatar of the celebrity chef, in the view of the historian and author Paul Freedman, began taking shape in the 1960s with the rise of the French chef Paul Bocuse, who propagated the image of "the chef as artist, as creator of things never seen before," Freedman says. "And then—this is further developed by Ferran Adrià at El Bulli—is the chef as genius." The media has played an indispensable role in creating these stars, just as it did in Smile's time. "The media's the oxygen," Freedman says. "But the media at different times wants different things in response to what it perceives what the public wants."

The question of what the American public desired from Smile has weighed on the author Vivek Bald for more than a decade and a half. "To simply describe Smile as a conman is to flatten the complexity of his situation as a dark-skinned Indian Muslim immigrant man in turn-of-the-century New York," Bald writes in an email. To believe it is to dismiss xenophobic, racist realities that Smile, and others like him, had to contend with in America at the time.

Bald, who's been at work on a book tentatively titled *The Rise and Fall of Prince Ranji Smile,* first came across a reference to Smile in 2004 when working on his 2013 book, *Bengali Harlem and the Lost Histories of South Asian America.* He was struck by the tone of *New York Times* articles he found on Smile. "It was as if Smile were the butt of some ongoing inside joke among New Yorkers," Bald says.

Bald doesn't deny that Smile did engage in a con on some level, using the "prince" designation to woo women (and workers). But Smile also "embodied a larger contradiction in Americans' regard for Indians at the turn of the century," Bald says.

"In Smile's day, South Asians appeared in the US imagination as mystics and yogis who possessed valuable 'ancient wisdom' or as elegant princes who lived in the enviable surroundings of lavish palaces, but, just as often, they were represented as heathens and criminals or as dour, turbaned migrants coming to take away 'American jobs,' " Bald explains.

Smile sat between the two. But he shrewdly played into those tropes—ones that Americans had inherited from the British. Doing so was part of the bargain that surviving in America required. "Smile was simply using the fantasy as a way to carve out a place for himself in a United States, where the popular agitation against Asian immigration was getting stronger and more violent with each passing year," Bald says. This is why Bald views Smile sympathetically: Smile "was always on the verge of having that all stripped away, and being revealed as 'just a cook,' 'just a servant,' 'just a laborer.' "

After all, Smile found himself working at the whims of white men like Louis Sherry and the Conklin brothers. They occupied a higher station in American society than Smile ever could by virtue of their whiteness and their access to capital. Smile's possibilities were always more finite than theirs for reasons he couldn't control.

Bald hasn't confirmed what happened to Smile at the end of his life, facts like when or where he died. He hypothesizes that Smile either went back to his home country under his birth name (which is still undetermined) or continued to eke out a quieter existence in the United States, far from the limelight. Bald has made peace with the possibility that he may not find firm answers. "In some ways, it may be fitting that he only existed in the US imagination—and historical record—to the extent that Americans could invest him with meaning and identity, and that he slipped away by becoming illegible to them again," Bald says.

Historians may never resolve the perplexing questions around Smile's life. But this much is certain: for a brief time, Smile served Americans exactly what they wanted.

ANDREW KEH

Tokyo Convenience Store Chicken Gizzards Saved My Life

FROM *The New York Times*

ON LANGUID BUS rides from one Olympic venue to another, a panorama of gustatory pleasures rolls by: noodle joints, skewer shops, sushi counters.

We stare at it all through tinted glass: it is like a mirage of the people we are not meeting, and the food we are not eating.

This is all for good reason. Japan is in a state of emergency. Coronavirus cases are on the rise. Unleashing thousands of foreigners like me, an American journalist covering the Games, into a city—to its restaurants and bars and stores—would be imprudent. But we do need to eat.

Enter the saving grace of these Olympics, the glue holding the whole thing together: Tokyo's twenty-four-hour convenience stores, or conbini, as they are known in Japan. They have quickly become a primary source of sustenance—and, more surprisingly, culinary enjoyment—for many visitors navigating one of the strangest Games in history.

All of us—athletes, team staff members, officials, and journalists—are largely prohibited from venturing anywhere but our hotels and the Olympic venues. Trips outside this so-called bubble cannot exceed fifteen minutes.

We can't traverse the galaxy of food outside the Olympic limits, but a conbini contains a culinary world unto itself, a bounty of bento boxes, fried meats, sushi, noodles galore, and all manner of elaborate plastic-wrapped meals and rare snacks.

While requisite health protocols, including a ban on spectators, have sapped the Games of both color and human connection, the stores have become a substitute arena of polychromatic cultural discovery for some.

"They are not Jiro Sushi," said Gavin H. Whitelaw, a socio-cultural anthropologist at Harvard who has researched conbini for two decades. "But they are equally Japanese in that they have a fifty-year history in the country now, and they have been indigenized, you might say, so much so that they don't look anything like their brethren in any other places."

In the lobby of the main press building, a Lawson store heaves each day with multinational crowds scavenging for their next meal.

The 7-Eleven outside my hotel hums with activity long after midnight, as people returning from late events gaze, frozen by choice, upon unending rows of ready-to-eat foodstuffs, looking to match component parts into a perfectly bespoke meal.

And even athletes have been spotted carrying overstuffed shopping bags of snacks.

I asked Matt Savas, one half of the pair behind the *Conbini Boys* podcast, to help me understand the spell we had found ourselves under.

"It's the quality, the variety, and the ubiquity," he said. "It's hard to convey how much better they are than American convenience stores."

It's true. Here, quickly, is a partial list of items I have plucked from conbini shelves that sparked at least a basic level of pleasure, and often much more: a runny boiled egg; mapo tofu (the spicy Chinese staple); french fries; a cup of cold corn soup (which I sipped through a straw); an unnaturally shaped, suspiciously juicy disc of fried chicken; lu rou fan (Taiwanese braised pork); Okinawa-style pig ears; hiyayakko (a cold tofu dish); soboro don (ground beef and egg over rice); spicy grilled chicken cartilage; a tuna salad sandwich; an egg salad sandwich; tonkatsu (breaded pork cutlet, which in this case came with a side of spaghetti); a hunk of salmon.

Just as important, as Savas noted, conbini are everywhere. My ten-minute walk to the press center takes me past three convenience stores, and barely a day has gone by that they haven't lured me in.

I grabbed sunscreen at a Family Mart after an early brush with

Tokyo's punishing sun. I picked up a handkerchief at Lawson upon realizing that bathrooms here often don't have paper towels. And I knew that if I somehow scored an interview with the prime minister, I could run to the 7-Eleven across the street to pick up a dress shirt and necktie.

"I've bought underwear there before," said Mike Markey, the other Conbini Boy, who works as a web developer in Kurobe.

Good to know. But food has remained my chief concern.

Despite their relentless schedules, the Olympics normally present little openings for epicurean adventure. In Brazil in 2016, I'd set up nighttime office hours at any number of botecos (relaxed bars with cheap food) around Rio de Janeiro, working my way through a checklist of small plates. In South Korea, I might have gone a bit overboard trying to squeeze in elaborate meals between all my reporting assignments.

As a longtime advocate of something I like to call meal-food fluidity—an elevated state of mind in which the time of day has no bearing on the dish you eat—I've found some emotional grounding this month in my hotel's breakfast buffet, which offers slabs of mackerel, fried chicken, noodle soups, and a selection of pickles each morning.

But dining at these Games has otherwise been an alienating experience. The press building has two restaurants: a cafeteria that serves Japanese lunch staples—udon, beef curry, and the like—and a pizza and burger restaurant called Pizza & Burger Restaurant. At both places, as well as our hotels, the menus are small and unchanging, and every seat is separated by a thick sheet of plexiglass.

It's no surprise, then, that people have been gravitating toward convenience stores for access to a wider selection.

Variety and innovation of this sort have been at the heart of the conbini experience in Japan for a half century. Whitelaw, the Harvard professor, told me that onigiri (rice balls) were the first traditional foods here to receive the conbini treatment. They're sold in clever packaging that keeps the seaweed dry, allows for easy assembly, and comes in seemingly endless permutations.

"They have taken a very handmade, homemade convenience meal—a ball of rice that has sustained Japan for eons—and wrapped it up and innovated it into something that is high cuisine, conbini cuisine, that is constantly changing," Whitelaw said.

Onigiri have sustained me through these Games, too. Popping one or two (or three or four) of them into my bag before running to an event has been a surefire way to stay fed.

My favorite conbini innovations were the simplest ones: a corn dog I bought at 7-Eleven came with a sauce packet designed so that a single pinch sent ketchup and whole-grain mustard shooting simultaneously from a spout, like two synchronized divers.

Some items, on the other hand, required more assembly than an Ikea desk. Cold soba noodles came stuck together in an unappealing, floppy brick. But after applying the many plastic-wrapped accouterments—tsuyu sauce, scallions, wasabi, frothy grated yam, a gooey egg—my hesitation melted into contentment.

It's important to pause and note that the conbini experience does animate some mental dissonance. First, extreme convenience of this sort requires an incredible amount of plastic packaging. Second, it's hard to ignore how these store clerks are perched on the front lines of Japan's unending coronavirus fight—in our case, serving customers deemed too risky to enter any other stores—and yet they are among the lowest-paid workers in the country.

A small consolation of this pandemic, Whitelaw said, might be greater appreciation for these businesses, which are heavily relied upon but sometimes taken for granted.

My own dependence on convenience stores began early. After a fourteen-hour flight to Tokyo, I spent another seven hours in the airport for coronavirus testing. By the time I arrived at my hotel, it was close to midnight—thirty hours since my last sleep, twelve or so since my last meal.

It was a cold pack of grilled chicken gizzards from Lawson that saved my life. They were peppery, like gas-station beef jerky, with a wisp of garlicky sweetness and a more satisfying chomp. Working through the pack, mixing in sips of beer, felt like meditation. I slipped on my hotel-provided pajamas and drifted into a peaceful slumber.

The biggest revelation for me has been the vinegar-flavored squid legs from the snack aisle at Lawson. They taste like salt-and-vinegar potato chips (my favorite), but squishy.

I have amassed a stockpile of them already. I'm wondering if I should check an extra bag for the flight home.

I Tasted Honda's Spicy Rodent-Repelling Tape

FROM *Haterade*

A WHILE BACK, after a series of car troubles too boring to enumerate, I learned about the existence of mouse tape.

Mouse tape exists solely to make Important Wires less delicious. Honda started selling rolls of the stuff a few years back to keep rodents from partying in their engine blocks.* You see, the thing about rodents—be they rat or shrew or vole—is that they really like to *gnaw.*

I don't know much about cars, but I do know you're not supposed to chew on them. So I nodded along while my mechanic explained that there was "rodent damage" on some mysterious bundle of wires beneath the manifold and that he would need to wrap the fresh, un-gnawed wires in a rodent repellent.

Then he told me the "rodent repellent" was a roll of gray vinyl tape printed with cute little mice silhouettes and coated in pure capsaicin. *Spicy mouse tape.*

When I got home, I googled it. I had a mad compulsion to taste it, but I didn't want to gnaw on my brand-new car wires. Plus, my head wouldn't fit beneath the manifold.

I found the tape immediately—OEM Honda part 4019-2317. It was outrageously expensive, like a white truffle or a tin of

---

* This proved somewhat prescient, as several class-action lawsuits would later allege that the soy-based insulation used in Honda's wiring attracted rodents.

osetra caviar. Fortunately, a reader had recently Venmoed me $50—almost the exact cost of a roll of mouse tape. I took it as a sign.

This is the *Haterade* promise: I will only ever use your money irresponsibly.

Almost as soon as the tape arrived, I began to have second thoughts. Each printed mouse had a little gray *x* on its head. This could mean only one of two things: either the mice were being poisoned, or someone was about to drop a piano on them.

Was the "repellent" really just capsaicin? Fearing the worst, I reached out to Honda:

> @Honda Is there anything toxic to humans in your chili-flavored rodent-deterring wire wrap (part 4019-2317)? I have acquired some, and I wish to lick the mouse tape.

Honda never replied to my tweet. To be fair, I hadn't really expected anyone in the company to get back to me, a clear and present danger, on whether their auto parts could be licked. That is a pervert's question.

Still, I fired off a couple emails to Honda's PR team just in case. My first went to Chris Martin, who was listed on the website as the media contact for "Safety, Regulatory, and Recalls."

To my great surprise, Chris got back to me the next business day:

> Liz,
>
> You have an adventurous nature. I have attached an Material Safety Data Sheet from the manufacturer of the tape, which indicates that there is "no data" about the potential for the tape to cause cancer, but it also notes "If swallowed: Consult the doctor immediately . . ." which isn't reassuring. The tape is subject to a California Proposition 65 warning, which intends to inform consumers about chemicals in a product that could cause cancer, but most consumer goods sold in the US also require such a warning these days.
>
> Because there is no reassuring information indicating that

it is safe to taste or eat the tape or its coating, I would strongly recommend against you or another human tasting it.

Please let me know if you need anything else.

Chris Martin
Automobile Public Relations
American Honda Motor Co., Inc.

. . . *wink,* am I right?

Look, I resigned myself a long time ago to the fact that I was going to die doing something so stupid, no one would ever mourn me—like French-kissing a komodo dragon or running the Kentucky Derby as a pantomime horse.

But for Chris, I scanned the accompanying Materials Sheet. There were no alarming skull-and-crossbones labels on "rodent-proof vinyl adhesive tape No. 347"—just one "Class 1 Designated Chemical Substances": bis(2-ethylhexyl)phthalate, better known as DEHP.

DEHP is a compound added to plastics (like vinyl tape) to make them more flexible. It's used in hundreds of household products, which means lots of people who bathe in Dr. Bronner's Useless Fluid think it will kill them. And sure—at high doses, DEHP can reduce both sperm count and sperm motility in rats.

But I scaled the dose up for my own weight and determined that I would need to ingest 36,000 mg a day to approach the Rat Contraceptive dose.

I licked the tape.

It smelled like a Band-Aid–flavored Rockstar Energy drink. It tasted like . . . *heat.* The capsaicin was subtler than I expected: nothing abrasive or punishing, just a blushing, ambient warmth like a string of white Christmas lights. There was almost a numbing, mala element, in the vein of a Sichuan peppercorn.

Mouse tape could have a future in modernist dining circles— you know, for the Willy Wonka, lick-the-wallpaper set. ("The schnozzberries taste like schnozzberries!" "The pepper mouse tastes like a pepper mouse!")

That might be a better gambit for Honda. I found a live shrew in my husband's slipper yesterday, so I'm not sure the tape is working as originally intended. (I am surrounded by rodents always, like a dumpster princess.) Plus, I really lathered my tongue with it and never felt like I was in any danger of being repelled.

As a culinary novelty, though? I can think of a few uses:*

This is not a recommendation, of course. You should not take any advice from this newsletter in general, but you should not lick mouse tape in particular. Chris strongly recommends against it.

When I am on my deathbed, wasting from Stagnant Rat Sperm Disease, my last words will be "CHRIS MARTIN DID EVERYTHING HE COULD TO TALK ME OUT OF THIS."†

I haven't emailed him yet to break the news. But I think he knows. I think he always knew. I think he will be unsurprised when this arrives in his inbox:

This Is Just to Say

I have eaten
the tape
that was in
the mice box
and which
you had probably
not intended for
human ingestion

Forgive me
it was delicious
so spiced
and so bold

---

* I was *always* going to make this into a Bloody Caesar rim.
† Followed by "NO, NOT *THAT* CHRIS MARTIN."

RACHEL LEVIN

The Grapefruit Spoon Makes Life Easier

FROM *Eater*

WE HAD TWO grapefruit spoons when I was growing up. Stragglers, clearly, from somewhere. They sort of scared me: with their sharp teeth, they were the sharks of the silverware drawer. Since only my parents ate grapefruit, only they used them. My parents had grapefruit spoons because their parents had grapefruit spoons, but those came with more pomp: they were sets of eight, sterling silver, each lying peacefully in its own slot in a felted wooden box. Whereas our serrated, stainless-steel duo lived unceremoniously jumbled among the teaspoons. Every so often I'd accidentally grab one and get a good cheek graze with my Honey Nut Cheerios.

Once I had my own home, and my own silverware, I forgot all about the citrus spoon, even though I came to love grapefruit. Instead, I painstakingly cut through the membranes with a versatile paring knife, until each wedge was wrested free. Using a grapefruit spoon to eat a grapefruit seemed akin to using an umbrella in a drizzle. A little ridiculous. Dainty. I was tougher than that. More practical, too.

Like fine china, specialized silverware seemed so antiquated. One-off utensils of yore. So Emily Gilmore–esque effete. So superfluous. Just more stuff in a drawer—in a world!—already cluttered. My kitchen had what it, and I, needed, and nothing more.

Until I met my mother-in-law, the queen of obscure, single-use culinary gifts of the inexpensive, unrefined kind: plastic square pan scrapers, strawberry de-stemmers, apple slicers—she's sent them all from across the country, with love. It was the pasta scooper that sold me. Serving spaghetti had always been more of an unruly spoon-fork-lift affair for me—and now here I was! Filling bowls like a boss, not a strand astray. It began to dawn on me: by dismissing such humble, hyper-specific inventions, I was actually making my kitchen more complicated.

But while the pasta scooper made me a single-use convert, there's no Grandma Ida's Kitchen Item I've loved more than the peanut butter knife. With a sturdy, thick red handle and perfectly curved seven-inch stainless-steel blade, the $12.99 utensil gets to the bottom of the jar, "saves your knuckles" from getting gooped (per the website), and spreads flawlessly. Its official name is the PB-Jife, and it has its own rather catchy jingle, or (ahem) jam, written and recorded by PB-Jife founder Landon Christensen. "It'll change your life," the lyrics promise.

Or at least change your mornings. As someone who eats peanut butter toast for breakfast five or six days a week, it has changed mine. Especially those mornings when I pull my toast hot out of the toaster (oven, always) only to realize I've got a brand-new jar that needs stirring, fast. And efficiently, sans the oily spillage that inevitably comes from a simple butter knife, or what I used to use: a backward-facing soup spoon. (Not a bad option, but it's no PB-Jife.)

Of course, the PB-Jife is not some priceless family heirloom, some marrow scoop passed down through generations. It's not a relic of another time. It evokes no nostalgia. Single-use silverware itself, on the other hand, does. Consider the Ortiz anchovy fork. That cute, dollhouse-sized prong that comes affixed to the jar of olive oil–packed filets, to keep your fingers from smelling like anchovies all night. A treat taped to a treat, since 1891.

Occasionally, I'll keep the Ortiz fork for a stint. To use with the cheaper jars, the lesser jars, that come without a fork of their own. I go through a lot of them. For six years running, I've been a jar-carrying member of an Anchovy Supper Club. Every dish must feature the bottom feeder, or its friends. My friend Samantha gussied up our most recent socially distanced backyard meal with a rare form of vintage fish flatware: a sardine fork. The squat, multi-tined symbol of Victorian refinement was used by oh-so-sophisticated people to horizontally support the slick and slender tinned fish. As did we, unpolished people, using it to bestow potato chip after potato chip with one marinated anchovy after another.

A collectible utensil, a single sardine fork can fetch upward of $900 on auction sites. Samantha found hers, etched and elegant, on Etsy for $30. A luxury, yes, but a little one. It left us swooning. Amortized over all our Anchovy Club years to come, we concurred: the fork was a worthwhile investment.

Did we need this wide-mouthed little-fish fork? Of course not. Specialized silverware is never necessary. That's what makes it special. A simple, affordable, and, yes, superfluous pleasure smaller than a bread box. (Also nice, but nonessential.)

The point is: the blissful functions of these forks and spoons and knives far outweigh both their price and the kitchen space they take up. Life is hard; single-use silverware makes it infinitesimally easier. It also makes me realize that maybe my grandparents, with their precious felted boxes, knew best.

One winter, a few years ago, I was reintroduced to the grapefruit spoon, and more specifically to its simple genius and true joys. My friend Lisa showed up to a shared Airbnb bearing breakfast fixings—bagels and cream cheese and coffee beans, and not only organic grapefruits but, being the overachiever that she is, a Ziploc of grapefruit spoons. All the freaking gear involved in packing for a family ski weekend, and this saint of a woman packed grapefruit spoons, too? "You can't eat grapefruit without a grapefruit spoon," she said, matter of fact.

She was right. The ease! The effortlessness! The neatly scraped rind! All that sweet satisfaction without an ounce of exertion. (And only $5.99 for a set of four at Bed Bath & Beyond.) She accidentally left them behind. They've lived happily among my teaspoons ever since, but lately I've been thinking they deserve better.

The other day, over a family text thread, I learned that my mother-in-law ate a grapefruit every single night for decades, until her cardiologist told her to stop. She never used a grapefruit spoon, though, she said. What! Why not? I asked. "Why would I?" she responded. "I had a grapefruit knife."

RAJESH PARAMESWARAN

I Was a Lifelong Vegetarian. I Decided to Taste What I Was Missing

FROM *Bon Appétit*

I WAS IN Argentina writing a novel when I decided—after a lifetime as a vegetarian—that I was going to have my first taste of steak. This was my plan: I would invite an acquaintance out for a meal. She would order a steak, I would order a vegetarian pasta or a salad, and she would give me just one bite of her food. And then I would finally know what meat was.

The idea had come to me when I couldn't get my horse to move. I'd taken a day trip to the Pampas, and the stubborn horse I was riding must have sensed I was a New Yorker who had no business riding horses. He slowed until we were far behind everyone else in our group, then turned sideways on the trail and came to a dead stop. I begged and I prodded, but he wouldn't budge. I had no idea what to do. Finally, I gave up and simply enjoyed the view.

It was a nice view. In the field abutting the path was a scattering of muscular cows, with hides of bright ochre and faces white as coconut meat, grazing in the dark grass. When the cows sensed I wasn't moving, they slowly raised their heads to see what the deal was. They stared at me with small ebony eyes, the curiosity in their faces rising only one or two degrees above indifference. *Who is this fellow staring rudely at us while we eat our lunch, who can't ride a horse and doesn't have the first idea of how to behave in the presence of dignified animals?*

Reassured of my insignificance, they returned to their meal. They had a dense, calm, powerful presence. I couldn't imagine creatures more casually imperious or coolly disdainful, more satisfied with life or sure of their place in it, more indisputable.

That was more or less the moment I decided I wanted to try steak.

Let me explain further. My whole family are vegetarians, going back generations. It's for reasons of religion and culture, overlaid more recently with concerns around climate change and factory farming. When I was growing up, if it was vegetarian, it was food, and if it was meat, it wasn't. It was a habit so deep it was thoughtless. But by the time I'd gotten to Argentina, I'd started thinking about it. Whatever the reasons for my vegetarianism, food is a part of culture, and it felt strange going through life without direct knowledge of what much of the world was eating. So I'd begun, kind of anthropologically, having a taste of chicken here, a bit of fish there. But I'd still never tried steak. Maybe it was an instinctive association of size with moral worth, or maybe it was inherited taboo, but steak was so bloody and thick and smelly and disgusting. It was meat itself, and I never had the slightest interest in it.

And then I found myself in the Argentine countryside, unable to get my horse to move, staring at these copacetic, gorgeous cows, so robust, well cared for, and content—at least while I was with them. They were not crowded into feedlots or cruel factories—certainly not yet. It seemed they had entered unwittingly into a noble compact: their premature deaths in exchange for living grandly on these endless plains and making their country famous with their meat. Of course, the endlessness of the plains required to feed them was part of the problem, environmentally speaking. But if ever in my life I was to have a taste of steak, just to know what it was, then perhaps it ought to be safely far from home, here in this place where the cows had the aura of minor gods. The idea thrilled me.

My first attempt was a flop. I invited a tourist I'd just met and found a restaurant on the internet. The bite she gave me was a chewy little nub that barely tasted like anything. But after talking with local friends, I concluded that this didn't count: I'd chosen the wrong restaurant and gone with the wrong person. So I decided to do it again and do it right.

This time I invited Pola Oloixarac, a brilliant, enthusiastic, and somewhat dramatic Argentine writer. We'd go to lunch at one of the best parillas in Buenos Aires on my last day of the trip. "It is an honor," she would say later, "to introduce you to the meat of my country."

Pola arrived at La Cabrera in a black dress and dark eyeliner. After kissing me on the cheek, she began charming first the maître d' and then our boyish waiter, and quickly the two men were grinning as they escorted us to a table by a window.

I explained my plan once more for good measure: a salad for me and just one bite of her steak. Pola nodded slightly. She stared with great focus and an air of appreciation at the menu, and I sensed already something feeble about my plan—about the presumption that I would be the one to make the plan—in the face of her intensity.

"Raj," she finally said, leaning forward, with confidential urgency. "We will order the steak, of course. That's why we are here. But there are things on this menu. Wonderful things. Things you will never find in New York or even anywhere else in Buenos Aires. Very Argentine things. I think we should order those things too."

"Ah." I needed to clarify myself. "I'm afraid I'm only up for one bite of steak. If there's something more you would like, please feel free. But I'm not used to eating meat, to say the least. And I have to catch a flight in a few hours—I don't know how my stomach will react."

"Of course." Pola settled back into her chair. "Just a taste. You don't have to finish everything."

"But do we really want to waste an animal?"

The wine had arrived, and I was sipping with nervous frequency because Pola's insinuations were worrying me.

"Look." She showed me the menu. "They have mollejas here. I don't think you can leave Argentina without knowing mollejas."

"If you want those, maybe you should get the half order, just for yourself?" I parried.

"And we also have to get morcillas. They are just wonderful. And then the steak, of course. And you also wanted a salad."

"Pola," I said. "This is starting to sound like an awful lot of food. Your instincts are generous, but I'm just here for one taste of steak. Please don't order anything if you're expecting me to eat it."

"Don't worry, Raj." She smiled; but I was, and I sensed that I should be. The waiter arrived. My Spanish wasn't quick enough to follow all that she told him.

The salad came first. Massive and mounded with grains, it alone would have been sufficient lunch for two people in my world. It was followed quickly by what I have recollected were the molle-jas. These were two charred, oblong objects, about the size and shape of mangoes or fists. To my nose they smelled noxious and intensely animal. In fact, the smell made me feel a little ill.

Pola began sawing one of them in half. She took that half and plopped it on a plate. She pushed it in front of me.

My heart began to beat faster and my neck grew warm. I couldn't stand the smell. "Pola," I said, "I can't eat all that."

"Just have what you like," she said warmly.

All I had wanted was to take one step across the line—put one toe across, really, to become slightly acquainted with the range of human cuisine and then put this behind me. But I couldn't become a new person entirely. And that seemed what would have been re-quired of me to eat the thing that was reeking on that plate.

What had begun as a limited experiment was spinning out of control. But I reminded myself that I was still responsible. In the-ory I believed that if an animal were going to die for your meal, it was better to eat every part of it. And my aversion to the food was matched by my reluctance to waste any kind of food: my im-migrant habits were at war with one another. And maybe there was also a wish to impress Pola, who was absolutely sincere in her enthusiasm. When you involve other people into the transgressing of your boundaries, you can't always control how the story unfolds.

"I'll have a taste," I whispered. I felt the blood leaving my ex-tremities, my head getting lighter, as I said this.

"What?" she asked.

"I'll have a little taste," I said, less weakly, gathering my resolve. The molleja, in cross section, seemed to be composed of a layer of charred skin around a pasty interior. "But before I taste it, please tell me, what is this I'm about to eat?"

"Oh, it's mollejas," Pola said. "I don't know how you say it in English. Hmm." She struggled for a moment. Then her big eyes brightened. "Oh!" She patted her sternum. "Do you know the *heart?*"

I stared back in horror. "Yes, Pola." My own heart was sinking. "Yes, I know the heart."

But this was the half order, and there were two of them. In what world did an order of heart come with *four hearts*?

"Oh, no, these are not hearts," she clarified. "But you know. Near the heart. There are, what do you call them in English? Ah. There are *glands*."

Glands? Is that really what she meant? Glands were things filled with hormones that swelled up when you got sick. You could eat those? I lost myself for a moment: was it better to eat glands or hearts? It seemed too generous to hearts to say that they were *better*, but right now it seemed indisputable that glands were somehow even worse.

"You look frightened," Pola said, with sudden sensitivity.

"Well, yes." My mouth was tacky and dry. "In fact, I am frightened. But I guess that's kind of why I came here. I'm going to do it."

Struggling not to smell the thing, I used a serrated knife to slice off a sliver as carefully as possible with my unsteady hands. The room receded to a buzzing haze. My arm moved, the fork came to my lips, my mouth opened, and . . .

. . . the molleja simply melted on my tongue. It was incredibly delicate, airy and light; at the same time it was somehow rich and sort of creamy. It was in every way different from what I thought the smell had suggested. The word *delicacy* flashed through my mind, and it had new meaning now. Here was something truly delicate and rare. Here was a great delicacy.

I'd done it. I'd had my taste. So now what was I doing having another?

Next the morcillas arrived. These were dark oblongs with little flecks in them. The smell was complex, deep, unfamiliar. "Morcilla," Pola explained. "You take some on a piece of bread. And you add chimichurri."

I asked again, although I should have known better by now: "But what *is* it?"

"Let's see . . . Well, do you know *blood*?"

"Oh, Pola," I said. "Yes, I know blood. You're telling me that this solid thing . . ."

"Oh, no," she said. "It's not blood. Not exactly. It's blood with *grease*."

I guffawed in grief. I vowed to ask no more questions for fear of more answers. I would just get it over with. I scooped a bit of the moist and crumbly dark matter onto a piece of bread. I spread it down and topped it with chimichurri, which had finely diced mango, cucumber, and cilantro. I brought it all to my mouth and sank my teeth in.

How can I describe it? The taste was complicated and layered, almost as if it had been flavored with cloves and other spices—savory but with a slight sweetness. There seemed something vaguely Indian about it. It was simply one of the most interesting things I had ever put on my tongue.

I hung my head down and took deep breaths. Somewhere in my veins I felt the molecules of my body transforming.

"My dear, you're frightened again."

"I just need a minute," I said.

"Yes, that's a good idea. Let's pause. Let's take a minute."

I was not frightened now; I was moved. A beast had been killed, one of those great orange cows of the countryside; and the people working in this kitchen had paid attention to it, to all of it, even the oddest parts, and made this art of it. It was a primal—but a very human—thing. It moved me.

I drank more Malbec and jettisoned my plan to take just a small taste of everything. The steak had arrived by now, sitting in what appeared to be a pool of blood; it was chewy and boring in comparison to the other marvels on the table. I kept eating everything, because I was amazed by the food, and felt some responsibility to the cow—half of which, virtually, had been served to us (there was also pig, I realized later; the morcillas are made from pig)—to not waste a bit of its sacrifice.

There are things of the mind and things of the body, and food is somehow both. It's an edible language, with its own grammar and local meanings, taught to us by our families. Like language, it's processed sensually in our mouths. Then one day we look around and want to learn what other people are eating. We realize food is created and contingent. What is incomprehensible can become intelligible; or what is familiar, strange. We can discover new appetites, hidden somewhere in our bodies, and someone can teach us another way of eating.

Halfway through our meal, Pola sent everything back to the kitchen to be reheated on the grill because one could do that here, if one knew to ask for it. "This way you can taste things both lightly cooked and medium." (There is an expertise involved in being a good diner, I saw, as much as is in being a cook.) In a few hours I would be back in New York, trying to reassume my vegetarian habits. This meat was knowledge that could not be unlearned, but I knew it would be less meaningful, less sustainable, without this richness of context, and my particular guide. How could I order glands in Manhattan and expect them to compare? But there with Pola, I kept eating until I simply couldn't hold any more. And on the plane home that night, I slept soundly, without even a murmur from my stomach.

In My Childhood Kitchen, I Learned Both Fear and Love

FROM *Bon Appétit*

R. STANDS AT the stove, studying the contents of a wok. *The oil has to ripple,* he says, *but not smoke.* And there it is, glistening like a Maine pond on an August morning. Leaning down, he flicks the meat until it hits all the sides of the sloped pan, a plume rising from the center island, a hiss escaping, born of the marriage of oil and water. I am eight years old, enthralled by the foreignness of the experience, the purity of it. Purity is still a possibility.

R. came into our lives in 1986. He'd been my mother's high school sweetheart, then born-again lover after my parents divorced. They eventually married, and we moved out of our Brooklyn brownstone and into a house in Massachusetts. Before R., my mother and I had our own way of doing things, and, despite her rigorous schedule as a public defender, she cooked dinner every night, mostly from a book called *365 Ways to Cook Chicken.* Our food was ordinary: gelatinous Wishbone Italian dressing over iceberg lettuce; boxed rice pilaf plumped with bouillon; chicken breasts swathed in breadcrumbs and baked beneath pats of butter. We were not culinary explorers. What we ate was enough to feed us.

But in our Massachusetts town, R. brought home ingredients I had never seen, like peanut and sesame oils for cooking and finishing, pink planks of pork foreign to my family's Jewish table, or long-grain rice that came in a burlap sack and not in a microwavable bag. R. had been to many places. His adventures felt outsized, and in the beginning, I wanted to know them all: his encounter with an upright cobra on the streets of Thailand, when he served in the Air Force; his college days skiing Alta; or his winding tales of Alice Springs, Australia, where he lived in his twenties, devouring pizzas topped with molten, runny eggs.

He was nothing like my father—a studious lawyer with an exacting, dark wit. R. was a towering, linear-thinking engineer. His working-class Catholic family was not ten miles down the road, but R. had accrued a certain indefinable sophistication from his travels. And while I had no true sense of who he was (what he loved, where his passions lay, or even the nuances of his personality), his food revealed a world I never knew existed. A promise rose like vapor; his shiny wok held a million stories. It said, *The world is so much bigger than this.* It said, *You can know the world too.*

I can't recall exactly when the shift between us started. I remember mostly twinned moments: R. at the stove, tossing jewels of pork. R. wrenching me up the stairs by my hair when I was eight. There were midweek ski adventures to catch the fleeting fresh snow, our downhill runs punctuated by pliable disks of fried, butter-bathed dough sold on the slopes. And then there was the day he ripped the phone out of the wall and chased me out of the house, his anger so igneous that it inspired the person on the other line to come, unasked, to collect me.

I didn't know how to comprehend these wild vicissitudes. R. could be tender, in ways that smoothed over our fiery fights. Every other weekend, he drove me to Logan Airport so I could visit my father in New York. On our way back home, R. often pulled into Papa Gino's, a New England chain that served my favorite pizza. We ate every slice of our pie, an act that defied our home's "no junk food" clause. Holding this secret meant we shared something that belonged only to us, something other than the violence we also secreted away. However fleeting the gesture, back then I believed that R. loved me enough to stop for pizza.

But our tenuous bond was just that. My siblings, born shortly after R. and my mother married, widened our family's arc, disappearing me into the background. He worshiped his children, gave them love in a way I didn't know he could, spun them around the room while the Hooters' "And We Danced" blasted from the record player. A decade into my life, I already knew that an order had been established: them over me, their needs over mine.

My mother may not have known our dynamics, though she seemed to understand R.'s temper and often encouraged me not to "push his buttons." R. and I existed in this set of frenetic circumstances, seesawing between a shared sense of obligation and ambivalence.

Yet, in the kitchen, there was mostly joy. I watched those cubes of pork take flight from his wok. I marveled at his stir-fries, and even the bold choice to serve springy ramen noodles as a side dish. These foods transported me to distant lands, away from the reality of life in that house. When he cooked, my narrow world cracked open. The possibility of more hopeful stories, elsewhere, sustained me.

I may have felt invisible at home, but at school, I asserted my existence by acting out. I was a throbbing nerve center of a child, a girl who came home with straight As—except in the "conduct" category, where my chattiness and attitude earned me demerits. In the third grade, I kicked a substitute teacher and spent the afternoon in detention while my classmates went swimming at the Y. My therapist asked my parents to stop sending me. So did my summer camp. My problem was that I wasn't able to articulate all that I'd lost: my home in Brooklyn, my father, the way my family once was.

I spent years imagining an escape. My plan was to return to New York for college, an adventure and homecoming, but one that felt distinctly far off—until one sticky summer morning, when I was fourteen. R. slapped me across the face in front of the babysitter. Before that moment, no one else had witnessed how he treated me. The truth suddenly snapped into focus. R. and I had vanished into something so dark and familiar, we didn't know how else, or who else, to be. If I wanted to exist, I needed to leave.

The purest agony of abuse is that you can hold both revulsion and love for the things that harm you. Love and abuse are vacuums, consuming one another. We love our abusers. We want them to love us back.

However complicated and bittersweet, through R., I gained an appreciation for food that would last long after I left home. After college, I worked as a bartender, then as a captain, and, finally, as a sommelier, eventually landing at a buzzy, critically acclaimed restaurant. The chef orchestrated a culture of toxicity that reminded me of life in my childhood home. Sometimes my boss was kind, and I leaned into those moments, as I had so many times before. It surprised me how easily I reentered that familiar space. I was hungry, had always been hungry, for even the smallest acts of affection and approval.

I still think, perhaps a little too often, of the dishes I loved at that restaurant: grill-charred sweetbreads with pickled chiles; chewy, spicy rice cakes slicked with ground-pork sauce; pucks of salty-sweet pork belly floating atop pillowy buns; a flurry of frozen, shaved foie gras that warmed in the mouth. It's possible, I've found, to keep affection and fear as paired emotions, to both appreciate a memory and revile its circumstances.

It's been a decade since R. was last in my life. But when I think of that time, pain is separate from the meals he set in front of me. Perhaps those were the only acts of love he could manage. Perhaps, too, what I needed he could never give me.

Now, when I cook for my own willful young children, they want nothing to do with my culinary exactitude. Most nights, they ask for hot, salty pasta. My four-year-old often reminds me, though, that what I serve doesn't matter. "You're the best cooker, Mommy," he says. And this isn't because the pasta I make is any better than the millions of other pastas he's ever eaten. My children seem to understand, already, that food can be a deliverance of love. At the table, they pick up rotini and fusilli with their bare hands, relishing each bite. It's messy and wild and perfect. They finish everything as I watch, moved by the purity. The possibility.

SAM ANDERSON

I Recommend Eating Chips

FROM *The New York Times Magazine*

OH, HELLO, NICE to see you, have a seat—let's stress-eat some chips together. Let's turn ourselves, briefly, into dusty-fingered junk-food receptacles. This will force us to stop looking, for a few minutes, at the bramble of tabs we've had open on our internet browsers for all these awful months: the articles we've been too frazzled to read about the TV shows we've been meaning to watch; the useless products we keep almost impulse-buying; the sports highlights and classic films that we digest in twelve-second bursts every four days; that little cartoon diagram of how to best lay out your fruit orchards in Animal Crossing. Eating these chips will rescue us, above all, from the very worst things on our screens, the cursed news of the outside world—escalating numbers, civic decay, gangs of elderly men behaving like children.

Please, sit down. I've got a whole bag of Cool Ranch Doritos here: electric blue, plump as a winter seed, bursting with imminent joy. I found it up in the cupboard over the fridge, where by some miracle my family had yet to discover it—it had slipped sideways behind the protein powder, back near the leftover Halloween candy—so now I'm sitting here all alone at the kitchen counter, about to sail off into the salty seas of decadent gluttony. The next few minutes of my life, at least, are going to be great.

Join me. Grab whatever you've got. Open the bag. Pinch it on its crinkly edges and pull apart the seams. Now we're in business: we have broken the seal. The inside of the bag is silver and shining, a marvel of engineering—strong and flexible and reflective, like an astronaut suit. Lean in, inhale that unmistakable bouquet: toasted corn, dopamine, America, grief! We are the first humans to see these chips since they left the factory who knows when. They have been waiting for us, embalmed in preservatives, like a pharaoh in his dark tomb. These chips might have even been produced in the former world, in the time before the plague, when people gathered in sports stadiums, filled concert halls, touched one another's faces, high-fived, passed around bottles and joints and phones and cash. But now they have been born into this world, into our doomed timeline, and they have absolutely no idea.

That is the great virtue of chips: they are here for us to eat them. So that is what we will do. I will put the first chip, now, into my mouth. I will set it delicately on my tongue like a communion wafer. Instantly, the flavor snaps against my taste buds—that earthy, cheesy tang—flashing like a firecracker, lighting up the whole wet cave of my mouth and radiating out, further, to fill my whole head, my whole being. These chemicals are transcendent, Proustian, as powerful as any drug: they trigger nodes of memory that stretch back years, decades, back to old Super Bowls and family reunions, back to the outside world that I am trying to forget. Another chip. Another chip.

What is the comfort of junk food? Why do we experience these very empty calories with such passionate sensual absorption? It is a question that predates the pandemic, of course, and probably has a prosaic answer—some proprietary formula hidden under fluorescent lights in a flavor laboratory in New Jersey. But even minor questions take on outsize importance these days. A pandemic, it turns out, produces a curious paradox: it not only creates a shrieking worldwide drama of existential dread—it also puts relentless pressure on the most mundane aspects of our everyday lives. For nearly a year now, many of us have been locked in a controlled environment, a closed lab of selfhood: the Quarantine Institute of Applied Subjectivity. Our homes have become biodomes designed to study the fragile ecosystems of Us. All our neuroses and addictions and habits are under the microscope. Willpower, productivity, resilience, despair. We have turned into scientists of ourselves. And so I watch myself eating chips.

The chips don't have to be chips, of course; they could be anything you binge in order to self-soothe. Maybe you do jigsaw puzzles instead of answering work email. Maybe you trade options all day on Robinhood. Maybe you walk counterclockwise around your home, over and over, tightening all the screws on every fixture. Maybe you read Twitter.

For me, a bag of chips is a way to defeat time. It brings temporary infinity: a feeling that it will never end. A chip. A chip. A chip. Another chip. The chips come like ocean waves, like human breaths, serial but unique, each part of a huge eternal rhythm but also its own precious discovery.

I hate to say this, to risk breaking the spell, but I have just noticed that my arm is reaching deeper and deeper into the Doritos bag. What used to be just my fingertips turned into my whole wrist, and now, although it seems as if it's been only five seconds, my whole forearm is disappearing into the bag. It appears that I have eaten one half of an entire bag of chips. Three-quarters, if we are being honest. Well, seven-eighths. The remaining chips are very small, just fragments, resplendent with flavor dust. I believe we have reached the point, in fact, where it would be shameful to leave only what's left. So we keep going. We must keep going. A chip. A chip. A chip. Keep going. A chip. If we stop, it will end, but if we keep going, it might last forever.

Contributors' Notes

Other Distinguished Food Writing
of 2021

Contributors' Notes

SAM ANDERSON is a staff writer for the *New York Times Magazine*. His writing has won a National Magazine Award as well as the National Book Critics Circle Balakian Citation for Excellence in Reviewing. He is the author of *Boom Town: The Fantastical Saga of Oklahoma City, Its Chaotic Founding, Its Apocalyptic Weather, Its Purloined Basketball Team, and the Dream of Becoming a World-Class Metropolis.*

LIZ COOK is a Kansas City–based writer and editor whose work has appeared most recently in the *Pitch, Eater, Defector,* and *Midwesterner.* She also writes the experimental food newsletter *Haterade.*

NINA LI COOMES is a Japanese and American writer, currently living in Chicago. Her work has appeared in *Guernica, The Atlantic,* and *Catapult,* among other places. You can find her on Twitter @nlcoomes, or at www.ninalicoomes.com.

CHRIS CROWLEY is a writer for *New York* magazine's Grub Street, where he covers New York restaurants, the people who work in them, and the city. He would like to thank Courtney Kennedy for her time and the opportunity to write about her.

SAM DEAN started his career in journalism as a blogger for *Bon Appétit,* then spent five years freelancing, frequently writing for the deceased food magazine *Lucky Peach.* He joined the staff of the *Los Angeles Times* in 2018, where he reports on business, technology, and (when the stars align) food. If you have any tips, or just want to say hi, you can contact him at sam.dean@latimes.com and find more of his work at samdean.com.

JOSH DZIEZA is a feature writer at the *Verge.*

JIAYANG FAN has been a staff writer at *The New Yorker* since 2016. She is at work on her first book, *Motherland.*

TOM FINGER teaches classes in American and environmental history at Northern Arizona University. His research focuses on environmental histories of food, water, and energy systems. He is particularly interested in how human economic relationships are embedded in natural systems, and how the materiality of resource flows contributes to human inequality.

WILLA GLICKMAN is an assistant editor at the *New York Review of Books*.

DR. CYNTHIA R. GREENLEE is an intentionally independent historian who's also a longtime writer and editor based in North Carolina. She was the winner of a 2020 James Beard Award and a two-time nominee in the 2022 competition. She coedited *The Echoing Ida* anthology about reproductive justice, and her work has appeared in publications as varied as *The Atlantic, Longreads, The Nation,* the *New York Times, Smithsonian,* Vox, *Vice,* and the *Washington Post.* She's also unspeakably angry that she does not own rights to her piece in this anthology and will likely hold this grudge until kingdom come. Check out her website at cynthiagreenlee.com.

ANDREW KEH is a sports reporter for the *New York Times*. He has written stories from more than twenty-five countries. He lives in New York.

ERIC KIM is a *New York Times* staff writer born and raised in Atlanta, Georgia, and the author of *Korean American: Food That Tastes Like Home.* He now hosts regular videos on *NYT Cooking*'s YouTube channel and writes a monthly column for the *New York Times Magazine.* A former contributing editor at *Saveur,* Eric taught writing and literature at Columbia University, and his work has been featured in the *Washington Post, Bon Appétit,* and *Food and Wine.* He lives with his rescue pup, Quentin Compson, in New York City.

RACHEL LEVIN is a San Francisco journalist who has written for the *New York Times, The New Yorker, Outside, Eater,* and elsewhere. She is the author of *Look Big: And Other Tips for Surviving Animal Encounters of All Kinds* and coauthor of two cookbooks, *Eat Something: A Wise Sons Cookbook for Jews Who Like Food and Food Lovers Who Like Jews* and *Steamed: A Catharsis Cookbook for Getting Dinner and Your Feelings on the Table.* Her first kids' book, a look at eating through the ages, will be published in 2023.

LIGAYA MISHAN writes for the *New York Times* and *T* magazine. Her essays have been selected for the Best American anthologies in Food and Travel Writing, and her criticism has appeared in the *New York Review of Books* and *The New Yorker.* The daughter of a Filipino mother and a British father, she grew up in Honolulu, Hawai'i.

SHANE MITCHELL is a journalist and author who frequently writes about problematic crops and food insecurity. Her essays have received multiple

James Beard Foundation awards, including the M.F.K. Fisher Distinguished Writing Award. "The Queen of Delicacies" is the seventh installment in her Crop Cycle series for *The Bitter Southerner.* She hates grits but loves her dog and husband. Maybe in that order on nights when he's playing the Allman Brothers or Grateful Dead too loudly.

RAJESH PARAMESWARAN is the author of the short story collection *I Am an Executioner: Love Stories,* a *Washington Post* Best Book of the Year. His work has appeared in *The Best American Magazine Writing, The New Yorker, Fiction, Granta, McSweeney's,* and *Zoetrope: All-Story,* and has been recognized with a National Magazine Award and the Jericho Fellowship Essay Prize. He has taught at NYU's creative writing program and at the University of Leipzig, and he has received fellowships from the New York Public Library, the Radcliffe Institute at Harvard, MacDowell, and Yaddo. He is at work on a novel.

TOM PHILPOTT is the food and agriculture correspondent for *Mother Jones* and author of *Perilous Bounty: The Looming Collapse of American Farming and How We Can Prevent It.*

JAYA SAXENA is currently the senior writer at Eater.com. Her most recent book is the essay collection *Crystal Clear.* She lives in Queens with her spouse and two ungrateful cats. You can find out more about her at jayasaxena.com.

LOGAN SCHERER writes about desire.

HANNAH SELINGER is a James Beard Award–nominated freelance writer and mother of two based in New York and Massachusetts. Her work has appeared in the *New York Times, Eater, Bon Appétit, Travel + Leisure,* the *Washington Post,* the *Boston Globe,* the *Wall Street Journal, Food and Wine,* and elsewhere.

MAYUKH SEN is the author of *Taste Makers: Seven Immigrant Women Who Revolutionized Food in America* (2021). He is currently writing a biography of the Indian-born Old Hollywood actress Merle Oberon, to be published in 2025. He has won a James Beard Award and an IACP Award for his food writing, and his work has previously been anthologized in the 2019 and 2021 editions of *The Best American Food Writing.* He teaches at Columbia University's undergraduate creative writing program and lives in Brooklyn.

JULIA SONENSHEIN is a forever Californian living and working in New York. Since the early 2010s, she has worked as a journalist, essayist, and editor. Her writing has appeared in *Catapult* and on Elle.com and Marie claire.com, among others. She is at work on a book about the evangelical church.

ADESH THAPLIYAL is a writer living in Berkeley, California. He contributes to the music blogs Tone Glow and The Singles Jukebox.

BRYAN WASHINGTON is the author of *Memorial* and *Lot.* He's a National Book Foundation 5 Under 35 honoree and a recipient of the International Dylan Thomas Prize, the New York Public Library's Young Lions Award, the Lambda Literary Award, and an O. Henry Award. He was also a finalist for the National Book Critics Circle Award for fiction, the National Book Critics Circle John Leonard Prize, the Aspen Literary Award, the Center for Fiction's First Novel Prize, the Joyce Carol Oates Prize, the Andrew Carnegie Medal of Excellence, and the PEN/Robert Bingham prize. He is from Houston.

Other Distinguished Food Writing of 2021

EXPLORE THE REST OF THE SERIES!

On sale 11/1/22
$17.99

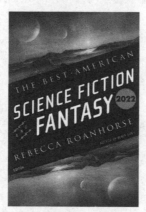

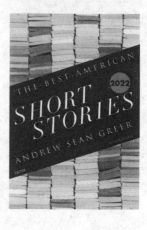